Steve Claridge is a football p
BBC television.

Ian Ridley is football columnist for the *Mail on Sunday*.

By Steve Claridge and Ian Ridley

Tales from the Boot Camps
Beyond the Boot Camps

Beyond the Boot Camps

Football, Inside and Out

Steve Claridge
with Ian Ridley

An Orion paperback

First published in Great Britain in 2009
by Orion
This paperback edition published in 2010
by Orion Books Ltd,
Orion House, 5 Upper St Martin's Lane,
London WC2H 9EA

An Hachette UK company

1 3 5 7 9 10 8 6 4 2

A CIP catalogue record for this book is available
from the British Library.

ISBN 978-0-7528-8320-5

Printed and bound in Great Britain by Clays Ltd, St Ives plc

The Orion Publishing Group's policy is to use papers that
are natural, renewable and recyclable products and
made from wood grown in sustainable forests. The logging
and manufacturing processes are expected to conform to
the environmental regulations of the country of origin.

www.orionbooks.co.uk

For Grace, who has filled the gaps in my life that I thought never would be

Acknowledgements

Having been in the mad world of football for more than twenty-five years, I can tell you that it takes a lot to survive. I would not have done so without my mum and dad, Anne and Alan, who have always been there for me. Much gratitude and love, too, to my wife Mandy for being so understanding.

I would also like to thank my co-writer, Ian Ridley, for always believing in me. Thanks, too, to all those friends and colleagues in the game who have helped him in the course of this book. They are named in the text.

Finally, my thanks to Ian Preece at Orion, who has patiently and perceptively brought this book into being.

Steve Claridge, January 2009

Contents

1. *Portsmouth – I started, so I'll finish*

Most players put together an autobiography as they come to the end of their career – if they are interesting enough for people to want to read about them, that is. Rarely do they have a second volume in them. Steve Claridge, however, is not most players. The evidence comes in the form of one of the most vivid and varied of footballing lives, on and off the field.

We first collaborated on *Tales from the Boot Camps* in 1997, just as Steve had finally worked his way up to reach the Premiership with Leicester City. It told of an itinerant career that embraced a gambling problem and a propensity for somehow getting into all sorts of scrapes. We thought the book was the culmination of a career that had begun with him being released as an apprentice by his hometown club Portsmouth as a teenager for what was perceived as a dubious attitude; few then were able to comprehend such a singular character who marched to his own drum.

That rejection triggered a realisation that his dream of being a professional footballer was in serious jeopardy before it had begun. It also triggered a determination to redouble his efforts. After kicking around Basingstoke Town and Fareham Town, he made it to Bournemouth under Harry Redknapp before going on to Weymouth, Crystal Palace (briefly), Aldershot, Cambridge United (twice), David Pleat's Luton Town and Barry Fry's Birmingham City before those days in the sun, encompassing joyous playoff-winning and League Cup-grabbing goals at Leicester City in the club's heyday under Martin O'Neill.

We updated the book regularly, as it remained in demand over the next three years, to include him scoring that joyous goal to bring Leicester the then Coca-Cola Cup following a replay victory over Middlesbrough at Hillsborough. Then came his move, via Wolverhampton Wanderers, back to Pompey, this time under Alan Ball.

He and the book certainly were in demand. At a well-attended signing session at a bookshop in Leicester, one man produced a picture of his cat and asked Steve to autograph it, saying that he had named the animal after him. "From one Claridge to another," Steve wrote.

The book was also made into a BBC Radio series and I drove Steve to a studio in West London for an interview. On the way, he insisted I stop immediately because nature was calling. I waited for ten minutes on yellow lines, anxious about traffic wardens. Eventually the penny dropped, and not the proverbial one for the public convenience. Nature had called. I found Steve in a bookmaker's shop, watching a horse race.

Since then, it has been a pleasure and a privilege for the best part of this past decade to watch him work his way through the gambling problem that once beset him, to see him change and mature, and even to work with him as his chairman for an eye-opening spell when he was manager of Weymouth, a period captured for the BBC2 fly-on-the-wall series Football Diaries.

But back then, at the turn of the millennium, Steve was 34 and we thought that would be just about that. Alan Shearer had always had a desire to return to Newcastle United while still fit and firing so that his Geordie people could see some of him. Steve felt the same way. The local hero had unfinished business. His career would wind its way to its back-home conclusion over the couple of years left on his contract and he would settle down to life back among the people whom he knew, and who knew him, best.

His long-suffering wife Mandy, who had always understood the lifeblood importance of football to Steve (or has had to), might get to see him more and experience more stability in their life together. He might get to enjoy the home he had had built next door to mum Anne and dad Alan, and which his father had christened "Wembley Heights", for longer periods.

With Steve, though, nothing pans out expectedly. As the old saying goes: "Life is what happens to you when you are busy making plans." We thought we had reached a full stop, but instead it was just a comma. There was a serious second wind left to his playing career – as he always believed there would be – and, astonishingly, he would go on to play for another ten clubs in eight years. Alongside it, he was building a media career. People asked us when we would be writing another book to bring it all up to date. Here is the answer.

We pick up the story in that summer of 2000, with Steve having returned to Portsmouth a couple of years earlier from Wolves and having been, during that period, through an interesting brush with the Football Association. He had bet on Pompey – and also the money of some of his team-mates – to win a home game against Barnsley. He scored a hat-trick in the match and revealed the wager in an interview afterwards. The FA fined him his winnings and told him not to do it again, although rules were changed afterwards so that it became no longer illegal to bet on your own team.

I recall going down to Fratton Park around that time to cover an FA Cup tie between Pompey and Leeds United and Steve invited me to stay at his house on the Friday night. He cooked roast chicken and roast potatoes with four different vegetables. The plate was piled about two feet high, with ne'er a drop of gravy to be seen. Steve liked his food plain and simple. The hospitality was typical of his generosity and singularity.

It would be a turbulent period. Steve's relationship with Alan Ball was becoming increasingly strained. At first both men had taken to each other. They were local favourites, after all, with a great passion for the game. World Cup-winner Ball was the manager who had let Claridge go back in 1983 during his first spell as manager – during which he got Portsmouth up into the top flight for just a season before being sacked the next – and he admitted to Steve that he had made a mistake in releasing him when he came to sign him from Wolves.

Come December 1999, Ball was sacked as Pompey slumped to the very foot of the table and Steve was left out of the side. The hierarchy at the club was not best pleased. Steve wanted to go out on loan, but it was the manager who departed instead.

Restored to the side by caretaker manager Bob McNab, and retained by full-time January 2000 appointment Tony Pulis, Steve would do much to get Pompey out of the mire and keep them up, scoring 14 goals, 12 of them in the second half of the season. He remained the fans' favourite for that memorable socks-down, shirt-out, heart-on-the-sleeve energy and wholeheartedness that had become his trademark. For his goals, for the way he led the attack and linked the team, he became Pompey's Player of the Year, as he had been the previous year in his first full season after his return from Wolves.

"He was quite a vision with his socks round his ankles. He had no airs and graces," recalls his strike partner Guy Whittingham. "Yes, his great strength was holding the ball up, but it was more than that. He kept it moving when it came up to him. It meant that a defender could never dare to get too close to him, which gave him time to distribute the ball.

"He was a good colleague to play with as well, though he could be frustrating. He was not a natural goalscorer – it was more that he combined goalscoring and being a target, but he wanted to be a goalscorer. He would twist and turn to create a chance for himself when he might have found you."

"You could trust him with the ball," adds defender Andy Awford. "As a defender it gave you breathing space. He was also very different, a fun character who liked a laugh and a joke. He would turn up scruffy for training, and would wear his kit home so you never quite knew what he was up to, whether he might be off to the bookies in a hurry or something. But he would never be late, for either training or matches. He was very professional like that."

Ball's revelation to Steve that he was on his way out came as a shock to him, but as with many he has had disagreements with in the game throughout his long career, Steve was not one to hold grudges and from then on he got on well with Ball. Several years later, Steve would even ask him to manage an International XI in his testimonial at Fratton Park. Ball's premature death in 2007 came as much more of a shock to Steve; the more so as the two men had spoken to each other the very day that England's youngest 1966 World Cup winner suffered a heart attack.

After the failing Ball era, during which Steve had also spoken out about what he believed to be assistant manager Kevin Bond's poor coaching methods, he initially welcomed the appointment of disciplinarian Tony Pulis as Pompey manager. However, for Steve, Pulis's methods would soon evoke too readily and distastefully the long-ball era of John Beck at Cambridge United.

"It was not a happy time for many of us," says Whittingham, who was sent out on loan to Peterborough and Oxford United. Pulis would last just ten months due to poor performances and even worse results as a new owner at Fratton Park was serving his apprenticeship in what would become an expert career of hiring and firing managers. That owner was Milan Mandaric.

Little was known about Mandaric when he first came into English football in 1998. A Serb, he had built up a car spare parts business in the old Yugoslavia before moving to America and creating another business career. There he became involved in football, deciding to branch out into Europe, first buying the Belgian club Standard Liege before taking on the French League outfit Nice.

The Serbian player Preki had been with Pompey around that time and talked Mandaric into buying the club, so the story goes, although Mandaric must surely have noted that the Premiership was fast becoming the rich man of Europe and that there were rich pickings to be had if mid-range, buyable clubs such as Portsmouth, could get a seat at the top table.

He had begun to give Ball some money to spend and had given Pulis even more, but had been disappointed by both. Mandaric looked inside the club for a new manager. And the man he turned to to succeed Pulis was ... Steve Claridge, for his first taste of management.

The money supply was being stopped for the moment, though, and Steve would also have to play, knowing that there were very few shining examples of men combining the roles of player and manager.

"The appointment was a surprise to me, yes," says Andy Awford. "Steve was very young, had no experience, and to be thrust like that into a Division One side was a daunting task. But you wouldn't say no, would you? He couldn't turn it down."

Steve, a man with a broad-brush approach to management, recalled Guy Whittingham – an embryonic coach with an interest in the nuts and bolts of making a squad tick – from Oxford and made him his assistant. He also promoted Neil McNab, the former Manchester City and Tottenham midfield player and now the youth-team coach, up to first-team coach.

"We were two totally different characters," says Whittingham. "To him, the game is more of an instinct thing, but he needed someone like me to do the detailed work.

"It's not to say he doesn't do his preparation, because he does, but he likes to think on his feet. There were times when me and Neil McNab would set up a training session and he would arrive five minutes before it started and say, 'No, I want to work on something else today.'

"We did share the same philosophy of how we wanted to play the game, though. We both liked width, through a 4-4-2 or a 4-3-3, to create space to play, and we spent a lot of time talking about that.

"Also, we both had a background of working hard," adds Whittingham, who came late to the professional game having been a professional soldier in the army until he was 24. "It wasn't just the army that gave me the discipline, though, I had self-discipline thanks to my parents."

Steve also found a role for Andy Awford. "Injuries were taking a toll on me," he says. "I was making noises about wanting to hang up my boots. Steve asked me to go and scout Crewe one week because we were playing them next and I did a report. The next week he asked me to do another report and, before I knew it, I was the club's youngest-ever chief scout.

"It was one of Steve's first tests as a manager, I think," Awford recalls. "Me and him were mates and it was difficult for him. He wanted to look after me, but also had a job to do for the club. In the end, I think he was fair to both of us, so you can't ask for much more than that."

At first, Steve took to his first managerial role as if to the manor born. Pompey won their first three games, and then went unbeaten in the next four, to prompt fanciful thoughts that they might even make the playoffs to reach the Premier League. But injuries bit hard into what, given Pulis's spending, was not as good or sufficiently deep a squad as it should have been. Results started to become mixed.

Steve was not unduly concerned, believing that Mandaric was allowing him to think ahead. He did as he was asked, releasing certain players to get the wage bill down and did not wish to spend the owner's money on replacements until the summer when he could get in decent ones who were then available, rather than the panic buys of mid-winter.

Awford even had to don his boots again, for a game at Queens Park Rangers. "We kept a clean sheet, drew 0-0, but I told Steve, 'I can't do that again.' I got back home and couldn't walk. My knees, back and neck ached.

"What I remember most about the game, though, was Steve telling the kitman he didn't like the socks we had and sending him to find another set. That was Steve; it had to be right for him, even if it wasn't for everyone else. He was very particular and very superstitious. The kitman came back with red socks because they were the only colour he could get in the right make. We had yellow shirts and blue shorts and ended up looking like Colombia."

Awford also recalls Steve accompanying him on some wild-goose-chase scouting missions. "We went to see some player at FC Gent, Dick Van Dyke or something, and it was freezing cold. We knew after five minutes he was no good." Awford and Claridge even had to share a hotel room to save money.

Next, it was a trip North rather than South. "I remember meeting Steve at the Solent Hotel at 2pm to go and look at a player at Huddersfield and the day never seemed to end," Awford reminisces. "Steve wanted to go to one of his old haunts in Birmingham afterwards for a curry.

"Nothing came of it with the player, but that's part of scouting. For every 50 rubbish ones you see there might be one you want. Steve was willing to do all the leg work, to be fair to him."

All seemed to be well. Whittingham believed that the relationship between the owner and the manager was a good one.

"They spent a lot of time on the phone, from what I could see," says Whittingham. "It was every single day. I saw that as a good thing at the time. It showed they got on. Steve also told me they did."

It would not be enough, though. After just five months in the job, early in 2001, Steve became yet another notch on the pistol of the trigger-happy Mandaric.

Alan Ball lasted just six months under Mandaric, Pulis ten, Steve five and Graham Rix, Steve's successor, would make it through only another 13 before Harry Redknapp moved across from director of football, recruited wily old Jim Smith as his assistant, and finally turned Pompey into a Premiership club.

In 2006, Mandaric eventually sold up for a serious profit and took over Leicester City, where he would get through six managers in a year. "I am not one for breathing down managers' necks," he would later write in a programme column.

"He did OK, could have done better," is the Andy Awford verdict on Steve's tenure as Pompey manager. "It was tough for him to make the transition from player to manager. He had always been involved in the social activities, the wind-ups and the jokes. In fact, he was sometimes the butt of them.

"Guy was a good foil for Steve. He was the sensible, more punctual one. He would be there half an hour early, Steve one minute before he was needed. But maybe Steve needed an older, more experienced man with him, because Guy was still a player there too. It probably came a bit too early for him and Steve would probably admit that too."

Maybe, but in the cases of Whittingham and Awford at least, Steve's judgement and vision proved to be accurate. The former went on to achieve his UEFA Pro coaching licence and became a coaching educator for the FA and the Professional Footballers' Association in the South-West, getting players through their coaching badges. He is also a commentator on BBC Radio Solent and a technical coach at the Portsmouth youth academy. The latter became reserve-team coach at Pompey before joining Oxford United as Jim Smith's assistant, moving on to a sports studies degree to become a PE teacher.

Who knows, had Mandaric retained faith and patience – actually make that discovered rather than retained – Steve might have gone on to have his judgement vindicated in other areas.

Steve was bitter at the appointment of Rix, it has to be admitted. After that, though, he was delighted that his club, under Redknapp, would make the Premiership. He would have loved, however, to have been the one given the licence to sign such talents as Paul Merson and Svetislav Todorov, whose creativity and goals would take them to the top flight.

He personally would simply get on with things and find a new footballing home where he could pick himself up. It is a theme that runs through one of the most fascinating of tales, one that weaves through every layer of the tapestry that is English football and which offers a portrait of both the game in this country and a variety of its characters. A portrait chiefly, of course, of one of its biggest characters.

1.1 Home Discomforts

Now, where were we? I'm not sure where you were that summer of 2000 when I ended the first instalment of my story in *Tales from the Boot Camps* – probably watching England struggle under Kevin Keegan at the European Championships in Holland and Belgium – but I was back where I wanted to be. That place was home, Portsmouth Football Club, where I had started my career and where I hoped to end it.

I had had enough of the have-boots-will-travel wandering and had returned to Fratton Park the previous year from Wolverhampton Wanderers. I was now 34, with a home built in the countryside next to my mum and dad's house a few miles out of Pompey. I also wanted my hometown fans to see the best of me for a few years after my apprenticeship there had fizzled out before I finally knuckled down and forged a pretty decent career in the game.

Dad had named the house "Wembley Heights" after the goal I had scored for Leicester against Crystal Palace in the playoff final that got them up into the Premiership. That and the winning goal for them in the League Cup final against Middlesbrough the following season had represented the twin peaks of my career thus far, after a journey that had taken me from Weymouth to Bournemouth, Aldershot, Cambridge United, Luton and Birmingham City.

Now I was back in the Championship, then named Division

One, hoping to have one last stab at the Premiership with Pompey. I didn't think it was going to happen, though, under the manager we now had at the club: Tony Pulis.

I had come back to Portsmouth two years earlier after an unhappy time at Wolves under Mark McGhee – and the two of us, it would prove, weren't finished yet either, though I had hoped to be – first on loan and then as a permanent signing. I was sorry I hadn't done better for Wolves and it was one of the few regrets of my career. They were such a great club with such passionate fans, but I never really got going there and McGhee never really fancied me.

In fact, I was so keen to get away that I took a pay cut of around 30 per cent, with my basic money falling from £5,000 a week to £3,500, with £500 appearance money. I did negotiate a contract that was a year longer than the one I had been on, though – as well as securing a testimonial that would be worth at least £100,000 to me. Still, I wasn't going back for the money.

I should have got on with the then manager Alan Ball who, in 2007, would sadly become the second of the 1966 World Cup-winning team to die after Bobby Moore, as we were both passionate football men and had a shared interest in horse racing. Instead, I always felt I had to work that bit harder to make it impossible for him to drop me, as there was something about me he didn't seem to like.

That much had been clear in the 1999/2000 season when before a match at Sheffield United in the December, he summoned me and my fellow striker Guy Whittingham to his hotel room on the Saturday morning. He told Guy that he would be needed the next season, but that I would not and I should find another club. Then he picked me in the 16 for the match and left Guy out. I never did quite fathom that out and Guy was also left scratching his head.

I was on the bench before the game when his coach Kevin Bond asked me what I was going to do now. Was I going to pack up or find another club? I didn't think it was the best question to ask someone as he was trying to prepare for a match. As it happened, Ball's first-choice striker Rory Allen, paired with Lee Bradbury, was injured early on – and Rory was often injured – and I soon got on the field.

Because there had been speculation about their jobs, I felt like saying to Kevin Bond that I would be at the club longer than him and Bally, but I bit my tongue and just kept working. Within a couple of weeks they were gone, after a run of 11 games without a win that included just four draws. Bally had become the first victim of a new owner at the club, a man by the name of Milan Mandaric.

Now everybody knew that Pompey had been in trouble for a while. Before I had rejoined the club, Terry Venables had even bought it for £1 from Jim Gregory because of the debts. Those debts may not have been serious, but they were mounting and the club was unable to compete with the growing sums being spent by other clubs in the second tier as they sought to reach the Premiership. That much was evident when they couldn't pay Leicester £400,000 for me and I went to Wolves, who then let me go to Portsmouth for what was to them a more affordable £175,000.

Mandaric had arrived in the summer of 1999, having paid Venables a sizeable old profit – believed to be around £500,000 – with nobody really knowing much about him. We read that he was originally from Yugoslavia and had made his money in business in America, but to be honest, as players we didn't take much notice. Players don't really want to get involved in that side of the club, unless it has any impact upon them.

Looking back, and with what I know now about football's finances, he got a fantastic deal. Yes, he was taking over a debt and a club losing money. But while people may have known Pompey were in trouble, they should also have known it was a big club with huge potential. If I could have afforded to underwrite the debts, I would have bought the club myself.

At the time, I'm not sure the fans took that much notice either.

This was well before overseas investment and ownership of clubs became an issue and people were not yet familiar with all the wheeling and dealing that is now commonplace on the sports pages. Back then, nobody really cared about the politics and economics of the game.

Besides, there had been so many false dawns at Fratton Park that Mandaric might well have been just another bloke in a boardroom; the fans weren't going to get too excited. They can be the greatest sceptics or the greatest optimists depending on results and those results weren't good. We were bottom of the table so, as far as they were concerned, this new bloke couldn't be up to much, could he?

Milan probably realised that's what everyone thought, too. He had given Bally a bit of money to spend, and Lee Bradbury was among those who had come in, though at £500,000 it was good value for the club as we had sold him for £3.5 million to Manchester City. But we were bottom of the table and although Milan and Bally had only been operating together as chairman and manager for six months, Bally had already been shown the exit door.

Milan got in Bob McNab, the former Arsenal full-back who he had known in America, as caretaker manager. He put me back in the side and the new boss Tony Pulis, who arrived in January, kept me in. I then went on a run of seven goals in seven games, including the hat-trick against Barnsley that would land me in trouble with the FA.

I saw the Barnsley team-sheet, fancied us to win and for me to score and told the Press as much afterwards. I was summoned to a hearing and fined – this happened in the days before a rule change permitted you to bet on your own team. I ended up badly out of pocket, as was usual with my gambling, of which more later. My fine was the winnings of £1,800, except that I had taken some of the lads' money to put on with the bookies and paid them out £900. No way were they going to pay it back. What was I going to do, sue them? Naturally they loved it all.

The funny thing was that I got on fine with Bally after he had left. In fact, I would ask him a few years later to manage an International XI in my testimonial match at Fratton Park, which he readily agreed to do. Our views clashed only when it came to football and whether I should be in his team.

Bally was a bubbly coach and did some good sessions working on team play with the ball. It was just that we did very little work for the times when we didn't have the ball and needed to win it back, which to me is just as important. He thought it was just a case of going out there and playing and he didn't pay enough heed to the balance and shape of a team. There was just not enough strategy and tactics, though you couldn't fault him for his passion and energy.

Perhaps our characters were also too similar. Perhaps he didn't like the fact that he had been unable to recruit any of the strikers he had really wanted the summer I signed and that he had been disappointed to end up with me who, according to the local paper, *The News*, seemed to be the fans' choice and someone who had been recommended to him by Terry Brady, one of the club's directors.

Later on, I would sometimes see Bally out shopping at the Lock's Heath Shopping Centre, near my home and his, in Warsash, and we would chat about the fortunes of Pompey and Southampton, where he also played and managed, and football in general. The night he died, I had seen him at Lock's Heath in the afternoon and had spoken to him for ten minutes, with him telling me about how he was moving up to Newbury way to be near his great mate Mick Channon, the former Saints and England striker and now a racehorse trainer. I also went for a run later that day, and the route took me past his house.

It came as a great shock to get a text from a club official at Portsmouth telling me the next day that he had died. It was a strange feeling. He had been at the club when I was a kid, had released me, and was there again as manager when I came back, being big enough to admit he had made a mistake all those years ago, even if he played me only reluctantly. I was actually a lot sadder than I thought I might be. Part of your past, our past, had gone, both in the Hampshire area and nationally, what with him also playing for Blackpool, Everton and Arsenal, as well as for England.

Like Bally, Pulis never seemed to like me much as a player either. Now there was a lot about him and his regime that was good. His teams were well organised and disciplined with two banks of four in defence and midfield and I did like the fact that he named his team on a Thursday so you could prepare properly on a personal level, as well as collectively as a side by working on set plays and team pattern.

Eight years on, he would bring it all together and get Stoke City up into the Premier League, so fair play to him, but he was fortunate to have a chairman in Peter Coates willing to invest and give him big money for wages and transfers. In return, Pulis produced a big, direct and physically intimidating side. He could do it at Stoke. The problem for him at Pompey was that this big, direct and physically intimidating approach did not square with my game nor that of the players he had inherited.

He was a no-nonsense sort of bloke who had also managed Gillingham and Plymouth Argyle, and he did manage to keep us up that season (1999/2000) as we hauled ourselves up to 15th at one point before eventually finishing in 18th. But I had misgivings about him right from the start.

I remember his first talk to us. It was straight and honest enough, after which he asked if there were any questions or if anyone had anything to say. Michael Panopoulos, an Australian-born midfield player who, having been in and out of the side, had had his own issues with Alan Ball, offered the opinion that it would be nice to be treated better.

I sat there shaking my head and thinking, "Uh-oh," as he said it. Long experience had taught me that it is always best to keep your mouth shut in these situations and wait to see how things develop.

Pulis's assistant David Kemp was quick to respond. He

made the point that they weren't here to treat people better but to get results. It was the sort of response to be expected. After that, the treatment you received depended on whether you were in the team or not. If you weren't, you didn't matter; you barely existed.

I was starting to take more in as a player at this stage of my career and had been for a little while. Management did appeal to me and I had become increasingly thoughtful about how and why managers did things, comparing what I might do in their positions.

In this situation, as a player, albeit one beginning to see a bigger picture, I reckoned that this supposed conventional management wisdom – about ignoring players who were injured or suspended because you needed to focus on those who were available to do a job for you – was outdated. One day you were going to need these suspended and injured players. I decided that if or when I became a manager, I would treat every squad member, regardless of their status, with respect.

Mind you, I did have some sympathy with Pulis over Kevin Harper. Kevin was once asked to play wing-back but refused and Pulis sent him from the training ground, with good reason, in my view. Managers may make mistakes over selection, tactics and formations, and you hope they see the error of their ways – if not you may have to move on – but you can't have players not co-operating like that.

Kevin was never my type of pro, though he did have fantastic powers of being able to predict the future. I remember him once saying that he would be getting three weeks off at Christmas and, sure enough, he had a groin strain that meant he was out. With that kind of foresight, I just wish he had shared some racing tips or football score forecasts with me.

That first day, Kemp marched out onto the training ground and started lining up cones in the corners of the pitch as we watched and wondered what he was doing. We soon found out. We were instructed to boot the ball into those coned areas and chase, the theory being that you turn defences, put them under pressure and force corners and throw-ins in their territory, then make something happen from the set-piece. It was just the same as Stoke would be doing nearly ten years later, although they would be doing so with better players.

If you did something wrong in training, Pulis would have you on your stomach doing press-ups. People resented it. Most of us were seasoned professionals and didn't need this kind of childish coaching. He had a reputation for having a temper on him and he did lose it once or twice, though there is nothing wrong with that if it is appropriate. It didn't bother me too much. If you are worried in football about a bit of shouting you should get out.

Like most players, I didn't mind being told what to do if I considered it was the right thing for the cause. If I believe in a manager I will run through brick walls for him. But I didn't believe in Pulis, his methods or his tactics. It was like the good old, bad old days at Cambridge United under John Beck and to me it was the sign of a limited manager.

The approach was basic. Defenders, for example, were urged to bypass the midfield and put the ball into the channels for strikers to chase and force corners, free-kicks and throw-ins, which could then be launched into the penalty box. It was all about second-phase possession and certainly not about building from the back, pulling sides around, using movement and width, as I liked, to create openings. In my view, you would be too predictable with the Pulis method and sides would find it simple to deal with once they had scouted you. The better the opponent and the higher up you went, the easier they would find it.

The only light relief came in the shape of a great lad called Lindsay Parsons, who we all thought was one of Pulis's assistants, despite the fact that the only thing he seemed to do was his party piece after training. It consisted of entertaining us by doing 100 press-ups on his knuckles. We thought he had a great life if this was the only thing he did. After six months, we discovered he was actually the chief scout, and he would follow Pulis around, going on to Stoke with him later.

Nobody really liked playing the Pulis way and the mood among the lads and the fans in pre-season was uninspiring. The jury was still out on him. It should have been buoyant, mind, since the owner was trying to signal his intent to the rest of the league. Milan had provided Pulis with more than £5 million to spend on players that summer, but there was no excitement as far as we were concerned, because we knew the style of play wouldn't be changing.

In came Lee Mills, who had scored only five goals for Bradford City the previous season, but who had still cost £1.2 million, and Shaun Derry, who arrived from Crystal Palace for £750,000. He may have been a player who liked to pass the ball by linking the play in midfield, but Shaun also had a tough approach to his game, which made him a Pulis player.

Fortunately, Shaun was not quite so tough off the field. I remember a group of us going out on the town after a game against Forest in Nottingham – which was Shaun's hometown – and he was delighted when he came across a bloke he reckoned had been his best mate at school. That changed to being mortified when the bloke said that he had never really liked Shaun and wanted to knock him out. So mortified, that thankfully it never occurred to him to hit the lad first.

Anyway, big Darren Moore also arrived from Bradford City for another £700,000 and goalkeeper Russell Hoult from Derby for £500,000. Nigel Quashie also cost £400,000 and Justin Edinburgh £250,000. On top of the spending, Pulis was also handing out some big contracts.

For all that, we knew the football would be boring and dour. We would surely not be in any relegation trouble this season with those sorts of players, or we shouldn't be if they were used properly, but from a playing perspective there was not much prospect of it being an enjoyable campaign.

I had damaged the anterior cruciate ligament in my knee

during the match against Charlton Athletic towards the end of the previous season, when I was again Pompey's Player of the Year for the second year in a row, even though Bally had left me out of the team for chunks of it.

It was a rare serious injury and happened as I went to trap the ball. As I put my foot down, a defender came in at the side of me and everything collapsed. My kneecap was flopping around; there was nothing holding it in place. At first there was just a numb feeling, even when I got up. When I tried to run, that was it, agony … and an early end to the season.

I spent the first six weeks of the close season on my back in bed or on a sofa watching television and waiting for the knee to heal. After that, it was rehab all summer. I have always been self-motivated when it comes to fitness and have never needed a pre-season, as I run every day in the summer anyway, but I stepped it up and really worked hard for three or four hours a day with the physio Jonathan Trigg at Fratton Park every day, doing weights and some steady running.

I also did pre-season to strengthen the knee, but though I love running and physical work, I can't say it was an experience I enjoyed. Pulis came up with a scheme where he wanted us to be able to run a marathon in a week. So it was running for one hour on the first day, then upping it by 15 minutes every day. It was boring – and that coming from someone who likes running – and often chaotic. I don't think the club's medical team were that happy, either, as we were doing too much work pounding on roads and gravel tracks.

We were, actually, in more immediate danger than that. Pre-season took place in the New Forest – near Pulis's home, so I think he could go in for a cup of tea while we were out – with us running in pairs 100 yards apart. But everyone got so strung out that people would get lost. Probably deliberately in Ceri Hughes's case, as he hated all the running – with Ceri, Pulis would have had time for a four-course meal. At one point, we found ourselves running alongside the dual carriageway on the A31 and a caravan had to swerve to avoid us. It caused a crash, fortunately not too serious, and we were quick to get out of there.

Not 100 per cent match fit, though still capable of contributing, I was not picked for the opening game away at Sheffield United, with Lee Mills and Lee Bradbury paired up front. At the time, I was a bit annoyed, but knew they would need me soon, especially as we lost 2-0.

Looking back, I can understand now why Pulis played them together, because they were a strong, powerful pair and that was his style and a sign of how he wanted the team to play. Back then, though, I had trouble grasping how the best striker in the club was being left out.

I was on the bench for the second match, at home to Grimsby Town, which was quite probably the worst game I had ever seen. As I sat there watching, I kept thinking someone must have been injured because the ball was going out of play that often. Surely the players had to be kicking it out deliberately, didn't they?

We scrambled a point with Lee Bradbury's late equaliser, then recorded another 1-1 draw at Gillingham in our next game. Two points from the opening three games. It was not looking good, either in the literal or artistic sense.

Now fully fit again, I was given my first start on the August Bank Holiday Monday and I was glad for it. The match was against Wolves at Fratton. I was really up for the game against Mark McGhee's team, as you might imagine. I wanted to show him what he had let go, and the Wolves fans what I could do. And, of course, I wanted to give the Pompey fans three points because we were struggling.

I was on the scoresheet within two minutes when a corner came in that was flicked on and I got ahead of Kevin Muscat to turn the ball home. Next, with half an hour gone, I scored with a deflected header. Then, two minutes later, barely believably, we were awarded a penalty and I converted it to complete a hat-trick with the game just one third of the way through. I went nuts and so did Fratton.

Though there was an inevitable anti-climax after that, and a Wolves revival, we held on to record our first win by 3-1, with the fans giving me a standing ovation. It was a point proven all round, both to Pulis and McGhee, not that either of them said anything to me. Pulis was not one for praising individuals. In fact, praise was usually in short supply for the team as a whole.

It was one of those rousing days you remember all your career, but a rare memorable moment under Pulis – the highest he took us to in the league was tenth. Despite my performance that day, I still felt he was always looking to drop me. It didn't take long. We lost to Preston and Watford and I have to admit I was not on top of my game, although I felt I had played OK against Watford. A few who had played as badly as me kept their places, but Pulis decided to pair Bradbury with Mills again up front.

Mills was having a nightmare settling in, though, and the partnership did not flourish. It was frustrating sitting on the bench watching the side slip to defeat at Bolton and at home to West Bromwich Albion. It was baffling, too. I had been top scorer for Pulis with 14 goals the previous season though my season with Pompey had only started in mid-October after having had another knee ligament injury. Not that I let it get in the way in the September when I was asked to be the starter at the Great South Run. After doing that, I fancied running it, so jumped off the stage and completed the ten miles in 57 minutes. The club's medical people were not best pleased.

Anyway, I wasn't too disturbed by Pulis leaving me out. By now I was an experienced enough professional to bide my time, knowing that he would have to play me sooner rather than later because I had confidence in my ability over his preferred partnership up front.

He duly threw me back in at the end of September when we were 17th in the table. It was out of desperation, I think, because he was really struggling and Milan Mandaric was putting the pressure on him. The chairman had gone to the Portsmouth local evening paper, *The News*, and warned Pulis that he had two games to show improvement.

I scored the goal at Burnley that rescued a point, and gave him a stay of execution, and it meant I kept my place for the trip to Stockport the following week, though I didn't make it through the 90 minutes; subbed in a 1-1 draw that saw us end up 17th again.

It was yet another grim performance. We were difficult to beat but were never going to win many matches. It was a silent, sullen coach home that night. The mood was subdued not only because we were struggling but also because of the dull football we were playing. Nobody was getting any pleasure from it. It was hard enough at Cambridge United when we were winning with these methods; when you're not, it just reinforces the negativity.

The results, but probably more importantly the performances, were just not good enough for Milan, whose trigger finger was getting twitchy again. The word was going round that Pulis could get the bullet and though it probably came as little surprise when Milan fired the gun, I certainly wasn't expecting it to be the starting pistol for my managerial career.

1.2 Managing Milan

The first call the next morning after the game at Stockport was from a reporter from *The News*, Mark Storey. He was a bloke I could trust and who had his finger on the pulse of the club. Tony Pulis had been put on "gardening leave", he informed me, and Mark wanted a reaction from me.

Pulis was apparently being given four months off to pursue a court case against a previous club, Gillingham, but we all knew what it meant in reality. Football was still getting to know Milan Mandaric – who would go on to put so many managers on gardening leave for so long that they could all have done horticultural degrees – but we all knew this was a sacking.

I wasn't that surprised, not only because of the results but because of the style of football we had been playing for the ten months he had been in charge. And I wasn't that unhappy, I have to say. I didn't dislike Pulis as a person, it was just that I wasn't enjoying my football and nobody else around the club seemed to be enjoying theirs. That wasn't right. I had always loved my football and so should everyone in it.

I couldn't really say all that to Mark. Let's not be naïve here. Some things in football you can't say in public, because it's just not appropriate at that time when a situation is raw, even though you might be able to later. I never lie, though. For public consumption, I just said that I was sorry it had come to this and that was true.

The second call came from a local television presenter. Fred Dinenage wasn't phoning me for a comment on the manager's departure, though. He was phoning me in his capacity as a director of Portsmouth Football Club and he did have a couple of questions for me. Did I reckon I could do the job and did I fancy it?

It took me a few seconds to gather my thoughts. Fred was an affable guy, who older readers may recall was a presenter on a children's show in the 1970s called *How?*. It involved the presenters showing you how and why things worked, like combustion engines or gliders staying in the air, or Tony Pulis's tactics. Actually, they didn't work. Anyway, I could never quite think of Fred without a picture in my head of him sitting there doing the show's trademark gesture of raising the right hand, like a native American greeting you, and saying "How".

It was clear that Milan Mandaric had got him to call me and sound me out before fixing up a meeting. I answered yes to both his questions. I knew I wanted to be a manager and had every confidence I could do it.

I have always believed that I am spot on tactically and felt that I could assemble a balanced team playing the game in the right way that would be entertaining and effective. I am not stupid, though. Given the position the team was in, I was concerned that if I failed, my managerial career could be over before it had started. No matter the circumstances, other potential employers were just going to see it as an unhappy interlude and proof that I couldn't cut it.

In addition, I still had a lot of football left in me and I didn't want to pack up just yet to become a manager. By then I wasn't your normal 34-year-old player looking to squeeze the last drop out of his career. I was fanatically fit and knew I could play till I was 40, but I also knew it was tough mixing playing with managing and there have been few successful examples down the years. I was close to the players and that also presented problems. For now I would have to keep playing because I was needed, but it was a situation I would have to rethink at the end of the season.

But how many times are you going to be offered the chance to manage your hometown team? And, let's face it, you're hardly going to get the job if the club and the team are in a good state, are you? You're there because it's in a mess. On top of all that, you can't turn something down just because you fear failure. That's a natural human feeling, but it mustn't stop you from doing things or taking risks. Besides, I backed myself to get it right.

And so when I met with Milan and Fred at the Solent Hotel near Fareham for dinner to talk things over the next day, I knew in my heart that I would take the job. I preferred, though, to talk about it in principle. I didn't want to look or sound too keen, which would make me a soft touch and could potentially weaken my position when I started. I also wanted Milan to be clear he was dealing with someone of substance, rather than just some figure he might have heard stories about.

It turned into a conversation between me and Milan, with Fred just there for company, I think, as he chipped in with the odd remark. Fred, I'm sure, was useful to have in the club and on the board for Milan, because he was a local personality and celebrity, with his big glasses and permanent tan. That alone probably made Milan feel comfortable and on familiar territory. When the owner was over from Florida, as he was now to sort all this out, Fred used to drive him around. In return, Fred got to fulfil his ambition of being a director of his football club and enjoying all the kudos and hospitality that went with it.

Milan, as has emerged over the last few years – with his profile in the game rising due to his hiring and firing of managers and his takeover of Leicester City – has an altogether more forceful, controlling personality. He is also a very emotional guy who wears his heart on his sleeve. I knew he wanted people who have got a bit about them running his club and that he likes characters, because he is one himself. I thought I fitted the bill.

After all the gloom around the place over the last few months, I think he also wanted someone who could bring back the feel-good factor. As Player of the Year for the past two seasons, and therefore popular with the fans, he knew that I would be a sound choice for him and that he would not get any stick off supporters.

I had always got on well enough with Milan on the few occasions our paths had crossed and knew he liked me as a player.

The one positive about taking on the manager's position was that the expectation that had been so high at the club in pre-season – with all the money that had been spent – had now disappeared. Milan conceded that reaching the playoffs with the squad we now had and the form we were in was unrealistic. Relegation was more likely but I knew we were too good to go down. It was more a question of rebuilding – both the squad and morale – and getting the club going in the right direction again, ready for a push the following season.

At this stage of proceedings, rather than talk about the money, I wanted to talk about being given time to do the job properly, to turn this around, about the staff I wanted, as David Kemp had also left the club with Pulis. I wanted to talk about playing styles and about which players I wanted to get in. When I looked at our squad, it was so unbalanced, with four right-backs, seven centre-backs and one left-back; and with plenty of left-wingers, but no right-wingers.

We talked for around three hours and I could have gone on all night. I was so passionate about doing the job and taking charge of the team I had always supported. I grew more excited and more animated about taking on the challenge and was still buzzing when I got home later, so much so that I was unable to sleep.

We ended on good terms, with a plan and a purpose. I was a bit concerned about being in a caretaker role, given that Milan had fired two managers in 16 months, but I could see why he had done it and, besides, no one knew for sure yet just how knee-jerk his decisions when it came to managers could be.

And he certainly gave me the impression that this was to be a long-term appointment. He told me to take my time and evaluate the club. He told me that he would be supportive. We would talk about my contract, he added, in the next day or two. I was more interested in the football, but I also knew that it would suit me to wait a little while to talk figures. By the end of the night, I had agreed to do it, making it look as though he had talked me into it. People in authority always like to think things are their idea, I have found.

Milan was at our Eastleigh training ground the next day when I first met with the players. I told them that Guy Whittingham, another former striker at the club and a coach I respected, was going to be my assistant. Guy had fallen out of favour under Pulis and was out on loan at Oxford United as his playing career wound down, but I called him back. He had always been interested in the coaching side of the game and had done his qualifications.

He was a man I trusted and respected, someone who was very organised, even meticulous in his attention to detail. He liked all the stuff about cones and bibs; making sure the team bus was on time and players' meals sorted. I liked to think about teams, patterns and shapes and preferred to leave all that stuff to someone else. Guy was also a nice bloke, whereas I have an edge to me, so thought he would be a good foil for me on the bad-cop, good-cop principle of managers and their assistants. He would go on to become a regional coach for the Professional Footballers' Association, facilitating courses for coaches, so my judgement must have been pretty good.

I was also promoting Neil McNab, the former Spurs and Manchester City midfield player, from reserve-team coach to the first team and did a deal with Andy Awford to come off the playing staff and become chief scout, as Lindsay Parsons had also left the club with Pulis.

I wanted to be called gaffer, I said, and I heard a snigger from the back of the room. It came from Ceri Hughes, but it was a nervous laugh rather than anything disrespectful. That was Ceri.

29

At least he would do it in front of you, rather than behind your back. He was an honest lad, who would later go through the pain barrier for me when he probably wouldn't have done for other managers.

But it did show the first problem I faced. I had been out on the town with some of these lads on Saturday nights. They had known me for a long time and we had all been through some, shall we say, adventures.

There was one senior player, for example, who I had better not name. I was out once for a walk around Manchester with him one afternoon ahead of a game at Bury that evening when we meandered down a back street and came across a brothel. He wanted to go in. I was less happy with the idea, but he persuaded me just to go with him and I sat in the reception area and waited for him. I was reading a magazine about home improvements – believe it or not, but it's true – when he came out sweating. I wished sometimes he'd worked up a lather like that when playing. He then wondered if we should ask a couple of the girls out for a drink after the match, because he had performed so well and thought the one he had been with had taken to him. I didn't think it would be wise, I told him.

Now I was trying to put distance between me and the players, while still being a player myself. That is one of the many problems of player-management and the initial one that had to be overcome. As for advantages to the role, there are none. The only possible benefit could be that I could do all the physical work as well if not better than them, so at least they would respect that. No one could complain I didn't understand how hard their lot was.

Even at this early stage I knew that in all probability my new position would mean I would have to give up my playing career at the end of the season to do the job with the single-mindedness it required. At that time, though, I thought the team needed me. I would get us to safety and then I would pack up to concentrate in the summer on making the changes necessary, including getting in a new striker.

I told the squad I understood what had been going on at the club, that nobody was having any fun. Consequently we were underperforming and underachieving. I wanted, I said, to put the enjoyment back into training and playing so that they all looked forward to coming in. That way, I believed, we would get the best out of ourselves.

Though there were some I wanted out and some new faces I wanted to bring in, which would have to wait until the summer, I knew I didn't have a bad squad of players and thought I could get so much more out of them if they were just given more freedom to play.

I sensed the majority were on my side, but didn't take it for granted. I knew it would be difficult to straddle the us-and-them mentality of management and playing staff and that some of the players would have trouble with my appointment. Some wouldn't consider me ready, some might be jealous or sceptical, some would worry that I might hold things I knew about them as a fellow player against them. Like that incident with the knocking shop.

I wouldn't, because although I am very big on proper preparation, I also believe in players being responsible for their own professionalism. And if they are doing it on the pitch on a Saturday, then you give them the latitude as men to live their lives as they choose, as long as none of it reflects badly on the club or lets the rest of the squad down.

In a way, it was only right that there was an element of suspicion, because I had to prove to them I could do the job. They know your weaknesses as much as your strengths. They have shared intimate moments with you that they wouldn't have done had you been the manager. And now I was. It helped a lot that I had been the best player at the club for the past 18 months, I reckoned, and one they had looked to on the field. Now it would be off the field as well.

I had a choice really. I could either stay pals with them and try to be popular or I could do the job properly and look to act with

31

authority, whether they liked it or not. Basically, they either accepted me and the situation or they walked.

I met with Milan again to talk numbers. I knew I was in a strong position now. I had only rarely needed agents, and only then to sound out clubs for me, and had no need of one now. I knew how to draw up a contract. And I knew I wanted a new player's contract, not a manager's. A player's deal is legally binding, thanks to the work of the Professional Footballers' Association, and has to be paid up in full unless the player and the club want to come to a mutually beneficial arrangement to facilitate his quick and easy departure. A manager's contract, on the other hand, can be cancelled and can then be liable to negotiation that can take months, sometimes even years, to be resolved after being sacked.

Milan agreed to the player's contract, and also to upping my money to around £5,000 a week. He was in no mood to haggle and just wanted it done. I think he is one of these chairmen who marry in haste and repent at leisure.

I also wanted appearance money if I was not playing, which I felt I should be entitled to as manager. Managers should share in the team's success; after all, they are responsible for it. In fact, I wanted everyone involved with the squad on a bonus – reserve- and youth-team coaches, kitman, the lot. They play a part in any success and deserve to be recognised, too. Not the same bonus as players get, but on, say, 33 per cent of it. It helps morale if a player sees contented faces around the dressing room rather than resentful, moaning minnies. Milan went away to get my contract drawn up. I was in no rush. My priority was sorting the team out.

My first game was at home to Sheffield Wednesday and, naturally, I picked myself. Actually, I had to, with Lee Mills having picked up an injury at Burnley that would keep him out for five months.

He had come to Fratton Park for big money and the expectation on him from both the club and the fans was high. It was expectation he struggled to handle, though had he been available to me, I would probably have picked him over Lee Bradbury as Mills might have suited my style and I also wanted to see if I could get the best out of him. He was a bit one-dimensional. He liked the ball to feet, rather than having to chase it, but it suited me, as I enjoyed working and moving.

I was also to be without the injured Gary O'Neil, who I rated as a terrific player for the club, and who went on to prove himself a Premiership player. A few years later, I was surprised when Harry Redknapp let him go to Middlesbrough.

We got an amazing reception that day against Wednesday. If there were elements in the crowd or within the club who resented this local boy getting the job, they were outnumbered many times over. At least 99.9 per cent of people seemed to be on my side, as they always were at Fratton.

The other 0.1 per cent? They are those two-faced fans and club employees you get in football, and who I would come to see more of as I moved from playing to working in management and the media.

There was, for example, a steward in the car park who was always all over me to get things signed, telling me how pleased he was that a local boy had got the job, and a club receptionist who was always nice to my face. A mate of mine sat near them in the stand and overheard them slagging me off, saying that I wouldn't be up to the job. It was nasty stuff, he reckoned. When I got back to the car park, my mate had a go at him while I just shook my head at the hypocrisy of the bloke. I did go in to speak to the receptionist and her husband, though, saying it wasn't on for a club employee to be slagging off the manager in public.

We won the game 2-1, to snap a streak of four without a win, with me scoring what proved to be the winning goal. After Thomas Thogersen had put us ahead at half-time, I poached a second three minutes after the break, Darren Moore heading a corner back across goal and me flicking it home. Wednesday pulled one back midway through the half, but we clung on in a nervy ending. Fratton was euphoric.

From a crowd of fewer than 12,000 at our previous home game against West Bromwich Albion, the last under Pulis, we pulled in 13,376. That would turn into 14,621 for the midweek game against Crewe Alexandra as the buzz, pleasingly, came back to the place. Those famous old chimes that the fans sing – "Play up Pompey, Pompey play up" – were ringing out again.

I scored again as we also beat Crewe 2-1– my late penalty being the winner – and as we overcame Crystal Palace 3-2 within the week. Happy days were here again. Nine points in eight days took us from 17th to the dizzy heights of tenth, which we had also briefly achieved under Pulis. I was tempted to send the kitman down to the shops to buy a consignment of handkerchiefs for all the nosebleeds at the club.

The win at Palace had been particularly satisfying, and amazing, as we fought back from 2-0 down, unheard of at that time for a Portsmouth side, especially away from home.

We took 5,000 fans to Selhurst Park for a fixture that has always meant a lot to Pompey. With there not being too many other League clubs around, the trip up the A3 and just a couple of junctions round the M25 to Croydon made it almost a local derby. The fans needed any bit of excitement they could get in those days with the club in the doldrums and the prospect of a match against Southampton, then doing well in the Premiership, seeming a distant proposition.

We let them down in the first half by conceding two goals in four minutes just before half-time, but I grabbed a goal right on the interval to put us back in it, when the keeper dropped the ball and it hit my ear, nose and throat before bobbling into the net.

At the break, I changed the system to go with three at the back and to get Thomas Thogersen breaking more from midfield. He then popped up with an equaliser – it was his third goal in three games – and Michael Panopoulos grabbed a winner. Strange pair, those two. Michael, for example, was a good player, an out-and-out winger but inconsistent and still learning the game fully. The problem with him was that he was fine if he was playing well, but if he wasn't, you had to work out a way of helping him to contribute more to the team. Sometimes, that is the distinction between good and average pros. If you're not playing well, you still have to make sure you are giving something, chasing and tackling, rather than just disappearing.

Expectations among the players had been raised, but given the underlying condition of the club it seemed to me it was unlikely they were going to be fulfilled. In Thomas Thogersen's case, I felt he was a very laid-back character. In fact, I think he might have ended up on Salisbury Plain at Stonehenge for the summer solstice, because he was a bit of a hippy who had various piercings around his body. As for the club, I knew that these results, achieved due to the impetus of a new manager, were unlikely to be sustained. You don't solve the problems of a club in a week.

That was the reason why I wasn't getting carried away and, to be fair, I don't think the fans did either. They knew the club was still evolving and that any thoughts of the playoffs were fanciful. Also, with injuries starting to intrude, it was getting hard putting together a fit team. Milan was also cool about things when we had dinner after the Palace game. He was never one to get too elated by winning, though did get down when we had lost.

And, having put Tony Pulis on that gardening leave, he could still find a cloud for every silver lining. "You'll have to be careful about winning all these games," he told me. "I'm having to pay the bonuses to Tony Pulis. He didn't get any when he was manager. Now he's getting them when he's not in the job."

At least the game had shown that there was ability and character in the squad, which was something Pulis had never tapped in to. A year or so later, when I was playing a game at West Bromwich Albion, their manager, Gary Megson, clearly a mate of Pulis's, would accuse me of getting him the sack and of agitating behind the scenes as senior pro.

Such an allegation saddened me and ignored two things: the first, that I was playing well whenever Pulis picked me and even scored that goal at Burnley to save his skin the week before he did get the sack; and, second, he engineered his own downfall, on and off the pitch.

As well as the poor tactics and results, Pulis was not popular with the lads over club fines. The biggest one concerned Aaron Flahavan, the goalkeeper who would be so sadly killed in a car crash the following year. Poor Aaron had got involved in a fight in TGI Friday and was fined £5,000. Michael Panopoulos was also fined £3,200 – two weeks' money – for some other misdemeanour.

On top of that, there was financial punishment for Ceri Hughes, who had been in a scrap with Shaun Derry, which left the former with a black eye and the latter – acting out of character – with a big nose. The easily offended Ceri was involved in another fracas at TGI's – it must have felt like Madison Square Garden to him.

The money went towards a lads' day out at the Cheltenham Festival (the horse-racing one, not the book festival), but it didn't seem to stretch as far as we hoped it would.

When I became manager, I also got to see the contracts everyone was on and they drove a coach and horses through the wage structure that I understood was in operation at the club. Sometimes you don't mind if great players are being paid a lot more than the rest of you, because they are doing it for the club and raising your profile and playing level, but at Pompey some very ordinary players were getting way over the odds for their contribution when others, who had been at the club for a while, were being underpaid.

With an unbalanced squad, and one that was vulnerable to any injury, it was inevitable we would falter after the three initial wins. A 0-0 draw away to Norwich was decent enough, as was a 1-1 draw in front of more than 15,000 fans at home to Birmingham City, who were then third in the table.

The game was notable, though, for another injury, one that stripped me of one more quality, experienced player – Justin

Edinburgh, the former Tottenham Hotspur left-back and the only real one we had at the club. He would try and return for a couple of games the following month, but the injury signalled the end of his career. Players must have thought I was the grim reaper.

Efforts to get another left-back in on loan failed, so I had to pick an overweight Andy Awford – not that he had ever been underweight – for our next match at Queens Park Rangers, which we drew again. Another draw at home to Blackburn Rovers, who were flying at the time and would go on to gain automatic promotion to the Premiership, made it seven games unbeaten and took us to a mid-table position. Then, in mid-November, we went to Fulham.

At that time, they were walking to the title. Under Mohamed Al Fayed's ownership and Kevin Keegan's management – before he took the England job – the club had invested big time and had surged through the divisions. Now, with French legend Jean Tigana as manager and Louis Saha leading the attack, they were streets ahead of anyone else in the division in terms of both budget and quality.

I had to go with a 3-5-2 – having recalled our full back Scott Hiley, who had been out of favour under Pulis, from a loan spell, to take his place in defence alongside Linvoy Primus and Darren Moore. We got battered early on, though, and fell behind to a goal by Barry Hayles.

But gradually we settled and played our football to reduce the 14,000 Fulham fans to near silence and stoke the optimism of our 5,000 travelling supporters. We grabbed a deserved equaliser just before half-time, when Ceri Hughes put in a low cross and I slid in at the near post to clip the ball over their goalkeeper Maik Taylor with a decent finish.

In the second half, Fulham were growing frustrated and started to hoist the ball long. In contrast, we were knocking the ball about well. Then it all turned. Linvoy Primus got himself sent off for hauling back a Fulham player, then Ceri Hughes was also dismissed, for a second bookable offence, and we were down to nine men.

Amid it all, Hayles scored again and Lee Clark added another to send us to a 3-1 defeat. It all got a bit out of hand when one of our outraged fans threw a snooker ball and it just missed a linesman, and then some trouble flared in the stands. Mind you, one of my Pompey mates, who I had got a ticket for, was hit by a missile. Someone above him in the stand dropped a steak and kidney pie on his head. He still had the crust in his hair when I met up with him later.

It was an undeserved defeat that resulted from the two red cards, but it was also understandable when you consider the state of the squad and its injuries, with players like Mills, Edinburgh and O'Neil out of the picture. Now we would be without Linvoy and Ceri through suspension. The one positive was that we had gone to the best side in the division and had outplayed them for long periods.

Reasons can be seen as excuses in this results-driven game, though. While scorelines remain, details are all too quickly forgotten. It can be unforgiving, no matter the validity of your protests.

My first defeat as a manager – eight games into my stint – was inevitable and it was no disgrace that it came against Fulham. In hindsight, though, that day would signal a turning point for me.

1.3 Fretting at Fratton

Players are selfish beasts. In many ways they have to be. They need to focus on themselves, their fitness and preparation, their game and their form, to make sure they are going to do themselves justice and be of the most benefit to the team. It may be a team game, but it is a team game played by individuals.

It is not really until later in your career that you start to think about anything wider than the next match, about training regimes, about which players work well together and why, or about what shape and formation best suits the group you are in. Those sorts of things come with experience.

For me, life had been changing anyway, mainly due to the natural ageing process. Being thrust into the highly responsible and intense position of manager of a Division One football club suddenly accelerated things. When you are a player, you can indulge your personality, as I had done in acquiring that reputation of mine as a "character". Now I could not be so single-minded – which may be a better description of a player than selfish – as I now had a whole squad of players to think about.

I had always been an inquisitive footballer, with an eye on how clubs function, on and off the field, but that interest had definitely been secondary to my own performances, which is as it should be. Now, though, I really did feel a different character. I felt ready for responsibility. Also, at that time I didn't have many opportunities to get into any mischief, or lose any money on the horses, since I was giving every waking hour I had to the club.

That's not to say it was all entirely a grind without its fun moments or that I couldn't see the funny side, or have a laugh about things. A trip to Belgium certainly provided some, um, entertainment.

Now, I hadn't been seeing too much of Milan as he was spending a lot of his time on business in Florida. Occasionally he would come over and stay at his flat at Port Solent, a nice little development of waterside properties by the M27 just outside of Portsmouth, and we would go out for dinner, usually to the Solent Hotel, talking things over.

He knew about the injuries and was supportive, even coming up with recommendations for players to sign now and then, possibly to get agents off his back. Having been in Belgian football for a while as an owner there, Milan put us in touch with an agent who had, he said, a decent left-back on his books.

And so Andy Awford and I went out on the Eurostar to Bruges, sharing a room to save money, what with some of the cost-cutting going on at the club. It's a good job it was twin beds, though, given Andy's size. There would have been no room for me in a double. The next morning, the agent arrived at the hotel and drove us to the game out in the wilds somewhere.

We knew after about ten minutes. This lad, Dirk Van Oekelen he was called, was probably the worst player I had ever seen. Andy and I just looked at each other and shook our heads. Out of courtesy, we stayed till half-time, but we had been wasting our time. I took a video of the player away and came across it a couple of years later when I was ferreting around looking for a film to watch. I taped an episode of *Miss Marple* over it and would have played her ahead of him.

In reality, I had little scope to bring people in, though I did get the former flying Manchester United winger Lee Sharpe on loan for a month, and he did all right for me. Instead I recalled people like Jason Crowe and Scott Hiley, who Pulis had let go out on loan and they also came back to do decent jobs for me.

The club had overspent under Pulis and was now looking to save money, since we wouldn't be challenging for promotion and gates, though they had improved, were not justifying some of the sums involved. We were, for example, paying £12,000 a week for the French defender Bernard Lambourde, who was not good enough and who would go on to languish in Chelsea's reserves.

I was getting to see more closely and starting to understand the politics and economics of the game better. And I was starting to experience things I had not thought about before – and was having to learn some things pretty quickly.

All of a sudden, for example, I had the club's former managing director David Deacon coming to me asking if I could help him get his job back. He was now just an advisor to the club, having been stripped of his powers, and wanted to be more involved, but I couldn't afford to get sidetracked into that.

As David's replacement, Milan had brought in a guy from Leicester City called Barry Pierrepoint, who I knew from my days there. He and Martin O'Neill, manager then, had not got on and Pierrepoint had tried to put together a consortium to take over the club. It hadn't worked and he had left. The whole episode had cemented Martin's position, as it should have done with all the success he brought on the field.

He is a great manager, Martin. Clever in managing men and squads, a huge ability to put square pegs in square holes, and a shrewd judge of a player. He assembled sides simply, putting them in straightforward formations, so that everyone knew their jobs. Whenever he bought a player, it was for a specific reason and he would just ask the player to do what he was good at, in a position he was happy playing in.

Quite simply, Martin did everything right and treated you properly, creating an environment in which you were comfortable and could flourish. Whether you were on £3,000 a week or £30,000, you would give your all for him, wanting to do well for him because he was doing right by you. It didn't surprise me that he went on to do good things with both Celtic and Aston Villa.

As Martin's experiences proved – and as I was quickly coming to see now that I was a manager – if you get results everything else melts into insignificance. It meant that you had to consider the alternative, mind. Bad results mean that even trivial things around a club can get treated with a non-proportional importance. But that is for later. After that seven-game unbeaten start, I still had some credit in the bank.

Given that I had admired Martin O'Neill, I was not particularly close to Pierrepoint and probably didn't give him a fair chance, but then I dealt mainly with Milan anyway. And Pierrepoint did not survive long with Martin Bishop, from the club's sponsors, a firm of printers, taking over. Bishop was now making cutbacks around the club, on everything from bread, milk, papers and water, to the flowers around the reception area. In that context, it seemed strange that we could spend £500 on a fool's errand to Belgium. But that is what football clubs can be like. They can penny-pinch on certain things, but be extravagant about others.

I didn't mind being asked to cut the wage bill, because I was happy to ship out some of the dead wood and was not fussed about spending big money either, just as long as I could get a few loan signings into the club to plug the gaps. It was all part of learning the trade of being a manager. And still Milan was talking about the longer term, so I didn't want to rush into anything, I preferred to hold back in reserve any money I was going to be given ready for the summer, when I could do proper business rather than panic-buy.

The season was effectively finished anyway. We weren't going up or down, not good enough for the playoffs but too good for relegation. And what with all the training and playing, as well as often sitting in my office all afternoon with Guy Whittingham talking and planning training sessions and our strategy on and off the field, I only had the odd chance to go and scout players. I mostly left that to Andy Awford.

Alan Ball had given Andy a too long and too expensive playing contract. I liked Andy a lot, but he was no longer going to do a job for us and when he was not playing, he was prone to putting on weight. In fact, he had an arse like Baloo the bear in *The Jungle Book* and could have done with a spell in what I call doughnut rehab. He had three years left on his contract, worth around £250,000 to him, but I persuaded him to become chief scout and take £40,000 a year. I thought that was good business for the club and fair to him. We would save money and he would get a job beyond his playing days.

I also got money in for Russell Hoult, our goalkeeper. He had made a series of errors in recent games and I had told him I was replacing him with Aaron Flahavan. I asked Russell to go on the bench, but he wouldn't have it and refused to be a substitute. I talked it over with Milan and he agreed that we should get rid of him. Neither of us wanted that kind of attitude around the club.

In these situations you fax every Premiership and First Division club to let them know of the player's availability and see who bites. West Bromwich Albion did and offered £300,000 for him – with me dealing with their former striking legend Tony Brown, who was now working for them in an administrative capacity, making the offer. But I held out. I knew the market and knew I could negotiate well, as my contract dealings had showed. Eventually we got £500,000 as a down payment, rising to £700,000 if Albion got promoted, which they finally did with him in goal.

Another reason I didn't want to waste money was that I had been back at the club for more than a year and had seen so many poor players come and go who had been no better than the ones we had. I had identified some targets, like Steve Guppy, a team-mate at Leicester who had a great left foot, and John Aloisi, who had previously been a hero at Pompey with his goal-scoring exploits and who was now playing in Spain with Osasuna. He might even have been my replacement.

John was a class act who came alive in the box and who would score pots of goals for us, while Steve had the sort of left foot that would create chances, as he would show in teaming up with Martin O'Neill again at Celtic. It was a question of being patient, though. These were players who would improve us and who were worth waiting for.

In hindsight, I suppose I should have made more of an effort to persuade the chairman to part with more money around this time – it being in the era before the introduction of the transfer window – as injuries were really biting. That, coupled with the imbalance of the squad I had inherited, meant we began to struggle.

My concerns increased when we lost 1-0 at Barnsley the week after the Fulham game, but worse than the result was the loss of our defensive rock Linvoy Primus – another who would go on to do well in the Premiership – to a long-term injury. That really was a crippling blow.

Things got so bad that I had to put Guy Whittingham on the bench against Wimbledon on Boxing Day. Fortunately, we got away with a 1-1 draw in which I scored. Guy also came on, and I challenge anyone to find another example at such a high level of both a manager and his assistant being in a squad together, let alone on the field at the same time.

Early in the New Year, Milan announced publicly that Tony Pulis's contract had been cancelled due to "misconduct". It ended any lingering doubts in the supporters', and perhaps even some players', minds that I was a caretaker, even if I was aware within the club, and secure in my own mind, that I wasn't.

We tried to get our FA Cup third-round game at Tranmere postponed due to all the injuries – I had just six senior professionals fit – but without success and a makeshift side was knocked out. Ceri Hughes was playing with a double hernia that made him look like he was auditioning for *Alien,* with two creatures looking as if they were ready to come out of his stomach. It was horrible and at Grimsby he literally could not run any more, so I had to take him off.

Results, as a consequence, were almost good, but not quite.

We had a useful 2-0 win at home to Norwich a couple of weeks after the Fulham game, but that and a 2-1 home win over Wimbledon were our only two victories in a 15-match spell from the Fulham game in mid-November through to mid-February. I did score goals to secure us points against Huddersfield and in that away game at Wimbledon, but it was a bit of a struggle.

That said, we lost only six of those 15 and never took a beating, despite the patched-up nature of the side. We were never in any danger of getting sucked into the relegation battle and I always felt we were getting the best out of the players available.

I was handling the training, both doing it and taking it, along with Guy Whittingham, with Neil McNab doing the warm-ups, although the three of us would arrive early to work out the things we needed to concentrate on. Them earlier than me, it has to be said. I'm not sure they were too happy sometimes when I changed their plans for the session, but I was confident I knew what needed to be worked on best.

Between us, I reckoned we were laying on good sessions, but I began to wonder if Milan perhaps didn't seem to think so. Strangely, one day I got a call from Graham Rix, the former Chelsea coach, offering to help me out – I suspected at the bidding of Milan. But I didn't want any help, certainly from someone I hadn't worked with before. Yes, we were an inexperienced management team, but that wasn't the problem. A treatment room with eight or nine players in it regularly – and 14 at one point – was the real problem.

On top of that, there were always other situations to deal with. Like Kevin Harper becoming embroiled in a dispute with a couple of women in a nightclub. They claimed he had insulted them and I had to defuse the situation before it got out into the press or before the police got involved. I rang them up and apologised, making sure both they and their families got tickets and hospitality for a game. Such are the unseen jobs in management.

I never really took to Kevin, who was a decent enough player, a Scottish international right-winger in fact, signed by Pulis. His lack of dedication, as I saw it, was completely at odds with mine towards the game.

I was overdoing things. Take the question of our training ground. Situated at Eastleigh near Southampton airport, it was owned by a school and was overseen by a groundsman who had his own way of doing things. You felt he didn't quite understand this professional football stuff.

Sometimes, if it was wet, he would just lock the gates and tell us we couldn't come in. We would have to go and work on the nearby all-weather surface, but then that might have been booked by students. Neil McNab had a mate who worked at Soccer City in Fareham, a private facility where they had synthetic pitches, but all this begging and borrowing wasn't ideal. It was a symptom of the club not being as professional as it should have been at that time.

I was charged with trying to find a new training ground in Portsmouth itself and spent hours and drove miles talking to people, the Royal Navy, private clubs – not that kind of private club – all sorts, but with no luck. It was another task on top of everything else that I let weigh me down.

My own preparation as a player was suffering. I had played well during the first seven or eight games, but with all the injuries, and not being as fit as I might have been, I had fallen off as a striker who needed support and service. I took a bad kick on my ankle in a match at Gillingham and was suffering from bone bruising, having to take painkillers to play. Often it would take me half an hour to get through the pain and settle into a game.

And when you are not at the top of your game, it is difficult then to dig out players at half-time. You can sense, quite rightly, they are thinking, "Well, what about you?" It was a shame because it was the one time I needed to be playing well.

I hadn't asked Milan about that phone call from Graham Rix because every day brought calls from agents and players, and even some coaches, looking for work and I tried to dismiss it as just another one. And although it had unnerved me a little, I still thought I was getting on with Milan, who listened patiently when I told him about the injuries and the balance of squad. I always got the impression he understood the problems I was facing.

He still demanded results, though. You may have noticed that chairmen can be a bit funny over things like that. We never fell out over tactics or players and he never interfered directly, even if he did want to hear every detail about my decisions. That was fine. It was his club and if it was mine, I would want to be consulted and kept informed. My only problem was that after games I would have to sit with him in a lounge and socialise for hours while he drank with his mates. I was beginning to get an inkling, mind, that he was becoming a bit less available when I wanted to call him after games when we hadn't done that well.

But he seemed grateful that I had slashed well over £1 million off the playing budget, including offloading the expensive Bernard Lambourde back to France, and as a result, with us slipping, he agreed that I could sign a defender. I enquired about Adrian De Zeeuw from Barnsley, but was quoted £1.5 million, which was way over the top for us then. In fact, in a few months' time, Adrian would join Pompey in the close season on a free transfer.

A new left-back was really the urgent call and so I made yet another inquiry to yet another manager about one. What happened next didn't exactly shock me, as little can in football any more, but it did take me aback.

Within an hour, the phone rang. It was an agent saying he represented the manager I had just been speaking to. He had a deal to put to me, he said.

"My client is willing to let the player go," he told me.

"That's good," I replied.

"He's going to need £25,000 to be deposited in a bank account first," the agent went on.

Perhaps he misinterpreted the unease in my silence at the other end of the phone for me awaiting a different offer.

"Now if you want to tell your chairman that it's more than

£25,000, then that's your business. It would mean a few quid for you and everybody's happy."

The manager, via his agent, was after a bung and suggesting I could get a piece of it too.

I told him very quickly that I wasn't interested, that I preferred to do everything above board, as I had done with the Russell Hoult deal to West Bromwich Albion. I suppose I could quite easily have let Russell go for £400,000 in return for £50,000 going into my bank account, assuming Tony Brown had agreed – which I don't believe he would have done for one moment – but it just never occurred to me.

Now there are not many who like a deal more than me, who enjoy the cut and thrust of doing a deal, and squeezing the best for myself out of it. But I have never and would never do anything devious, like take or offer a bung. It was a topic that became hot when Mike Newell said that during his time as manager of Luton Town it was rife. The allegation prompted the Premier League, FA and police inquiries into transfers since the introduction of the transfer window. This was actually the only occasion I have come up against it.

I can see the temptation, I have to admit, though more in agreeing to pay out rather than to take one. Take a situation, for example, where your club is struggling and badly needs a certain player. The only way to get the player – and maybe keep your job – is to pay the bung to either a manager or an agent to ensure the deal gets done. But that is panic, really, and you probably shouldn't be doing the job anyway, having allowed the situation to get that desperate. Personally, I would rather lose the job, because I wouldn't deserve to keep it. As for taking a bung, you know the money has been ripped off. The thrill for me has always come in earning it properly, or simply negotiating a deal that is good for you and which is all above board.

These days, people say that because deals are often done from chief executive to chief executive, or chairman to chairman, there is less scope for bungs to change hands, as was the case in the old brown-envelope days, when cash would be passed over at motorway services or in hotel rooms. Managers still have a big say in deals, however, and are still heavily involved. They will put the pressure on their chairman if they really want a player who is going to make a difference, but will back off if it's one that will do a job but is not going to change your team.

In the end, I simply asked Andy Awford to tell me who was the best available out there. He came back with the name of Jamie Vincent, who I had known from his Bournemouth days before he went to Rangers in Scotland. He was now at Huddersfield and I agreed to pay £500,000 for him.

As it turned out, however, he would play only one game for me.

Given everything Milan had told me, things should have been fine, but my instincts alerted me that all was not well after a 2-2 draw at Watford in early February, which, on top of two recent defeats by Grimsby and Preston, had dropped us from 12th in the table to 16th. Weakened once again through mass injuries, we had gone 2-0 down before fighting back with a lot of spirit to get the point. I was very proud of the boys and the performance and expected Milan to be pleased too.

After talking to the lads, getting changed and speaking to the press, I couldn't get hold of him on his mobile, though. It took an hour and a half for him to pick up and I could sense his coolness. I could tell he wasn't listening to what I was saying about the team and the squad, and that I had run out of players. For the first time under him I felt uneasy.

Next, we were at home to Bolton Wanderers, who were flying and would get up into the Premiership that season via the play-offs. Before the game, Sam Allardyce was getting stuck into the referee and it didn't stop all game, including half-time. It was a bit of an eye-opener for me as a new, young manager, but I was determined to fight our corner and had my own two penn'orth with the referee, just to urge him not to let himself get bullied. He said that he wouldn't, but we lost the game 2-1.

It was no disgrace, but after having reached a high of tenth just after I had taken over, we now found ourselves down in 17th, the position we had been in when Pulis went. Sam came to see me in my office after the match to offer some advice.

Having seen all the scouting reports and the list of people we were missing due to injury, he said he understood the situation I was in, but that I should get stuck into my chairman to release money to buy players. People won't thank you for not spending it if the slide continued, he said. They would thank you for not letting the team slip towards relegation.

I told him I was biding my time for the summer and didn't want to waste the club's money, and that I was sure we wouldn't get sucked into a relegation battle. We were eight points clear of it, after all. He told me that you needed to look after yourself, protect your position and your job, as well as the club in this game. He should have known what he was talking about, going on to survive so well and so long with Bolton in the Premiership, although it didn't do him much good at Newcastle, where he lost his job after just half a season.

After talking to Sam, I then went up to the lounge with Guy to see Milan. I could tell straight away that something wasn't right. He was curt and unhappy with us. I didn't want to stick around too long in such an atmosphere. I drove home with more concerns eating away at me.

With the next round of the FA Cup coming up – a competition we were already out of – our next game against West Bromwich Albion was ten days away. The next week was a tough one with the press, who were saying that I was close to losing my job. When these things hit the papers, people can talk all they like about it just being speculation, but there is usually no smoke without fire and they must have been getting their stories from somewhere. Then, on the Thursday before the West Brom game, Milan called me and Guy to the boardroom at Fratton after training.

He was straight to the point. "It's not working," he said, and told me he was letting me go.

I was stunned, gutted, but didn't rant or rave in response. I suppose I had seen it coming and was ready for it, not because I deserved it, but because I was starting to be able to read Milan. My instincts are usually sharp, as they had been after the Watford game, and I sensed he had made up his mind after Bolton.

I always had the feeling with Milan that he was a bit like a cushion – he bore the imprint of the last bum to have sat on him. He was quick to respond to public opinion and to deflect any flak. In my opinion, he was not always the best judge of character. In some ways he was typical of football club owners and chairmen. I don't think they would have reacted with such short-sightedness in the businesses in which they had made their money. If they had, they would never have been so successful.

That's not to say Milan wasn't a smart guy, though. He obviously was. Portsmouth had been in administration and he had picked it up for a comparative pittance. In several years' time he would be selling the club on as a Premier League going concern for £32 million. He certainly saw the opportunity.

And whenever he started getting some stick, he came out with a public relations stunt. He dressed well, was very open in interviews and was even on TV and in the papers more than me. He was clever with the fans, too, once sitting with a group in a local pub to head off a little rebellion. I also had to smile years later when he bought Leicester and told the fans what a good club it was and that he felt as though he had been here all his life. It was just what he said at Pompey. Looking back, I couldn't help but like him and I hope he feels the same about me.

In a strange way, my sacking came as a relief. I had been under so much stress that I was wrapped in a bubble of worry. I was spending every afternoon at the ground with Andy, Guy and Neil McNab, but they would go off to pick up their kids from school and I would still be there mulling things over on my own, hitting the phones till six or seven at night. One of the ironies was that I had been working that week on the pre-season programme for the summer and had been making arrangements to go and scout players myself at the Toulon international Under-21 tournament.

Milan actually asked me to take the team to West Bromwich and I agreed, though having been humiliated, in retrospect I can't think why. At the time, I was in a bit of a daze and maybe I thought that if I did it, he would be more accommodating with my severance package. Besides, it was my team and club and I still cared a lot about it. I saw them as my players and I had a duty to prepare them properly.

It was eerie the next day at training and on the trip up to the West Midlands. The players knew I was going and that all my power had gone. Some of them, like Linvoy Primus, Ceri Hughes and Shaun Derry, told me how sorry they were about the situation and that they had enjoyed having me as manager. I just tried to prepare the team as best I could with Guy, who would also be out of a job.

Having been in pain with bone bruising in my foot for some time, I named myself as substitute for the West Brom game, which we lost 2-0, but I went on for a farewell appearance. I clapped the fans, who knew what was going on. It was touching as they responded with applause in return and it prompted a few tears. And that was that. After just 22 games and four-and-a-half months in charge, my debut in management was over.

Sadness, however, would give way to a mix of anger and stubbornness over the next few weeks.

I had heard a whisper about who the new manager was going to be: Graham Rix. It started to make a bit of sense now – although it shouldn't have done. I would not have employed Rix and I don't know how the club did. He did have a top playing career at Arsenal and had been coach at Chelsea, but had recently been convicted of indecent assault concerning a 15-year-old girl and had served six months of a 12-month jail sentence. He was struggling to get back into the game.

Then again, his agent was Dennis Roach, once very powerful in the industry when he worked for Glenn Hoddle and Chris

Waddle, and who had obviously been talking to Milan on his client's behalf. I don't suppose Rix wanted to take over for a difficult away game at the Hawthorns, which was why I had been asked to stay in charge for another couple of days.

Now I was feeling used and it would make my severance negotiations a lot easier. Milan was stunned when I told him that I wanted to leave now. He thought I would simply stay on as a player. But having been manager myself, I simply couldn't play under another and with lads who I had been in charge of the previous week. I had my self-respect and I don't suppose the new man would have wanted me around anyway.

I had been in the game long enough to know that the sack could always be just around the corner for a manager. It was why I had insisted on a player's contract, and one that showed improved terms, as I was in effect doing two jobs. I had spent so long trying to please Milan, to cut the wage bill and had been working all hours, but now I was ready to play hard ball. He would have to pay off a contract that still had two and a half years left on it. It totalled around £190,000 after tax.

He baulked at the sums involved. He was, I think, still paying off Alan Ball and was in the process of sorting out Tony Pulis's money. Now he had me. On top of that, Pulis's old chief scout Lindsay Parsons was suing the club for arrears he was claiming. I was being called as a witness on his behalf until it was settled out of court.

Milan passed the buck to Rix, but he was either too weak or otherwise pre-occupied to bother. The chief executive Martin Bishop also had to get involved. It started to drag on.

I got the feeling in my limited dealings with him that Rix would not be strong enough to make a good manager. In fact, under him they would win only three of their last 13 games and finish 20th, narrowly avoiding relegation by a point. We had been eight points clear of relegation when I got the push. I even ended up as top scorer again, with 11 goals, despite missing the last two-and-a-half months of the campaign.

Rix got the sack quite early on the following season when matters didn't improve and Milan installed Harry Redknapp, who he had brought to the club as director of football, as manager. It started the Pompey revolution that I really believed I could have done given the chance and if I had been given a summer – and the transfer funds that Alan Ball and Tony Pulis had been granted – to make changes for the better.

At home waiting for my pay-off to be sorted, I went over and over in my head where I had gone wrong. I wished that I had spent money, that I had been able to retain more balance instead of being obsessed about the job, but I came to the conclusion that there was very little more I could have done given both the circumstances and the resources available. After all, Milan told me I had time. Though he was now putting it about that I had always been a caretaker manager, never at any time did he say that directly to me.

I hate making injuries an excuse, but they really did cripple me. The initial seven-game unbeaten run showed what we could do without too many of them. And looking back, I think some of those long-term injuries might have been a legacy of Tony Pulis's hard-running pre-season and his direct, physical style of football.

Thinking now, as a manager, it was strange that I could understand Milan's timing. We were – or should have been – clear of the drop and were coming into a series of winnable games against Stockport, Tranmere, Crewe, Sheffield Wednesday and Burnley. If I won them, he couldn't have got rid of me. If a new man came in, he would have a straightforward start. Except that Rix turned it into a tough one.

As I kicked my heels mulling it all over, consoled by around 250 letters from everyone, from kids to pensioners, forwarded to me from the club and sympathising with me, I heard that Milan was saying I could rot in the reserves. Chairmen quite often say that sort of thing, in anger and to try and send out tough messages, but you know they will settle on a deal once they have calmed down, just as they know you will settle because you don't want to waste two years of your career on a point of pride. It's nothing personal, or at least it shouldn't be. It's just business.

It was a game of bluff, one that I had become very good at through all my financial dealings. It was another example of being a pro who knows how to survive. You think it's just about talent and ability? Attitude, mental toughness and savvy come into it as well. The pubs are full of talented amateurs who never had that.

I had become good at knowing how far to push it and how far to go; I knew what I could and couldn't get away with. I even told Rix that I would come back to training, if that was how the club wanted to play it. He could see, though, that it would be counter-productive, as I would be a distracting figure around the place.

I was training on my own by going to the gym and running the lanes around my home and did so for the whole of March. I was not going to go to another club before I was paid up, as then the process can drag on and may never even get settled to your satisfaction. They would just have to sort it. So unprofessional had been the club's administration, the terms of my contract were stacked in my favour, incredibly so. I almost felt sorry for Martin Bishop, as I knew I was the one holding all the cards.

They were having to pay me full money and I even had a clause in my contract saying that if I went to another club and they could not afford to pay me £200,000 a year, Portsmouth would make up the deficit. Thus if another club offered me £500 a week, and I agreed to the move, Pompey were liable for £3,500 a week. It was a cock-up on their part really. What kind of amateur outfit does that?

As the season's transfer deadline day approached, Pompey said they were ready to do a deal with me. Soon we were £10,000 apart, then £5,000, at which point – I was doing the negotiations on my mobile on a day out with Mandy down in the West Country – I accepted their offer.

Now I was free to find another club. I was doubly sad because

I would be leaving my hometown club once more, at a time when I had hoped to finish my playing career there and to get off to a great start in my management career by having a tilt at a place in the Premiership. But you have to move on quickly in this game or you can stagnate or even go under. It can be a ruthless occupation like that.

Around half a dozen clubs had phoned to register their interest in me as a player, but I now wanted to join a club that was on the up. After a gloomy couple of seasons at a club bent on survival – even if I was always up for the cause as it was my club – I needed another one with passion and excitement. And there was one that fitted the bill perfectly.

2. *On The Road Again*

Steve Claridge has some enviable character traits. There is an absence of self-pity about him whenever he encounters a setback. Depression is a concept to be kept at bay by staying on the move so that it doesn't catch up with you.

People have dived under duvets for days for a lot less than happened to him at Portsmouth. He had been at a club – for him THE club – where he hoped to kick his last ball in front of his fellow Frattonites, had been given the chance to be its manager, only to see it all snatched away with the panicky impatience that is the stuff and curse of football.

After all, he was almost 35 now, a dangerous age for a player. Most pros are already out of the game by then. And he was a sacked manager. Needing a pause before resuming attempts to make a good manager himself, Steve wanted to keep playing, but it was not the most attractive of combinations for any prospective employer.

He knew what it was like on the other side of the fence. Perhaps he would be critical, either in front of the rest of the team or, even more damagingly, behind your back. He might be a disruptive influence in the dressing room. He might even not try and thus get you the sack, being in situ to take over your job. Such can be the insecurity and paranoia in what is frequently a dysfunctional game.

Against that, Steve has always been younger than his age in physical terms – emotionally too some would also joke – and as fit as a flea, being obsessive about running and working out in the gym on his own way past normal morning training. Not to try, not to do his best for his own personal pride, is against his constitution. Managers with any savvy in the game knew that about him, that whatever other things people said about him, they would be getting a still-dedicated professional. And, as such, he would be more likely to keep a manager in a job.

It was probably why the Millwall manager Mark McGhee was willing to add him to his squad that transfer deadline day in March 2001.

The pair had history at Wolverhampton Wanderers, with McGhee having brought Steve to Molineux from Leicester City. It was an ill fit, with Steve earmarked as the replacement for the irreplaceable Steve Bull, probably only second in Black Country legend to the former England captain Billy Wright. Never responding to McGhee's management, Steve was out of the club within six months and on his way to the then safe harbour of Portsmouth.

McGhee had not lasted much longer at Wolves and was now looking to rehabilitate his managerial image in South-East London. And he was doing it well. He had inherited an outstanding crop of players from the youth team – players like Tim Cahill, who would go on to make a top-quality Premier League player for Everton – and had taken them to within touching distance of promotion from the old Third Division, now League One.

Now he needed a striker, an experienced head up front among the youngsters to hold it together, and hold up the ball, as well as grab a few goals that might just cement their elevation.

Steve's recruitment actually came via Bob Pearson, the wizened and highly respected academy director who would find and develop players such as Cahill, Steven Reid, who went on to Blackburn, and promising young Republic of Ireland striker Richard Sadlier. Because of that success, Pearson became the confidant of chairman Theo Paphitis, owner of the Ryman stationery company and La Senza lingerie company and who would go on to become more widely known as one of the business entrepreneurs putting would-be tycoons through the mill in the BBC2 reality series *Dragons' Den*. Pearson recommended Steve and suddenly McGhee had two new strikers, having also brought in Tony Cottee, formerly of West Ham and Everton.

"I think Bob was clever," says Richard Sadlier. "He did scouting and youth development and became assistant to the chairman. He was Theo's employee, so basically no manager could sack him.

"When Steve came in with Tony Cottee, they were the first players who joined that we knew a lot about. That quality of player was not available to us before. There was a bit of a buzz about the place because they were famous. But my first memory of Steve is that he was really open and approachable. I warmed to him straight away." Steve warmed to the New Den as well.

Millwall have always been one of the, shall we say, earthiest clubs in the game. In the old days of the rough-and-ready old Den – situated in the evocative Cold Blow Lane – in the 1970s, the Irish midfield player and now outspoken pundit in his homeland, Eamon Dunphy, wrote a diary of a season called *Only a Game?*. It captured perfectly the rawness of life with the Lions and, yes, the potential for violence in one of London's poorest areas.

The new, all-seater stadium, completed in 1993 just a mile away in Bermondsey, was supposed to have produced a civilising effect and indeed Millwall did much to shake off their fearsome image that had players joking about not wanting to take corner kicks at the home fans' end. They were in the vanguard, too, of anti-racism campaigns and community initiatives.

But while the Premier League basked in its new-found corporate wealth, Millwall would never lose touch with their blue-collar support, who demanded honesty and industry of their players. It was why they would take to Steve Claridge and he to them.

And it was he who would come through to become the partner for Sadlier, with his talent and consistency helping to ensure that Millwall did not lose another game again that season.

It was Sadlier who actually thought his were the days that were numbered. "I thought, 'That's me finished' when they came," he says. "I either accepted it or moved on. But it actually gave me a kick up the arse to sort out my own game and my attitude."

The other striker at the club, Neil Harris, would fall ill with testicular cancer the following season – thankfully he went on to make a full recovery – and Claridge and Sadlier became a partnership to rival heroes Teddy Sheringham and Tony Cascarino from 20 years earlier in fans' affections.

It was at that time, as football feared Millwall – or more particularly their fans – being in the top flight that the chant went up, "No one likes us, we don't care," a line that has stuck.

Just as then, the front pairing would lead a charge for promotion from Division One as Millwall took the league by surprise, dovetailing neatly. Sadlier was a young target man and willing worker, with good feet and a powerful head; Claridge a wily old campaigner who would drop short for the ball and feed it wide or set his partner free.

"It was strange," Sadlier remembers. "I don't recall us doing any extra work on the training ground or analysing what we did, or saying things like, 'If you go near post, I'll go far,' but we just seemed to complement each other. We just knew when to respond to each other's movement. I always worked hard, but there just seemed to be less work involved when I played with Steve. I just seemed to work a little bit better with him than any other partner."

The two did communicate though. "I remember him saying to me in the pre-season that we were on a hiding to nothing with Neil out," adds Sadlier. "Neil was rightly popular with the fans and in the dressing room and we might be wrongly compared. But we saw it as a challenge and as an opportunity as well."

And they did talk, too, during breaks in games. "Steve would always wander over to me and have a chat, either to whinge and moan about the service we were getting that day or, less often, to praise the supply. In among all the swear words there would always be an observation about the game and I would think, 'Yes, he's right. Jeez, that's insightful.'"

The pair clearly had great affection for each other's game as well as an understanding, with Steve saying that Sadlier was among the best he ever played with. Indeed, Steve was hoping that Manchester United would make good on the word that swept the New Den that Sir Alex Ferguson was ready to make an offer of £7 million for Sadlier. Steve has always insisted that it was him who made Emile Heskey look so good and that it was he who got Heskey his £11-million move to Liverpool from Leicester. Perhaps with Sadlier he was hoping for a cut of the deal.

After a slow start, Sadlier hit the goal trail and the two ended the season as a potent pairing, leading Millwall to the brink of the Premier

League. Steve would be the fans' Player of the Year, an award he has received at virtually every club he has played for.

"We didn't really sign too many people and we were a young side, except for Steve, with most of us under 24 but everybody improved and we had the momentum from the previous year," Sadlier remembers. "It was no coincidence that I had the best spell of my career playing with Steve."

The following season would illustrate again how football, like investments, can go down as well as up. Having endured controversy, even violence, Millwall struggled as both a team and a club.

Sadlier would develop a hip problem that would preclude him from playing for virtually the entire season and which would eventually, sadly, end his career ridiculously prematurely when a top club and a long international career beckoned. He would go on to study sports science and return to his native Dublin to write a column on football for the *Sunday Independent* and co-commentate on the Irish TV station RTE as well as work towards a Masters in sports psychology.

In that anti-climactic third season, his second full one with Millwall, Steve would tire more than ever of playing for a manager in Mark McGhee whose methods would never impress him.

"We knew that the two of them didn't have a rapport," says Sadlier. "Steve would tell us. He would say, 'He must hate me.'

"I don't know what it was about, maybe something from Wolves, but I got on great with McGhee. He was not a man for tantrums, a bit more controlled and measured, and that suited me, but maybe it didn't suit Steve. Still, professionally it was a good link-up for both of them."

"I always thought McGhee liked him," says Robbie Ryan, Millwall fullback at the time and Sadlier's house-mate. "If he didn't I don't know why, because Steve was our best player."

"Steve's a bit odd," Sadlier offers, looking for explanations for a host of things. "He has a million different superstitions. He could be anonymous in training, as if he was knackered. Then when training was over, he would be on the treadmill for 40 minutes. It would be a blazing hot day, but he would keep a rain jacket on. I know he had sensitive skin, but you wondered how he did it. Sometimes, at the end of training, he would just run off somewhere. Perhaps he was off to the bookies."

"He was a funny character," adds Ryan, though with the same affection in his voice that emanates from Sadlier. "He would be straight in before training and straight out. Sometimes I'd be driving home and I'd see him running on the roads. He was always as fit as a fiddle."

Ryan is another on the list of people amazed by Steve's cars. "He had these nice motors, like a BMW," he recalls. "But the car was always full of clothes, boots, papers and pillows. All sorts of rubbish."

Ah yes, pillows. It remains one of Steve's many idiosyncrasies. Wherever he stays – at hotels or as a guest at your house – he brings his own pillows with him. If you think about it, it actually makes sense to anyone who has to stay away from home a lot. It means you are more likely to be comfortable and sleep properly; it was something Steve recognised in his playing days – the value to a player of rest and sleep – and, no doubt, did much to contribute to the longevity of his career. Many of Steve's eccentricities have their own simple logic.

Ryan also recalls nights he had out with Steve and Sadlier – and another trait peculiar to Claridge.

"He could be quite strange," he says. "I'd go out with him and with my girlfriend, we would be in a club and Steve would get up and dance on his own. He never drank very much, but once he'd had a couple of beers, he would like dancing and didn't care if it was alone. My girlfriend and other girls would often get up and he'd have the women dancing all night then." More method in the apparent Claridge madness.

Ryan, who went on to work on the London Underground in maintenance and play part-time for Conference South club Welling United, remembers one particular Saturday night out. "Steve was staying with me and Richard at our place in Bromley. We all went out for the night together after a match and sometimes he would just go off on his own. This night he did. We got home about two or three o'clock and wondered where he was.

"At 4.30am he comes rolling in. We asked him where he had been and he said he was out for a walk and came across a bloke having a fight with his missus and he stepped in to sort it out. Actually, I think he sorted the bloke out. He had blood all over his shirt."

Sadlier is another who reckons too many people underestimated Steve due to his image of tardiness, gambling and the – let us describe them as – unusual events that seemed to befall him.

"There is this image of him being a little bit scatty, and it's easy to pigeonhole him as shabby, but he has a real knowledge of the game," says Sadlier. "You can discuss a game with a team-mate, but when you discussed it with Steve, you really discussed it. A lot of older pros will go through the motions, but he has a real passion and love for the game. That must be why he had such a desire to carry on."

Carry on Claridge, indeed.

2.1 London Calling

I am one of those rare animals in football – I love Millwall. I had always enjoyed playing at the New Den because of the passion and the atmosphere – actually, I am old enough to have played at the previous Den – so when the chance came to join them I seized it. It meant dropping down a division to League Two, but I didn't think it would be for long. They had been in the top two since Christmas and I reckoned I could help seal the promotion place they deserved, as well as get back to where I thought I belonged.

Millwall inspire all sorts of emotions in people and, during my time there over the next two-and-a-half seasons, I would start to have a greater understanding of the area and for what is a unique club in English football. The mix of that part of South-East London and the working-class roots of the club make it a social phenomenon. Much of the culture is understandable and admirable, more of it still a mystery and some of it prone to producing behaviour and incidents that are just not acceptable. I would witness it all.

It just felt like my type of place from the start, full of proper people who scream and bawl because they know and love their football. I love all that. I want to be able to walk into a stadium and know whether the home side is three up or three down just by the fans' reaction.

And people like that love people like me because they know I am going to give them everything for their hard-earned admission money. I am a good player, with ability as well, but it is my attitude that has always set me apart. I am like they would be if they were out there wearing their club's shirt, fighting for every lost cause.

My agent, Phil Morrison, had a good relationship with the Millwall chairman Theo Paphitis, whose company Ryman sponsored non-League football, which I think was his first love, but he had decided to get involved with 'Wall, as they were also known, when they went through a period of financial trouble.

Because it was late in the season, there was very little chance of me getting a management job anywhere else, as clubs were trying to stay settled either to go for promotion or avoid relegation. Not that I was considering it anyway. I was certain that I still had plenty of playing years in me and was not ready to give that up yet. I did want another crack at management in the near future, but playing had always been my comfort blanket and, after my experiences at Portsmouth, I needed comfort right now.

My link with Millwall came largely through Bob Pearson, a wise old football man who looked a bit like one of the old gits from *The Harry Enfield Show*. Bob had been chief scout or assistant manager at various times and now he seemed almost to have become Theo's personal footballing assistant. His stock was high with the chairman, I think, because he was overseer of the club's academy system; one that was producing a lot of players for the first team at that time and which would go on to produce a lot of revenue in transfer fees.

Bob always seemed to like me as a player and obviously recommended me to the club, so it was Theo who basically signed me and did a deal for £2,000 a week until the end of the season, with an agreement for a proper contract worth £4,000 basic if they got up. To do that, Bob and Theo knew the club needed a new striker and, from what I understand, they virtually foisted me on the manager, whose own choice was Tony Cottee, the former West Ham and England striker, who signed on the same day as me. That manager was Mark McGhee, who had let me go from Wolves.

My deal was not done until about 11pm that March deadline day, just an hour away from the last chance of signing players before the end of the season in those days before the transfer-window system, mainly due to getting the deal I wanted. I was never worried it wouldn't go ahead. Both parties wanted to make it work – as did Portsmouth, if only to offset some of their own costs.

The arrangement included £1,000 an appearance and £1,000 a goal. I have always been a believer in productivity incentives in football – if I do well, I should be rewarded; if I don't, I don't cost you as much. Fair enough all round. I knew my worth and held out and, in the end, got what I wanted.

Anyone who would later go on that BBC show *Dragons' Den* and who wanted to get the better of Theo should have contacted me first to know how to deal with him – financially at least. Our paths would cross again in the future – although a quite different relationship developed, one that would change everything for me. For now, though, it was about knuckling down and playing.

The other reason for the late signing was my concern about joining up again with Mark McGhee. I always got on OK with him away from football and there was nothing personal between us. In fact, he was pretty straight with me when it was not working out at Wolves and he let me go to Portsmouth. It was just that he never seemed to rate me that highly and I always had to work hard to impress him. I was not his signing here, so I wondered how he might treat me.

I was also at that stage of my career where I was looking at managers and what they were doing, in terms of formations and strategy, just to test what I might do in their position. I had not been impressed with McGhee, particularly in an FA Cup semi-final with Wolves against Arsenal, which we had been lucky to lose only 1-0 after being overrun as a result of the strange system he played, a sort of 4-3-3, but without the right players in their right positions.

Bob Pearson reassured me that it would all be fine, though, and my agent, having talked to Theo, went further: "Don't worry about McGhee," Phil Morrison said. I sensed that the manager's instinct was to play Tony Cottee ahead of me, but I would always back myself to be the one who would prevail. He may have played higher for longer than me, but after arriving at Millwall from Wigan after Everton, Tony was coming to the end of his career. Having also been a West Ham boy, I thought he might also have a bit of trouble winning over the 'Wall fans.

I knew, too, when I saw him walking on the treadmill in the gym – when I would be running – that Tony would struggle. When McGhee put him in ahead of me for the first game at Wycombe, he pulled a stomach muscle, though to be honest it was hard to see a muscle around his midriff. Tony would not figure again. The injury prompted him to pack it in.

People who thought I might be at the end of my career just because I was of a similar age to Tony were well wide of the mark. I had kept myself fit with my own regime – running every day around the Surrey Quays area of South London after training, where Millwall had put me up in a hotel, and was desperate to play, despite the bone bruising in my foot that was still giving me some gyp. McGhee had no choice but to throw me in the next week against Rotherham. It was a massive game. Rotherham came to the New Den top of the table; Millwall were second.

The moment I walked into the dressing room, I knew I was around good characters. They were full of confidence and not a single one of them was a big-time Charlie. When you look at them now, it was an astonishing team. And it was an exciting time.

There was Tim Cahill, who would go on to play for Australia and get a big-money move to Everton, where he became an out-standing attacking and goalscoring Premiership midfield player. There was Lucas Neill and Steven Reid, who both went on to Blackburn, Lucas on to West Ham after that for big money, as well as Paul Ifill, who joined Sheffield United. Then, up front, there was Richard Sadlier, a Republic of Ireland international, who may well have gone on to be the best of the lot, but who was to suffer cruelly with injuries. The goalkeeper Tony Warner also went on to play Premier League football with Fulham.

Therefore McGhee was lucky when he took over from Keith Stevens and Alan McCleary, who had been joint managers: he had inherited an outstanding crop. They were all the product of an astonishing youth team, one of those remarkable happy events where a whole group come through at the same time, which is why Bob Pearson had so much clout at the club. He must have been a good judge of a player. He liked me.

You see it happening now and then; at Ipswich once, at Southampton, when Theo Walcott was playing. The most famous example was probably up at Manchester United in the mid-1990s with the Gary Neville–David Beckham group, who would go on to be phenomenal for more than a decade.

I think at least five of that Millwall side would go for a million pounds or more to keep the club in business over the next few years. One of their problems became, I think, that they thought it would happen every year, that there would be a production line of players from South London. The reality is you should treat these things as rare windfalls.

Looking back, it was an uneven Millwall side actually, with six or seven really outstanding players and the rest making up the numbers. In defence, Matt Lawrence was a good player but, to be honest, Stuart Nethercott and Sean Dyche got away with plenty as centre-backs. They always wanted covering players around them, yelling at people to come back and help. That's the trouble with defenders. They always want more like themselves in a team. There are always too many attacking players in the team for their liking.

For now, the blend we had was good enough, and it was good to be at a place where you knew you had a chance of winning something. Every game for Pompey had been special to me, but I had endured two years of making do and mending there, knowing we weren't going to be challenging for any honours.

This was a strong unit, as a rousing 4-0 win in that huge home match against Rotherham proved. Reid and Ifill gave us a 2-0 lead inside half an hour and when I scored a debut goal just before half-time, it was game over. It was a good goal, too. I turned Guy Branson, who I had been at Leicester with, and chipped home a left-footed shot from 20 yards.

To seal the day, I added a fourth in the second half with a simple header after a shot had hit the bar. I left to a fantastic reception from the crowd of more than 16,000, who were delighted to see us go top of the table. I took the place that day of Paul Moody, who had a sideline in house-painting, and he did one of mine in Southsea for me. He was good, too, though I'm not sure he ever forgave me for having him out of the side.

It was good to be playing again and especially so given that I had got off to such a great start. I was absolutely shattered at the end after my first game in six weeks, but I was an instant hero and loved it. I thought to myself that if they love me like this when I am not fully fit, what's it going to be like when they see me running around properly?

In fact, it felt like it did when I joined Leicester City from Birmingham City a few years earlier. I was the final, missing link in a side that was confident and on a roll. I had fitted in perfectly then, scoring that memorable goal against Crystal Palace at Wembley to win the playoff final that took us up into the Premiership.

Now, like Leicester then, we were on an unstoppable run. We would not lose another game and won the next three against Port Vale, Swindon and one of my former clubs Cambridge United, with me scoring a sweet goal in a comprehensive 5-1 win, when I got the ball wide, turned inside the full-back and shot home across the goalkeeper.

Then came a 1-1 draw at Wrexham, in which I picked up another anterior cruciate knee injury. It just popped. I had not been doing the same physical work as I had been doing at Portsmouth. This was a wake-up call to work harder.

I was gutted to miss the promotion party at the final game at the New Den, watching from the stand in a crowd of 18,510 that saw us beat Oldham Athletic 5-0. I was satisfied, though, that I had done enough to play my part – and earn that contract for another year. Millwall were back. And so was I.

It was back to a summer of rehab – with my wife Mandy thinking I was doing it deliberately to get out of taking her abroad on holiday, knowing how much I hated the sun. After promising her a fortnight, in the end I got it down to a long weekend. With the injury being similar to the one I had suffered a year previously, I followed the same programme of rest, then running and weights down in Portsmouth, just going up to London once a week to get the knee checked over.

The work was interrupted one morning in early August when my mobile rang. It was Karen, who had been my secretary at Portsmouth when I was manager. She told me that Aaron Flahavan, who had been my first-choice goalkeeper back then, had been killed in a car accident. I was stunned.

Flavs was a lovely bloke away from the football pitch, very happy and bouncy. When he got a drink inside him, though, he would be on his knees, very morose. Talk about alcohol changing people.

Apparently, he was three times over the limit as he was driving along the A338 towards Bournemouth and doing 100mph when he lost control of the car, crossed over the central reservation into the other carriageway and rolling the car over before ending up in a ditch. It took two hours before he was found because the wreckage was so spread out. It was all very shocking and sad and, as I sat at his funeral in the village of West End near Southampton a week later, I couldn't help wondering what had got into him to get so drunk, so down, and to drive his car like that.

That summer was also the time I also became fully aware of what Millwall fans could be like.

Still not match-fit, I went up to watch a testimonial match for

'Wall legend, player and manager, Keith "Rhino" Stevens against Tottenham Hotspur, which was also a pre-season friendly. Wanting to miss the traffic, I left five minutes early. Out in the car park, I was amazed how many Millwall fans were about, hundreds of them. They were massing, ready to try and get round to the Spurs end to ambush them.

"Hello Stevie, mate," one of them said to me. "Fancy coming to have a go with us?"

Now I know some of the episodes in my life might have made some funny, offbeat film scenes, but this was ridiculous. I thought about that moment in the movie *Mike Bassett, England Manager* when one of the players starts brawling with fans. I decided that discretion was the better part of valour. Besides, my car was in the firing line and I wanted it moved.

One of the things about a lot of the 'Wall fans is that they do not hero-worship players in the conventional sense, though they can come to revere them – if they earn it, that is. These fans are "geezers" and it is not cool to hero-worship. They treat you as one of them, not apart from them, and while they might be respectful towards you, and never abuse or harm you, they are not going to put you on a pedestal. Once you are one of them, though, they really take you to their hearts, as my visits back there down the years have always proved.

You are never lucky if you get injured for long periods, but after two cruciate injuries in 18 months, I was as lucky as you can be. Both of them had happened towards the end of the season and I missed only seven competitive games, despite being out for a total of seven months.

It meant I was fit enough to start the season and we were quick out of the blocks. Our first game was against Norwich City at home. It was an interesting clash and one that showed just how big a part confidence plays in this game. We were just promoted, keen and enthusiastic; they had just been relegated from the Premiership and were still shell-shocked.

We blitzed them 4-0 and I got the season off to a flying start with the first goal. Norwich certainly got a rude awakening about life below stairs. The luck certainly went with the buoyant team; everything went for us that day.

The euphoria didn't last long, though, as after that we went on a terrible run, starting with a 4-0 defeat at Birmingham in our next game. If we had ever had thoughts that this League One was going to be a stroll, we were quickly disabused of them. This game does have a habit of lifting you up one week and bringing you back down to earth the next.

It was at this point that McGhee fell out with Lucas Neill, and often if you fell out with McGhee that would be it. The previous season Lucas had been in and out of the team and had often been played out of position. Although he would end up at right-back in the Premiership, he was a good central midfield player at a lower level. He never found a regular slot, though, and started to grow disillusioned.

After being dropped following the Birmingham defeat, Lucas asked for a transfer and was soon on his way to Blackburn for £1 million, with McGhee saying it was best to cash in now rather than let him go for nothing at the end of his contract the following summer. In fact, Lucas, who was the club's longest-serving player at the time, might well have stayed and been a key figure in our bid to reach the Premier League. However, after being messed about by and then falling out with the manager, he was on his way. It was a sad, and potentially costly, loss.

We did have Dave Livermore and Tim Cahill in the centre of midfield forming a classic and formidable partnership, one holding, one going; one a breaker-up of the play with a hard tackle, the other great at getting in the other team's penalty box, though both worked hard and could do either job when called upon. But Lucas could and should have been accommodated in the team, maybe even at centre-back, and we would have been even stronger.

It was strange, but I knew that there but for fortune it could have been me, even if no one, least of all in the Premiership, was going to pay a million quid for me these days. McGhee was never warm towards me at the best of times and I also knew that I would be dropped if I wasn't at the top of my game. You know when managers like you or don't. He was quicker to praise others and was more friendly and open towards them.

Then again, curiously, he would seek my help at one point later in the season, perhaps as senior pro, perhaps because he knew the chairman liked me.

After one game, he was in his office, which could be accessed from the dressing room through the physio's room, and getting a coating from Theo about something or other. McGhee came into the dressing room and called me into his office, where he got me to back him up over some issue, the detail of which eludes me. I did stick up for him, but I wasn't sure if I had done the right thing to ally myself to him.

Perhaps, subconsciously, I was thinking it might keep me in the side, because I knew what he could be like with me, even though I should have been an automatic choice. When we lost to Burnley and Crewe, I thought I might get left out for the derby match with Crystal Palace at the beginning of September, but he kept me in the side and I produced a performance that meant he couldn't drop me.

In front of a crowd of more than 21,000 at Selhurst Park, which included 6,000 Millwall fans, we went a goal down before Richard Sadlier grabbed an equaliser right on half-time. Then, early in the second half, I bundled home a scruffy goal – a mistake by their goalkeeper and a defender, with the ball bobbling into the net off my knee – to give us the lead. I then confirmed victory right on full-time by chasing down a long ball and stabbing it through the keeper's legs with my studs. They were two of the worst goals scored in the history of English football, but no one cared.

I got some stick off the home crowd about being a Palace reject, due to the short spell I had there early in my career when I was well behind Ian Wright and Mark Bright in the pecking order, but it was strange because I never played a league game for them. It was probably more to do with having scored the playoff goal that put Leicester in the Premiership, but which condemned Palace to another season in the First Division. Our lot naturally loved me, mind. It was a sweet day as we suddenly clicked. We had so many fans there that day that I think some of the Palace were glad that we won.

I have to say I never really got the worst type of abuse or really minded the abuse I did get. Certainly I never felt tempted to react the same way Eric Cantona had done at Selhurst with his kung-fu kick at that Palace fan who had verbally abused him. Early in your career, you would get the personal stuff off opposition fans about your mother or something like that, but that stopped as you got older and gained more respect.

The worst I've really had to endure was being billed as a pikey or a gypo, because of my scruffy demeanour on the pitch. Naturally, I've heard "Where's your caravan?" All together now …

The one I have had trouble understanding is "You fat bastard". I have always been among the leanest of specimens. Perhaps I have looked a bit blobby sometimes in midwinter down the years because I have to wear several T-shirts under my shirt. I feel the cold so badly, due to having an under-active thyroid gland as a result of taking pills for that heart defect I was diagnosed with when I was a teenager.

Thankfully, I have been able to shrug off the abuse, though it can get out of hand. I know most people see me with some affection or respect, as they tell me so, and I haven't had the nasty stuff, though even I, who likes to think he understands football fans, do despair of some of the things you hear.

Much as I like West Ham and the fans there, Upton Park can be an unforgiving place. I was once there to see them play against Newcastle, then managed by the former Hammers manager Glenn Roeder – who had undergone surgery for a blood clot on his brain. He had to hear chants of "Tumour Boy" behind him from those who used to sing for him, which also tells you something about the potential for hypocrisy among fans in this game.

West Ham seems to be among the worst places, actually, from what ex-players say. When I was at Leicester, the coach there, Steve Walford, used to talk about having been a Hammer and hearing some of the stuff shouted from the old Chicken Run terracing. It did for many careers, he said, and had the effect of causing some players to ask to swap wings. He was a central defender or left-back and on the days he played wide, found himself next to the Chicken Run. He said that, such was the abuse, he was only too willing to move infield to cover for the centre-halves. Steve reckons he did his knee in by bending his run away from the Chicken Run.

Our next match after the Crystal Palace win took us to Gillingham in the League Cup, then called the Worthington Cup. It was on 11 September 2001.

We were sitting in the canteen at the training ground in Bromley ready for our pre-match meal that afternoon with the television on in the background. All of a sudden we saw two jet planes flying into the Twin Towers in New York. At first, we thought it was some disaster movie. Then we realised the seriousness and the severity of the situation.

It was a strange feeling having to get on a coach and go to a football match after that. I suddenly got an insight into how Liverpool must have felt after hearing that some of their fans had been killed in the Heysel Stadium disaster before being told to go out and play the European Cup Final against Juventus back in 1985. It was the only time I have not wanted to play a match. We lost 2-1. Gillingham again.

We lost again the following Saturday, by a single goal at Preston, but it would be just an aberration. We knew the team was bedding down now. That game up at Deepdale was the only time I ever saw Tim Cahill bossed during his time with us. His opposite number in midfield, the Nigerian Dixon Etuhu, was a powerful player who ended up in the Premier League with Sunderland and I took note of him that day and have followed his career since then.

After that, we beat Barnsley and Sheffield United in our next two matches and were on our way up the table, with me scoring twice in the 3-1 win over Barnsley. That was a strange night. I had overslept in the afternoon in my hotel room and left it too late to have a pre-match meal, so I felt really bad as I stepped out on the field. I have always believed in preparing properly and this was not good, particularly as I had had an anxiety dream about being late for the game.

It took me an hour to get going, but when I finally did, I headed home a free-kick and followed it up ten minutes later by touching home a deflection off a defender. I thought that maybe I ought to sleep late more often, but then I thought about that first hour and how rough I had felt.

The win signalled the start of an eight-match unbeaten run that would take us up to a heady sixth by the middle of November. We were beating some good sides, too, notably when Richard Sadlier scored twice in a 2-0 win at West Bromwich Albion.

That was the night their manager, Gary Megson, had a right go at me from the sidelines, shouting at me that I was the bloke who got Tony Pulis the sack at Portsmouth. I was just trying to concentrate on the match – I wasn't some kid whose game he thought he could disturb – and let it go. I was a bit baffled by it and wondered what Pulis had told him about me.

Not that I was going to let it bother me. In the next game, at Stockport, I scored twice in a 4-0 win – one of the goals a penalty, the other a neat finish after I had nutmegged a full-back. However, a return to the West Midlands proved less enjoyable.

I felt the 1-0 defeat at Wolves a bit more keenly than the rest of the lads – and probably even Mark McGhee – and not just because it was an old club of mine. I didn't take the elbow from supposed hard man Kevin Muscat personally, though. Playing for Australia, he once twatted two Brazilians, so I was in good company.

Kevin had been at Wolves when I was there and he was OK off the pitch. On it was a different matter, though. He had that bit of spite in him. Personally, I never thought of him as a real hard man in the true, honest sense of the expression. He only did you when there was no chance of him getting hurt. He would later sign for Millwall.

The loss didn't dent our confidence because by now we realised we were a decent side with a serious chance of making the playoffs. We bounced back with a 3-2 win over Coventry, in which I scored again – with a goal that was too good for me, a left-footed half-volley – and then went on to record another home victory, by 1-0, over Rotherham, who had been promoted with us the previous season.

Then it was up to Grimsby, and a last-gasp 2-2 draw with my bundled-home goal. With the point we gained taking us up to sixth, it felt like a win – particularly given we had gone behind after 86 minutes – and it made the journey home from such a far-flung spot so much less gloomy. Actually, it can be horrible going to Grimsby, let alone coming back. Blundell Park seems to have its own micro-climate: the wind howls in off the North Sea no matter the time of year. This was November. You don't even need to paint a picture. Just the words Grimsby and November should tell the story.

Richard Sadlier had scored the first goal and we were developing into a top partnership. I was really enjoying it. Normally, I found myself playing with a striker who was a leader of the line, with me in the withdrawn role, holding the ball up and creating chances for my partner. Richard was such a good player that he could play either role. He would run the channels, allowing me to get in the penalty box more and, consequently, I scored more goals than I might otherwise have done. We were a really strong, balanced pair.

It came as a bit of a shock losing at home to Gillingham, but then they had always been a bit of a bogey team for Millwall. I suppose it was the closest thing Gillingham had to a derby, so they were always up for it, while 'Wall always look towards the bigger London clubs. In fact, they have the Cockney view of the Kent club's fans as pikeys, possibly because they might have gardens.

After that, we were beaten 3-2 at home by Manchester City, which was no disgrace. Kevin Keegan's adventurous team were the best outfit in the division and would win it by a mile – no wonder with players like Shaun Goater, Darren Huckerby and Shaun Wright-Phillips, their three goalscorers, in the side.

I bagged a penalty, with Richard scoring the other goal, but it was a strange midweek night with only just over 13,000 inside the New Den. City always had a big following, and a lot of exiled supporters in London, but the two clubs had agreed not to admit away fans for the two fixtures between us, because there was huge potential for combustion between the two sets of supporters.

Perhaps a lot of the Millwall fans didn't bother to turn up because there was no one to sing songs against or to have a go at. It was funny at the New Den sometimes. There was often a delayed reaction after we had scored a goal because so many of our fans were looking at the visiting fans and were busy giving them grief. Then, when they might have heard a roar at the other end, they would turn around and say, "Oh, we've scored have we? Who got it?" and only then would they start to celebrate.

In all seriousness, Millwall were still suffering from bad publicity and it was that which kept our gates lower than they should have been for such a good little side who were putting together a real challenge to get into the Premiership. Especially when you consider the form we were in. We were a tight unit, too, with virtually the same side playing week in, week out.

In fact, if you look at the teams that win things – and this may be why Chelsea, Manchester United and Arsenal have been the more successful clubs in the Premier League these last few seasons – they keep a nucleus of seven or eight players in their side all the time. The League Cup is a different matter and provides a good opportunity to give fringe players a run-out, but I believe that for the serious stuff you need familiarity. It was a lesson Rafael Benitez finally came to learn as Liverpool mounted a title challenge.

And with the form we were in at Millwall, everyone wanted to play – the injuries players picked up seemed to heal that little bit more quickly. It is strange how that happens to a winning side. We all especially wanted to play at home to Crystal Palace on Boxing Day. Me more than most, I think. I've always loved Christmas football.

After a goalless first half, and despite McGhee playing a system I didn't like, which featured three strikers, I broke the deadlock early in the second half when I seized on a backpass, rounded the goalkeeper and scored from an acute angle. Within five minutes, Richard Sadlier had added another couple. It was game over. The New Den was rocking. The Millwall fans now had bragging rights over their near neighbours for the New Year. We had done the double over the Palace, with Richard and I sharing six goals in the two games against them.

There was a marked difference in the support that day by the way, and it was one that mirrored how different the two clubs were. While we had taken 6,000 fans for the game at Selhurst, Palace had only brought 1,300 across South London to the New Den.

When we won at home to Crewe three days later and then went on to beat Watford 4-1 on New Year's Day to get up to fifth place, we all felt that we could really challenge for promotion again. It was going to be a big second half of the season.

Such was our form and the quality of the side that we knew Sadlier, Cahill and Ifill were being watched by the big clubs. And we were made only too aware that Millwall had been in the old First Division back in the 1980s when they had Teddy Sheringham and Tony Cascarino up front.

However, in this day and age, when money talks the loudest, reaching the Premier League would be a different thing altogether. Working-class, comparatively tiny old 'Wall, with all their troubles and the way they were perceived – that "No one likes us, we don't care" syndrome – surely couldn't gatecrash the corporate elite of English football, could they?

2.2 Strife with the Lions

It has been known at various times as the old Second Division, then the First Division or Division One, even League One, and now the Championship, but no matter the name and no matter what the critics say about its quality, I reckon that, in terms of sheer competitiveness, the second tier of the English game is a great league. For intrigue, twists and turns, it is hard to beat.

We all know these days who the top four in the Premier League will be, barring a serious blip, or maybe one club having a season when they muscle in as one of the others slips up. We also know who are going to be challenging for the UEFA Cup places and who will be in contention for relegation.

One step down, though, while you may have a good idea of who the big clubs are and that the strongest should be those who come down from the Premier – because they will have the "parachute" money to be able to keep a bigger wage budget – there are no guarantees.

And the gap between escaping relegation and making the playoffs never seems huge right into the final third of the season. The beauty is that while three defeats can suck you down into trouble, three wins can put you right back in the frame. Anyone can really beat anyone and the bottom side beating the top is never the shock it would be in the Premier League.

The upside is that things need never be as gloomy as they appear. You always have a chance of hauling yourself out of the mire. The downside is that, although you may be flying, you can never afford to take anything for granted and you are always vulnerable.

We found it out the hard way in March when we lost four games in a row as nerves and a bit of fatigue kicked in. Until then, we had been doing OK, without quite showing the form we had displayed around Christmas. I picked up an ankle injury at Norwich in January and missed five games, during which we lost at Manchester City and at home to Wimbledon but beat Nottingham Forest and West Bromwich Albion and drew with Walsall. Not quite playoff form.

I was replaced by Neil Harris, who obviously didn't impress McGhee too much as I was recalled as soon as I was fit and my two goals against Preston North End proved both decisive and a vindication of the manager's decision to recall me.

But the March run really was a shocker. We were beaten by both Sheffield clubs, Wednesday and United, Gillingham – again – and Portsmouth.

It was a gloomy return to Fratton Park for me as we were well beaten 3-0 and I took fearful stick. "Who the 'effin hell are you?" they were singing. I had got tickets for some of my mates and my dad and I'm sure I saw him leading some of the chanting. I took consolation in the thought that I was an old girlfriend they had been in love with and they were now jealous I was with someone else. At least that car-park steward and club receptionist would have had a good day, I suppose.

I even missed a late penalty against Dave Beasant in goal, with the home fans saying I had done it deliberately because I was a Pompey lad. I just smiled and nodded, because it would make going out on Saturday nights around the city a lot easier, but they couldn't have known me that well. I would never turn down the chance of a goal, no matter who it was against.

Actually, nerves weren't the only thing blighting us. A hip injury had afflicted Richard Sadlier and he was a huge loss at what was a worrying time. Fair play, though, McGhee did manage to get Dion Dublin in on loan from Aston Villa and he made a difference.

Dion and I had been together at Cambridge United years earlier and we were a good pairing, even if we now had a combined age of around 70. He had this amazing ability to leap for a ball, stay up there to have a look around and see where he wanted to head it on to. I think they call it "hang time" in basketball. Les Ferdinand also had it, as does, believe it or not, Tim Cahill. He has got a great spring, which is why he scores so many headed goals for Everton, even though he is not the tallest of players.

Dion made an immediate impact by scoring in a 3-0 win over Stockport at home that stopped the rot. We had dropped down to sixth in the table, but were still in the picture, hanging in there with a 0-0 draw at Rotherham, when I was not best pleased to be on the subs' bench, after McGhee decided to pair Dublin with a fit-again Sadlier. I spent most of the afternoon running up and down the touchline with the Rotherham sub Mark Robins, who I had been at Leicester with, moaning about being left out and about our respective managers, as well as recalling the good old days at Filbert Street.

Richard got injured again at Millmoor and McGhee brought me back for the home game against Wolves, which was a massive, nerve-racking occasion. They were going for automatic promotion, us for the playoffs and there were more than 17,000 at the New Den.

Wolves were a good side, with Paul Ince their driving force at the time, but I scored a sweet winner from the penalty spot, which was probably just as sweet for McGhee against his former club as it was for me. My arse was twitching for that one, I have to admit. It was a major, major result and one that would condemn Wolves to the playoffs and cement our place in them.

I had a mate in the stand that day who told me what a tense and poisonous atmosphere it was. And after the game, I saw a Wolves player giving V-signs to the milling Millwall fans as their coach pulled away. I could have said he was a brave man, except for the fact that the coach was in third gear at the time and picking up speed.

The only thing that soured the day for me was that I picked up two broken ribs, which left me in agony. With just two games left and with the playoffs in sight, though, I was not going to let that keep me out of the next match at Coventry. With some padding and pain-killers, I duly made it on to the field.

And my goal midway through the first half, a scruffy effort, would prove to be the difference between the sides. I had to come off after scoring, because I was in so much pain. I had hardly been able to run or breathe, and I had been getting banged in the ribs all the time. When you have an injury like that, you realise how much physical contact there is in the game, just in the normal run of play.

I think it was probably the only time that McGhee and I were both happy at the same time: him because he could bring me off and me because I was coming off and knew that the pain would stop.

With my ribs strapped, I found myself on the bench for the final game, at home to Grimsby, but three goals in the first half an hour by Dion and Neil Harris, who scored twice, made it comfortable for us. I didn't begrudge Neil his appearance or his goals because it had been a tough season for him, after having been diagnosed with testicular cancer, although fortunately they had caught it early and he went on to make a full recovery.

We had finished fourth, a fitting reward for a hard season's good work, and we reckoned we had an excellent chance in the playoffs, in which we were paired with one of my many old clubs in Birmingham City, with the first leg due to be played at St Andrews. They had taken four points off us in the matches between us during the season, but against that, we had battered West Brom, who finished runners-up to Manchester City, so we knew we were more than capable of going up.

McGhee went with Dion and Harris again up front as a result of the Grimsby game and I suppose he could justify it on the grounds of not changing a winning team. But this was a different kind of challenge and one that he should have known was made for me. My ribs were still sore, but with the strapping, I was ready to play.

This was one of my stomping grounds and I was really up for the occasion. There were more than 28,000 fans in the ground that night – though only 1,900 of ours, which was the amount of away tickets the two clubs had agreed on for both legs – and I always revelled in matches like that. The atmosphere was tasty, edgy even. I don't think the Millwall fans liked it that one of the songs always played at St Andrews is Del Shannon's "Runaway". They would never run.

Finally I came on for Neil, who I always considered a decent lower-division striker but not in the same class as me at this level, and my name was announced to the crowd. "Who?", they screamed. I just stood there with my hands on my hips, smiling. St Andrews started laughing as if to say, "All right, we know who you are." They should have done. Trevor Francis and I were the only post-war strikers to have scored 20 league goals in a season for them.

We were a goal down, scored by Bryan Hughes, when I arrived into a tough, uncompromising game, but gradually we got to grips with it. We deserved it when Dion grabbed an equaliser with ten minutes to go, looping home a header from a cross to round off a move I started. Now we were well set for the home leg.

McGhee knew I now deserved to start that one and I did. It was a crackling, cracking night. It also turned out to be a long one.

We started brightly but the game then developed into a tense struggle and one you knew would be settled by a single goal. Our chance of that winner came with ten minutes to go. Over comes a cross that gets deflected and Dion is alone with the ball at his feet eight yards out. He sidefoots wide, though, and everyone associated with Millwall has their head in their hands.

Then, in the very last minute, Stern John grabs a goal. Now

there was no way back, no time for it. Birmingham City, not Millwall, were through to the playoff final.

When the goal went in, we stood looking at each other in disbelief. Time stood still. I just wanted someone to say it hadn't happened, to press the rewind button on the remote. We had worked so hard and, after 48 games, our season was all over in a second.

Around 14,500 Millwall fans in the crowd of 16,391 were silent; the 1,900 Birmingham fans, on the other hand, jubilant. That might sound a very low attendance, by the way, but in fact three sides of the ground were near full, with one side having to be given over to those Birmingham fans to ensure that, for their own safety, they had plenty of space around them. Despite all those empty spaces at an end, though, it was a powderkeg of an atmosphere. And one that was about to explode.

After our own fans had got through their shock and the final whistle had blown, that should have been that. Instead, the stunned silence turned into a cocktail of anger and disappointment and it would all kick off as the rage of our fans spilled out into the narrow streets surrounding the stadium.

While we were sitting numb in the dressing room, the silence pierced only by the odd angry shout of a frustrated player, the Birmingham fans were being held in the ground and would be until approaching midnight. I was staying in a Hilton Hotel no more than ten minutes drive away from the ground, but we were advised not to leave and it was around 11pm before I could get away.

From the car park I could see the skies around lit up with the orange of fires. I drove round the back roads trying to find a route out, but the police had closed a lot of the streets and we were being diverted miles out of the way. It was very frightening. I don't suppose anyone would have had a go at me as I had been the season's top scorer with 17 league goals, 20 in all competitions, but I didn't want to risk it. I had just been part of a team that had lost a playoff semi-final and I was glad I had a few mates with me in the car.

I drove past a kiddies' playground that had been levelled; those little rocking horses had been ripped up to throw at police cars. With no visiting fans to get at – they were well protected as they had been bussed out – the police became the targets and the local area the battleground for what was genuinely a riot. I remember later seeing some news footage of a woman at her front door screaming at a bunch of yobs not to smash up the local area. It made no sense fouling your own doorstep like that, but such was the red mist that had descended in the wake of our defeat.

There was also talk that a lot of the trouble was down to fans of other clubs who had jumped into it and stirred up trouble just to darken Millwall's reputation. The argument made some sense. Why would you do this to your own patch?

Now, there are few with more affection for the 'Wall than me but if there were Lions fans doing this, it was something you just couldn't defend. There had been some tasty encounters with some big clubs who have tough followings, from Birmingham to Cardiff, but this was completely different.

You can only try and grasp what the area and the club have to deal with. It is an old-fashioned part of London, less privileged than neighbouring areas, still very working-class, down to earth and short of the investment other parts of the capital seem to get. Chelsea it ain't and, sometimes, there are chips on shoulders.

Nearby, Crystal Palace and Charlton are such different, more family kinds of clubs who enjoy a day out at the game. In the middle of the two, 'Wall are a magnet for some of the worst geezers around, lads who fancy themselves as being a bit handy and who seem to like being in the centre of something a bit edgy and dangerous. People talk about a lunatic fringe following the club. I think it's bigger than that, I have to be honest having seen a lot of them, because of the violent hangers-on who aren't gen-uine followers of the club.

The club has also had a reputation for racism, despite being in a multi-cultural area and working hard at the Kick Racism Out campaign, but in one example I can think of, it's hard to see it completely as such, more born of ignorance and an easy expression of anger and resentment.

We were playing Coventry City at home and I was standing next to their defender Richard Shaw during a break in play. All of a sudden, a metal bolt hit me on the shoulder. I looked into the stands and saw a bloke making his way ten rows down the aisle to the front. He was shouting, "You fucking black cunt," at Richard, who I guess was supposed to have been on the receiving end of the bolt.

One of our own black players, Paul Ifill, who was also standing alongside took exception and let the bloke know. "Sorry, Ifes," he said. "I didn't mean you. You're great. You're one of us."

I stood there scratching my head. Paul looked at me and laughed. Richard had once played for Crystal Palace but, with great irony, would sign for Millwall a few years later and even went on to become their Player of the Year. That fan probably even voted for him then. The double standards of some football fans can be almost ludicrous at times.

When I contemplated our playoff defeat in the cold light of the following morning, the fires having been dampened down, I was distraught. Everybody remembers me for reaching the Premiership with Leicester via the playoffs, but I had also gone out with Cambridge United. This was the second time and the feeling didn't get any better.

Birmingham went on to win the final at the Millennium Stadium on penalties over Norwich City, who we had beaten 4-0 on opening day and who had overcome third-placed Wolves in their semi-final. I was asked to go down to Cardiff for Sky Sports and it was tough watching it all.

I did meet up with Karren Brady, the Birmingham chief executive, and her husband Paul Peschisolido and had a good chat about the old times. I didn't bring up the subject of my fractious contract negotiations with her though, ones which prompted her to get her solicitor to send me a writ after mentioning the episode in *Tales from the Boot Camps*. Nothing came of it, though.

Brum were not a great side, certainly no better than us, even though they probably had a deeper squad. We had 12 players really who pulled it together and we were fortunate to steer clear of injuries, apart from Richard Sadlier at a bad time, although we filled in around him. Tony Warner was a good keeper, and although Stuart Nethercott and Sean Dyche were not the best central defenders, we had good players around them, like full-backs Matt Lawrence and Robbie Ryan.

Then there were Cahill and Livermore in the centre of mid-field, with Ifill and Steven Reid either side and me and Sadlier up front. When we were all fit, it was quite some starting XI, and looking back it was a privilege to be among so many who would go on to have excellent careers at the top level.

It was a strange summer, the first for three years I hadn't spent recovering from an injury with my ribs having mended by now. Most of the time I moped, I think. When we got back together for pre-season, our playoff defeat was still very much in our systems and I sensed there could be a long hangover. The mood at the club was very downbeat.

Quite often, coming so close but being so far away can mean the break-up of a team, and so it would prove for us, if not imme-diately. It is tough to recreate the intensity and desire to have another shot at it. On top of that, the game's authorities had, understandably, come down heavily on the club following the post-playoff defeat riots and the club introduced a new member-ship scheme to try and keep troublemakers out.

The trouble was it would come to seem as if they were trying to keep everyone out. So weird were the conditions, I think you had to be 5ft 6in tall and have ginger hair and a limp to get a membership card. And you had to apply in person for member-ship between midnight and 12.30am on a Monday night. Whatever hoops they put you through, you couldn't get in with-out a membership card and a ticket on a Saturday afternoon.

And few away fans now wanted to venture to the New Den. After what had happened, you couldn't blame them.

Dion had gone back to Villa after our playoff exit – and had scored for them on the last day of the Premiership in a 3-1 win over Chelsea – and we would also lose two major talents, in Cahill, who would get injured in September and not return until April and, even worse, Sadlier. He had been a substitute on opening day but was not properly fit and although he came back for four games the next March, his hip was never right. He tried again the following season but, after two appearances as a sub, he was forced to retire at the tender age of 24.

It was a great sadness above all to Richard, but also to me as his partner up front; I am a lover of the game and I love to see young talent coming through. I had really enjoyed playing with him and it was no surprise to me that the papers were talking of Manchester United's interest in him.

Richard could do anything. He was great in the air, quick and had two good feet. A nice lad, he had a good temperament, too; everything, in fact, to go right to the top. Back in Ireland, they used to call him the next Niall Quinn, but I thought he was better, quicker and more mobile, as well as being strong.

I had negotiated a new one-year deal at the same money of around £4,500 a week back in the spring while the going was good. I suppose I could have got more, but I loved the club and didn't want to leave, which they were aware of and so probably knew they could get away without paying me more. Some of the boys were on more than me, but I was happy.

And so I went in for pre-season training but did the running with such ease – as was always the case as I kept myself fit in the close season – that Mark McGhee and his first-team coach Ray Harford told me to go home and report back a week before the season. They knew they could trust me to keep myself fit, and to be fair to McGhee he was really good with me like that.

Ray had been Kenny Dalglish's No. 2 during Blackburn's title-winning days in the 1990s before taking over as manager himself and had now taken over from Steve Gritt, who was a good bloke but seemed to have been made a victim of the previous season. Ray was a smashing guy, bubbly as coaches should be, and it would come as a shock and real sadness to me a few years later when he died of cancer. He once told me as we ran side by side on the treadmills as we often did that he and Kenny had tried to buy me for Blackburn when they were winning promotion out of the old First Division.

Very little felt right going into the season. There was an uncertainty to the squad with a few still waiting to sign contracts and none of the bonuses for the season sorted out. There was also a suspicion that Theo and Bob Pearson, who had previously had a lot of input into picking the team, had become less involved, as McGhee's power base had grown following the run to the playoffs the previous season.

Not that Theo and Bob were entirely out of the picture. I remember one time that season when we were having a pre-match meal ahead of a game at Watford and Ray Harford got chatting to this player who he thought was a new Watford signing in the hotel because his club were putting him up there. Ray was then a bit surprised to see the lad get on our coach, asked him what he was doing, the lad replying that he was with us. Ray went to speak to Mark McGhee who knew only slightly more, that the lad had been told to report with the first-team squad.

The squad needed a boost with new blood and there was not much coming in. Andy Roberts, out of contract at Crystal Palace, trained with us but, as he was so overweight, he looked a bit like that marshmallow man in *Ghostbusters*. The squad, by contrast, began to look a bit thin. We had hoped to be kicking on, what with having come so close the previous season, but we desperately needed a fresh injection of players. We had played as well as we could have and needed a fresh impetus, but it didn't look as though it was going to happen. Not that it would have been worth saying anything. You never felt that McGhee was the sort of manager who would go to the chairman to voice any of the players' concerns.

When we kicked off against Rotherham, he fielded an unbalanced side, with two left-backs, Robbie Ryan and Ronnie Bull. Everything that could go wrong for us did – and everything that could go right for Rotherham did – and we were beaten by an embarrassing 6-0. Now I have heard plenty of swear words in my time but I learned a few that were not even in my vocabulary that day. When they turn at the New Den, they turn big time.

I don't know about the fans singing "No one likes us, we don't care", it should have been the players.

You could hear most of the fans' complaints pretty well, too. Due to the new membership scheme, there was a crowd of only just over 7,000 to watch us play against Rotherham; it reflected the downbeat nature of the club following that night against Birmingham a few months earlier and it was a huge contrast to the optimism that had gone before it.

As a player, you could only try and be professional and let this feeling of "us against the world" wash over you and not let it affect your preparation or performance. But that is easier said than done. A TV documentary that was aired about the club and its reputation around that time didn't help. You could say that we should have used all the adversity to bond us, but the stuffing had been knocked out of us and it would be a struggle to get it back.

You could only put the opening-day thrashing down to experience and hope that a 0-0 draw in our second game at Watford was going to be more reflective, although an exit from the League Cup – then the Worthington Cup – at the hands of Rushden and Diamonds on penalties, did not bode well.

That night, the kit manager had forgotten to load the boot skip on the coach and the club had to borrow some money off Rushden to go out and find a local sports shop to buy new boots for all the players. The Doc Martens of the sponsors in the club shop just wouldn't do the job. It was lucky the shoewear company's boss Max Griggs was still putting his money into the home club at that time otherwise we might have struggled. I was all right, mind. I always kept my boots with me in my kitbag. It is just another example of there being method in my madness.

I seemed to be made the scapegoat for us failing to score in our opening couple of league games and was dropped to the bench for Ben May – a decent enough young kid coming through, but by no means better than me – for the next game against Gillingham. We lost 1-0. Them again.

I was starting to get the hump with McGhee and it took two more games, a draw at home to Ipswich and a defeat at Sheffield United that left us in the relegation zone, before he recalled me to partner his favourite Neil Harris. I obliged with both goals in the 2-0 victory over Grimsby, our first win of the season.

All through the autumn I was in and out of the team and it became an unsettling, frustrating period. I was friendly with Andy Roberts, who got bombed out when he struggled to keep his weight in check, but then got on well with Dennis Wise, who had come to us after being sacked by Leicester following a fracas on a trip abroad with Calum Davidson, who got his jaw broken.

Dennis was always fine with me and I have been friendly with him ever since. You can only judge someone on how you find them and I had no desire simply to judge him on his reputation. Too many people in football do, but I figure that if I want people to make up their own minds about me rather than believe all the far-fetched stories, then I have to be open-minded myself.

I don't think McGhee wanted him at the club and he was, like me, more of a signing by Theo Paphitis. Dennis was now in his mid-30s and was looking to go into coaching in the near future, so I think the manager might have felt a bit threatened by him.

Eventually, it would surprise me that Dennis ended up at Newcastle as a director in charge of football, with a brief of recruiting players. He might have had trouble finding the place as we once had a conversation where he talked about Barnsley being off the M25. Neither did he strike me particularly as a student of the game, or as someone who knew a lot about players and where to get them, but he was good mates with the property developer Paul Kemsley, who was a big friend of the Newcastle owner Mike Ashley. Often in this game it's about being in the right place at the right time. I get the feeling that Dennis is a bit like me – he never quite knows where life is going to lead him.

We had some other names in on loan, like Kevin Davies, whose career was in the doldrums at Southampton after a big-money move to Blackburn but who finally went on to be a success with Bolton, and Glen Johnson, who had been farmed out by Chelsea to get some experience but who ended up at Portsmouth and did well to rehabilitate his career. We could never get firing, though, and with Tim Cahill also struggling to score goals now in this opening period before long-term injury, we got stuck in the relegation zone for the first half of the season.

It was not enjoyable now for many players. McGhee was chopping and changing the side so much and the fans were now getting on his back. The whole place was crumbling, the situation was slipping away, and you could feel it.

I did enjoy my return to Leicester City just before Christmas that season, even though we were beaten 4-1. I scored in the first few minutes and the home fans broke out into their "Super Stevie Claridge" song that they used to sing when I was at the club.

I had a good Christmas again, scoring in a 3-1 win at Rotherham that turned our opening day result against them around. It prompted me to ask about a new contract but after consulting with the chairman, McGhee told me I would have to wait. We had drawn Southampton, then of the Premiership, away in the third round of the FA Cup – let's see if we get through, I was told, and we'll have more money and can make some decisions then.

The game at St Mary's proved the highlight of the season for me. McGhee let me stay at home overnight on the Friday and I drove the few miles to link up with the team at the Solent Hotel on the Saturday morning. I was feeling up for this one – Saints were the old enemy for this Portsmouth lad.

I missed a great chance to open the scoring for us early on, with Paul Ifill getting in my way, and the home crowd gave me some fearful stick. I soon shut them up, though, by making amends with a poached goal ten minutes later and loved it. I turned my shirt around and showed them my name on the back of my shirt. They knew it well enough anyway, though, and hated it, which I enjoyed.

We should have won but Kevin Davies – who had been on loan with us a couple of months earlier – grabbed a late equaliser, prompting me to give him a kick up the arse as we left the pitch. It took the tie back to the New Den where, as often proves the case, the Premier club prevailed at the second attempt by 2-0.

It was funny. I played well against them and found out the following season that their then manager Gordon Strachan had considered signing me in the next summer. He needed someone to hold the ball up, play 15 or so of the less intense games the following season to ease the burden on his first-choice strikers.

That would have been quite something. Me getting back in the Premiership at the age of 37, and with Southampton. That would have taken some thinking about. I might never have been able to show my face in Portsmouth again. But then again, there are plenty of Pompey fans who go and work in Southampton every day.

After that, the season petered out for me as once again I found myself in and out of the side. There were some good moments, too. I got the ball rolling with a goal in a 4-0 win over Watford and scored both goals in a win over Grimsby that took us up to mid-table, but my relationship with the manager was now patchy at best.

The end really came for me in early March against Burnley, when McGhee dragged me off after about 50 minutes. I had not been playing that well, but didn't reckon I had been that bad and finally I cracked. I was tired of being messed around and had a right go at him in the tunnel. I told him that this was a joke and that I was fed up with him. It was the first and only time I lost it with him.

He had apparently been a very fiery and feisty centre-forward himself during his playing days with Aberdeen under Sir Alex Ferguson's management but as a manager he was a laid-back sort. He never panicked and never lost his rag, which many may say is a strength, but I prefer a boss who has changes of tone, so that players can see what is serious and what is not. You can't constantly keep beating people up, but equally you can't remain laid-back all the time or the players won't be able to sense differences in situations. You need a range.

And so he said nothing back to me, but he knew he had all the power. Between then and the end of the season, I would start only twice more, in games when he needed me due to injuries and the rest of the time I was on the bench. He got a big striker in from Brentford, Mark McCammon, to partner Neil Harris and I knew which way the wind was blowing.

The club did have a decent finish to the season, mainly thanks to a run of games against teams who had little to play for, and finished a respectable ninth, but we were past our best, could never reach the heights of the previous season and although too good to go down, were never again challenging for the playoffs. You sensed this would signal the break-up of the side; that the club would probably look to cash in on the likes of Cahill, Reid and Ifill, which they duly did.

Now aged 37, it was time for me to re-evaluate my future, too. I had always given up a lot for football and had always been prepared to do more than most, but travelling up and down from Portsmouth to London, then staying in a hotel for part of the week, was not ideal. At first, I travelled up and back every day with Paul Moody, who lived near me, but he was getting a bad back sitting in traffic on the A3 every morning so started to stay up there.

I started to do the same, just trying to get home for two days a week. I spent a lot of time on my own watching telly, using the gym and spinning out meals. When I checked out at the end of the season, I asked them how much my bill had come to over the previous two-and-a-half seasons. They said around £100,000. I had asked Millwall several times about the possibility of renting a flat for me, which probably would have cost about £30,000 over that spell, but it never happened. Such are the false economies football clubs think they are making sometimes. Actually I should have bought a flat around there myself. At the time they were going for £175,000 and more than doubled in value over the next few years.

There was a similar false economy regarding me and my salary. By now they had offered me another year, but at a reduced wage of £125,000 for the next 12 months. I thought I was worth more and that it would cost them a lot more than that to get another striker of my ability. Besides, I wasn't sure if I could face another season of being mucked about by McGhee, even though he was being decent to me at this point. He told me I should take the offer because the club would not be handing out the lucrative contracts it had been doing in the past. It seemed to indicate that he wanted me to stay.

I wanted to take my time. I had a testimonial to organise as well, with Pompey having agreed to let me have Fratton Park on a Bank Holiday Monday that May. They had moved on and done well under Harry Redknapp by now and had just won promotion to the Premiership, so the place was in party mood.

The club had guaranteed me £100,000 from the testimonial when I took the deal to go to Millwall, but I worked really hard to get players and auction items off my own bat and ended up making around £120,000 from a good, appreciative crowd of more than 12,000, so saving the club a fortune. When you are organising something like that and need favours from people you have done them for and get a no in response, you certainly find out who your friends are, as I did over those few weeks.

Against a Pompey side, Alan Ball managed my International XI, which included Emile Heskey, who played a blinder for me by flying down from Liverpool in a day and back, Dennis Wise, Ray Wilkins and Ally McCoist. In fact, the way some people put themselves out for me was amazing and I was very touched.

The PFA certainly did their best for me as well. Teddy Sheringham and Robbie Keane had agreed to play in the match but on the Sunday night I got a call from Tottenham Hotspur saying that they were not insured to play and that I would have to get cover. I checked out some prices and the premiums were just astronomical. When I phoned Gordon Taylor, the PFA chief executive, he said he would sort it and was as good as his word. The premiums were paid.

"If we can't help you after all you've done in the game, we wouldn't be doing our job," Gordon said to me. It was something I really appreciated.

As well as Ted and Robbie, I had Matthew Le Tissier on my team and he had agreed to play the role of the pantomime villain. Because he was from Southampton, he played with the word "Scummer" – Portsmouth fans' nickname for that lot up the road – on the back of his Pompey shirt. He insisted on wearing a Saints shirt underneath it and revealed it after he scored from the penalty spot. The game ended in an enjoyable 5-5 draw.

I must have been in a good mood then when my old co-writer Ian Ridley phoned me and asked if I would play in another testimonial that week. Ian had just taken over as chairman at Weymouth, one of my early clubs, and was offering the princely sum of £200 out of his own pocket for me to turn out for David Laws, the club's striking legend, against a Yeovil Town team who had just been promoted to the Football League as Conference champions.

I took pity on him and agreed, but was a bit shocked by the state of the club as Weymouth lost 5-1, with me creating a consolation goal for Lawsie. The pitch was in a terrible mess, the stadium was crumbling and the crowd of 1,500 was the biggest they had seen for a fair old while. I told Ian I didn't envy his task down there.

After that, it was a few weeks off. And a stand-off with Millwall over the summer about a new contract, but I was in no rush.

Despite my age I was still really fit because I lived to a proper regime.

I think I proved that when I agreed that summer to take part in the BBC series *Superstars* at the La Manga resort in Spain. The programme had been a big hit with massive audiences back in the 1970s as it pitted sportsmen from different backgrounds against each other in a series of disciplines. The judo player Brian Jacks became a national celebrity as a result of winning it. Footballers generally did badly, and many people's lasting memory of the programme is of Kevin Keegan wobbling about on a bicycle around a track before falling off.

Now the Beeb were bringing it back and I was invited out for six days' filming that turned into ten as I did better than they or I imagined in reaching the final.

In my heat, I had the cyclist Chris Boardman, rugby players Rory and Tony Underwood, cricketer Dermot Reeve, runner Iwan Thomas and world champion boxer Steve Collins, who was a very intimidating man; when he talked about how much he loved fighting, I believed him.

I managed to win the heat, though. It was my type of event as I am very competitive and love trying any sport. We had 100- and 800-metre runs, target golf, rowing, cycling, swimming, archery and gym tests, although I wasn't eligible for the football skills. I was flattered when the former Scotland rugby union player Gavin Hastings said he had never come across someone with all-round abilities like mine.

I gave it a good go in the final – the only footballer ever to get that far – and won the tennis, the golf and the 800 metres, but I tailed off and struggled in the technical events, like the archery and rowing. Still, at least I did better than Dennis Wise, who enjoyed the social side of it in the evenings even more than I did. He dived off a stage one night and was fortunate that a group of people caught him.

In the end, I finished fifth and was pleased with how I had done. The athlete Du'aine Ladejo won it, with another athlete,

Jamie Baulch, not that far behind, along with the skier Alain Baxter. Incidentally, before the competition, I thought footballers gave each other serious stick. They don't come close to the athletes.

Once I got back home, I waited for the phone to ring, figuring that Millwall would improve their contract offer or that a new club would give me a better deal. Someone did come in for me, but it was neither who nor what I expected.

3. *In Dorset? Not sure that I would*

I had always said – and repeated it at the end of *Tales from the Boot Camps* – that if I ever became chairman of Weymouth, Steve had the job as manager. I never thought that either part of that would come to pass, particularly the second.

I had first met him when he was a player for my hometown team back in 1985, on loan from Bournemouth. He was not finding regular favour with the then Cherries' manager Harry Redknapp at Dean Court, but was proving a revelation for the club I supported – who went by the nickname of the Terras due to the terra-cotta and blue strip they once wore – and they were sufficiently impressed to buy him for £10,000. The club had money then, having just moved from their town-centre ground to the Wessex Stadium, and were pressing for a place in the Football League from what was then the Alliance Premier League, now the Conference.

I encountered him again during my work as a football writer a decade later – he was at Birmingham City at the time – and we became firm friends as his itinerant career wound its way through the Midlands back to Pompey and then on to Millwall.

Now I had grown tired of watching Weymouth lurch from crisis to crisis since being relegated back to the Southern League – even falling into a regional division of it – at one stage – a few years after Steve's departure to Crystal Palace on a free transfer as a result of the club missing a deadline to offer him a new contract.

Returning to the town now and then to take my father to games, it was demoralising seeing the long-ball brand of football on offer as the

100

team finished 17th and narrowly avoided relegation. The gates had fallen to around 600. I offered to help, seeking to become chairman and to use my contacts and experience to try and turn the club around. After a three-month power struggle that should have forewarned me of the politics around the club that was to follow, the board of directors agreed.

My first act was to sack a manager in Geoff Butler whose brand of direct football had been unpopular and I cast around for managers. Steve was always top of the wish list, but a wish seemed to be all it would be. He was out of contract at Millwall and, though contemplating management soon, as the fittest 37-year-old in English football he was still capable of playing in the Championship; in fact there were 27-year-olds who were less fit. He looked, quite literally, out of our league.

As I kept meeting candidates that summer of 2003, I would ring him for input and advice. Eventually, I was ready to appoint Shaun Teale, another favourite son of the club who had gone on to play for Bournemouth and Aston Villa. I asked Steve one last time. He asked me to go and see him. I was intrigued.

To my surprise, all of a sudden he had become interested and, after a five-hour negotiation that would bring him a basic salary of £1,000 a week with the rest in bonuses – about a third of what he had been getting at Millwall – we had a deal. Or nearly. Over the next 24 hours he would be back on the phone for such deal-sealers as a season ticket for his dad.

It was astonishing news really: Steve Claridge was to become player-manager of little old Weymouth. *Sky Sports News* ran it as "Breaking News". The press conference drew a bigger crowd than the club had been getting for matches.

I told everyone that if Sir Alex Ferguson and Arsene Wenger had both applied for the job, I would still have given it to Steve. What we needed was a figure who would galvanise the club and the town and he had the charisma to do that, as well as the ability, through playing and managing, to turn the team around. In addition, his name would help to sell sponsorship. The phrase these days is "ticking the boxes". Steve ticked more boxes than there were boxes.

First, he would score goals for us, in tandem with the good striker we already had at the club, Lee Phillips. Second, he would bring the crowds back. Third, he would attract revenue and sponsors to the club. For that level, we were paying him well, yes, at £1,000 a week with the rest based on bonuses for results and gate figures, but we would recoup that money in spades.

That night we also held a fans' forum in at the upstairs bars of the Wessex Stadium. The place was packed and Steve drew a huge cheer when he asked the rhetorical question of whether they wanted to "live the dream". The phrase stuck and became our slogan. I had forgotten that it had also been Leeds United's under Peter Ridsdale and should have known better.

Later in the season, an ITV film crew would come down to record a feature for their Saturday lunchtime football show and I would tell them the story of the "live the dream" moment. When interviewed, Steve insisted that "it was the chairman's idea". It prompted Andy Townsend – a former Weymouth player himself as a youngster – to comment that the two of us were obviously on the same wavelength.

I had been happy to give Steve a five-year contract not only because I knew he needed security should I leave the club – and since I was certain he was the right man for the job even if I departed – but also because if a bigger club came in for him, Weymouth would be due a wedge of compensation.

He would also lead by example. "Steve was, hands down, the fittest player I have ever played with, and that's not taking into account his age," says John Waldock, a Wearsider who had joined the club years before and who had stayed because he liked the area, becoming club captain.

On a limited budget, Steve attracted some good players to the club, notably Lee Philpott, who had played with him at Leicester City and who had latterly been at Hull. Then there was Paul Buckle, a feisty midfield player who took a pay cut to join us from Aldershot.

"I knew what he had achieved in the game and knew that if he was at Weymouth then he must be ambitious and the club must be ambitious," says Buckle.

Results were immediate. "Steve was very tactically astute," Waldock recalls. "He knew what formation to play against what opposition and what style of football to play in which areas of the pitch. He knew every detail about everyone we were about to face, so he knew how to adapt the team to win the game."

Adds Buckle: "He wore his heart on his sleeve and was operating playing below his level. He made me team captain and I knew I had made the right move. I was impressed by the club and the players and the great team spirit he provoked. He was always very fair.

"Early on I had a big row with John Waldock at half-time over some incident or other that happened in a game. John was a good man and it was just a professional thing, but I think Steve knew then that I was not there for the ride, that I was going to be honest, and I think he liked that. He liked honesty in the dressing room. He was the same. We were both passionate people. If you are honest, you are going to have an impact."

As we surged to the top of the table, it was an astonishing time, one of those periods in your life that you will always look back on as a time you felt really alive. The whole town was abuzz. For the first time many people around the club could remember, everyone was pulling in the same direction.

And all this was going on without a big backroom staff. "He never really had a first-team coach and used to phone me every day," Paul Buckle recalls. "He was always open, asking me how the players felt. He needed that. It can be a lonely place being a manager and I was happy for him to bounce things off me.

"We talked about it and I think he wanted to make me first-team coach. He knew I had been coaching at the Centre of Excellence at Exeter City and was gradually letting me take some sessions. He takes a while to trust people, but if he does, he shows you loyalty.

"I think that's what he needed, because he was best as a manager who man-managed and used that 'wow' factor pre-match and in the golden ten minutes at half-time. And when he walked in wearing a suit, he had that. I was always inspired by him in the dressing room. But he was playing as well and you can't do it all and be fresh for the talks at half-time. Tactics are important, but those talks can make a massive difference."

Coming from another angle, John Waldock did not always see it that way. He had not played in the full-time professional game as Buckle had with Colchester and Brentford and felt that Steve had been over-the-top on occasions with players who were not used to the intensity of the pro game. It is something Steve would come to acknowledge, but defended his approach by saying that, compared to football higher up the scale, it was nothing unusual.

"Steve's management style was the one and only thing that let him down in his time at Weymouth," Waldock believes. "To say his style was brutal would be an understatement. The Alex Ferguson hairdryer would be described as a subtle breeze in comparison with some of Steve's post-match debriefs."

I had persuaded a television production company to follow us for the season, to bring in some much-needed revenue, and they had sold the series, entitled *Football Diaries*, to BBC2. It captured the frantic fun surrounding a club that was being turned around, and also the knockabout nature of some of my own dealings with Steve. One TV critic saw us as Terry and Bob from *The Likely Lads* – no prizes for guessing which was which – another as Jack and Vera Duckworth from *Coronation Street*, a married couple at war.

Some of it you wished they hadn't captured, like arguing with him when he arrived late – a rare occurrence, I have to say, despite earlier lapses in his career – for a testimonial golf day for John Waldock. Some of it you were glad they hadn't, like me having a go at him after one of the players had left pornography at the house I rented in the town, which was found by my then 14-year-old son, Jack.

The property at the end of the beach road, and which overlooked the sea, was also used to put up players and it became something of a mad house in which Steve would hold court and cook pasta and chicken as the team members who came from afar and who needed accommodation watched daytime TV.

Lee Philpott would be teased for bringing fresh eggs that his wife supplied from their chickens. Luke Nightingale would be ridiculed for his French O-level and quiet nature. One time, they were watching some reality show when Luke, uncharacteristically, piped up to tell them who had won it, knowing it to be a repeat. He was bombarded with cushions and plastic water bottles.

Going out in the town with Steve was also an experience. Because he had an engaging common touch, he would make conversation with anyone in bars. In nightclubs, I would see the truth of his Millwall colleague Robbie Ryan's description of him dancing alone at first hand. Not that I stayed. I recall one night when he came home at around 3am, waking me up in the process, and kept a taxi waiting outside. Half an hour later he was gone again. When I asked him about it the next day, he said he didn't like the toilets in the nightclub and needed to come home.

The high point of the mad whirl arrived with an amazing 8-0 win over our local rivals Dorchester Town on Boxing Day in front of a remarkable crowd of 3,728, with Steve and Lee Phillips both scoring hat-tricks. The turning-point time was not far behind, though.

On New Year's Day, in a controversial return match that saw Steve sent off for only the second time in his career, Dorchester rediscovered their spirit and held us to a draw. Two days later, we lost at home to Crawley Town who were becoming our closest rivals. Steve missed a penalty in the match.

You couldn't be upset with Steve, though, as it was he who had carried us to those heights. My assessment was the same as Paul Buckle's: "The great thing about Steve," he said, "was that you knew he was always giving as much in every game for Weymouth as if he was playing a cup final for Leicester."

In truth, due to a limited squad Steve had been papering over cracks on the field and, behind the scenes, so had I.

At the start of the season, the old board of directors had resigned en masse, believing that Steve was too expensive and that the whole thing would go pear-shaped, at least financially. I had managed to recruit a new group, though, both from local businessmen and moneyed supporters who lived away from the town.

Between us, we had put in more than £100,000 in the form of share-buying, but with the stadium in need of work to get a safety certificate and pressing debts from the previous regime to pay off, that money had long gone. A couple of the local directors now decided against buying the shares they had promised and money became tight. Our challenge faltered.

Steve was performing miracles but, as the results started to turn, it was hard to get people to see just what a great season we were having. Even with a record turnover of almost £500,000, the club had lost money, as we knew it would in its first year of being virtually re-launched. In cash terms, though, when you considered the amount of money the directors had put into the club, the loss was less than £50,000. Given the progress we had made, though, it was worth it. Now we had two choices: we either had to cut back and run the club along strict income-and-expenditure lines or we had to seek new investment.

An old friend and board member, Charlie Lesser, offered to buy up around £300,000 worth of shares in return for control of the club, but he expected to revamp it and was looking to make a profit. The board declined the offer and although Charlie would have rethought his plans to make a more acceptable offer, several members – mainly those who had declined to invest the previous season when we needed them to – had been wooing a new man called Martyn Harrison, a local hotelier. He was willing, it seemed, to put in a no-strings-attached sum of money.

At first I was happy that Steve would get the increased playing budget he needed to have another title tilt, but as decisions were now being made without me being consulted my position as chairman became untenable. The fun was going from the club, I sensed. And there had been a lot of fun.

Steve's fondness for fruit – and I once presented him with a pineapple as a birthday present in the dressing room before a game, much to the amusement of the team – was well known among the players. John Waldock certainly recalls it.

"It was a Friday night before an away game in a hotel and I had just been out to buy strawberries and grapes to eat that night and bananas for the match the next day," he says.

"I was settling down at 8.30pm to watch a film before bed when he knocked on my door. I let him in and wondered what he wanted. I feared he was about to tell me that he was dropping me.

"He started asking about the film, and I told him it was *Godfather II*, when he spotted the strawberries, wondering where I got them from and how much they cost. As I answered, he interrupted to tell me to turn the telly up and keep telling him what the film was about. I got up to find the remote to turn the telly up, kept talking then turned round to find him gone. Along with the strawberries, grapes and bananas."

What Steve and I had established – and which Harrison had coveted and was now dismantling – was being eroded. I felt guilty knowing that Steve would now be in the firing line from a new, more aggressive but less knowledgeable board – two of my other appointees as directors having also now resigned – but for my own sanity and integrity, I had little choice.

Steve, meanwhile, endured a patchy start to the season, but gradually started to turn it around to the point where the team was looking like likely challengers for the playoffs. All of a sudden, though, Harrison had other ideas.

3.1 Close-season Encounters

Ian kept phoning me about Weymouth. I had first got to know him there when I was a player and he a supporter around 18 years earlier. I thought he was a bit mad, but fair play to him for wanting to give it a go at what was once a more than decent non-League club, one actually with Football League potential, but which had fallen on hard times. They were in the Conference when I had a spell there and once even finished runners-up in the days before automatic promotion to the old Fourth Division and playoffs. Now they were back in the Southern League, a level below.

Ian had just sacked the manager Geoff Butler after a season in which the club had barely avoided relegation to a regional division of the Southern League and, according to Ian, had played some dire football. I could understand why he did it, though you never want managers to lose their jobs. I had played a testimonial match down there for David Laws and Butler had not particularly impressed me in the dressing room with either his personality or his knowledge.

It was now early June and Ian was offering me the job as player-manager. I told him I was flattered he was asking me, but no thanks. I did want to be a manager one day soon, but I reckoned my full-time professional career was nowhere near finished. And though it was a full-time commitment to a management job, the football was part-time, semi-professional, with training two nights a week.

Besides, even allowing for Millwall's stingy deal on the table at around half of last season's money – and I still reckoned I could get them up to at least £3,000 a week – he couldn't come anywhere near the money I could still command just for playing, let alone the added burden of management.

He went out looking for an alternative and kept ringing, though, seeking my advice, mainly about appointing a manager. He would put a name to me and, if I knew them, I would offer an opinion. He told me that he was close to appointing an old team-mate of mine at Weymouth back in the late 1980s, Shaun Teale, a strong defender who went on to have a good career with Bournemouth and Aston Villa before managing in non-League football with Burscough of the Northern Premier League. In what was quite an achievement, he had just won the FA Trophy with them, the top knock-out competition for non-League clubs, when they were really no more than a village side.

I told him that it sounded good and to go and get Shaun, because I was sure he would do a good job. Before doing so, Ian asked me again whether I was sure I didn't want the job. I thought about it for few seconds and then told him to come and see me at my home.

I was disappointed with Millwall. They were mucking me about again. I had been joint top scorer with 12 goals the previous season, even though I had not played in half the games, and I was still popular with the fans, who had made me player of the season the year before. I suppose I could have signed thinking that McGhee may well get the push if we had another start like last year's, but is that really a reason to re-sign for a club?

On top of all that, I had rung Theo Paphitis a couple of times off my own bat to ask him if there was any room for negotiation on the contract offer. This is the time of your career, remember, when agents can suddenly go missing. They know there is not much money to be made out of you any more and suddenly start devoting themselves to the younger lads on their books. You do expect them to stay in touch at least, mind. Theo, however, said no. You know then that this a club that doesn't really want to keep you, although I suppose, to be honest, I would have gritted my teeth and taken the deal had nothing else come along.

And although there was plenty of time to find another club – it was now the end of June and pre-season training didn't start for another week or two, which was the time managers started getting twitchy and phoning you up – I wanted a bit more certainty and stability in my life.

Ian outlined the state of Weymouth to me. At around 650, gates were still pretty good for a club at that level, but around half of what they would be if the team had been in any reasonable shape. There were only around half a dozen decent players left at the club, he reckoned, most of them who were out of contract and trying to get fixed up elsewhere.

On top of that, after doing all the sums, he said that the most he could pay any manager would be around £600 a week and that the wage bill could be no more than £6,500 a week. There were individual players at Millwall on more than that. He was a crap salesman.

Or maybe he was a good one, because I found myself thinking about it really seriously. Ian was very sincere and passionate about it and I admired anyone in the game with those motivations. They had been mine throughout my career. I began to think it was an interesting challenge. I remembered Weymouth as a good club and had enjoyed my three seasons there. It's a bit like thinking about a holiday years later, I suppose. You remember the good times, the sun and the sand, and not the family rows. We had a good team at that level back then, too, with several of us going on to enjoy League careers.

And when someone keeps asking, it means they really want you. We all know it is nice to be wanted. It was like when David Pleat kept trying to get me for Luton. I have always believed you should go to where they believe in you. On top of all that, I wanted to work with someone I could trust and I had always thought Ian was a straight sort of bloke – too straight for his own

good sometimes, as he was too trusting of people. A fringe benefit was that I could live at home for a change.

One drawback was that my media work, mainly with Radio 5
Live and Sky Sports, was taking off and I thought being a
Southern League manager, rather than a Championship footballer, might harm my profile and that they might not want me
any more. Ian checked it out with them and told me that they
were more interested in what I had to say than what I was doing.
It was still going to mean more travelling up to London, though.

What with the money Weymouth were going to be paying me,
I would need everything I could earn from media work as well. I
was going to be taking a serious pay cut to take on this job. Ian
knew that and agreed to it. He said he liked the idea of me being
in the media, anyway, as it would get our name known and
maybe increase crowds and sponsorship.

I wasn't going to do it for nothing, though. I could guarantee
him goals as well as my management and I said I wanted a basic
of £1,500 a week. He took a deep breath and shook his head. It
was half of what I could get from somewhere else, but a good
sum for them, I realised, with their previous manager having
been on a few hundred quid and the top player on £400. I also
wanted bonuses for promotion. Ian came back with a figure of
£1,000 basic a week, with other sums added on a productivity
basis. If crowds and league positions were good, I would get
bonuses. If I made plenty of appearances and scored goals, I
would also benefit.

If we averaged around 2,000 spectators a match and I scored
40 goals, I could earn around £100,000 for the season. But if that
was the case, the club would also be making profits from the
attendance and the increased revenue through the bar and food
outlets. And if I got promotion, then I would be due a bonus of
£20,000, which the club would then be able to afford from all the
new sponsorship money that comes from being in the
Conference.

I didn't have too many problems agreeing to the low basic. It is how football should be, we both agreed. If clubs were making money, so should those who create the wealth. If they weren't, they just got the minimum affordable. It was an incentive for me to get the crowds up and, hopefully, create a team that could challenge for promotion to the Conference.

I did insist on a five-year contract, though. Ian had a good vision for the club, of getting up into the Conference within three years, by which time the club hoped to have a deal for a new stadium. Back in 1987 when I was a player, we had moved from the old Recreation Ground by the harbour out to the new concrete Wessex Stadium on the edge of town. The Asda supermarket chain had bought the old Rec to build a supermarket.

Now they had outgrown that site and wanted to build a superstore on the Wessex Stadium site, agreeing to build a new stadium in return. Ian had inherited the deal from the previous board and was in the process of trying to negotiate for more money, but it would leave the club with about £1.5 million surplus after the build costs to put in trust to provide a future income.

If it came off and with that sort of money at his disposal, he wanted to think about going full-time and making a push for the Football League. It all sounded promising to me. I knew he saw the big picture and wouldn't panic about half a dozen bad results and sack me, but he couldn't guarantee he would always be chairman. He didn't own the club, so would be vulnerable and I knew that. And so he agreed to the security of a long contract for me.

We had a deal and after a few more phone calls about getting a signing-on fee of £5,000 and a couple of season tickets for my dad and his mate, I agreed to go down to Weymouth for a press conference to announce me as the club's new player-manager.

It took around, ooh, half an hour for the regrets to kick in. That was the time it took for the M27 to run out the other side of Southampton before it turned into dual carriageway after Bournemouth then winding, single lanes through Dorset. The

112

traffic down there was a nightmare, as it always is in the summer months with all the holiday traffic heading along the South Coast, even though this was midweek and not even the Saturday of game days when every caravan in the land seems determined to cause a late kick-off.

Where I hoped to be an hour early for a meeting with Ian's board, I only arrived five minutes before the press conference, which we had to put back but only by 15 minutes. The board seemed a mixed lot. There was Dave Higson, a decent, open sort of bloke from Bolton, and his partner from the club's sponsor, Park Engineering, Mick Archer, who I took to less.

Then there was Peter Shaw, who Ian had made his vice-chairman. He published magazines and had been on the board during my first stint at the club. In those days he seemed affable enough, and a couple of times paid me a couple of hundred quid to make some guest appearances for a *Punch* magazine team, one of them at Fratton Park.

He was certainly different now to how he had been then. He started asking me if I was going to do something about improving the throw-ins this season, as the team kept giving the ball away from them last season, he said. It struck me as a bit of a daft question, one that showed a man who wasn't appreciating what the real issues at the club were. I thought he might have been better worrying about the sorry state of the place, which Ian had told me about.

I didn't have any time to form relationships with these men, though. Within weeks, they would all be resigning. It gave me my first glimpse of the politics inside the club. They seemed happy enough to meet me that day and seemed content that I was at the club, but soon they were saying that I was costing the club too much and that they didn't want to be associated with it all. It left Ian having to find a new board with just days until the start of the season to go. There were factions at the club and in the town, which is not how it should be if it is going to be successful.

The press conference was fine that day and we attracted a

good crowd both regionally and nationally. I was a dab hand at all this stuff, with TV crews and radio, daily, Sunday and local papers. We had created quite a stir and it was gratifying to be in demand when I thought I was going to a backwater. It took a couple of hours to satisfy them all.

It was the tour of the ground that Ian then took me on that was so worrying. I was prepared for something a bit run-down, but not this. Nothing seemed to have changed since the day I left. It seemed as though it had not even been cleaned. The dressing rooms were a disgrace, filthy and bare. These are a player's place of work and he deserves better. It also helps when you are trying to sign a player. If he can see that the facilities are going to be decent, that can help you to swing a deal.

First off, the home and away dressing rooms were in the wrong place. The current away one was bigger than the home one and was next to the physio's room, with the smaller one at the end of a draughty corridor. I had them switched. I also got Ian to arrange for them to be painted and for some proper floor covering to be laid and new baths and showers to be installed.

The pitch, meanwhile, had weeds and deep, bare gouges all over it. It looked dangerous and I couldn't see how it was going to be playable in a few weeks' time. The training ground at the back of the stadium was unusable. When Ian said he had plans to allow a local speedway promoter to put a speedway track round it to bring in revenue for the club, I feared for the safety of the riders.

The whole thing was a shambles and I began to think I had made a mistake. Later that year, in the December, Millwall would sack McGhee and appoint Dennis Wise. If I had known that was going to happen, I might well have stuck around, bad deal or not.

For now I had made my decision and was going to abide by it. But it was such a shame the way the club had gone. I knew Ian was working hard behind the scenes, having to spend money that could have been better used building the squad on getting the place painted and patched up so that we could get a safety certificate to start the season. The local authority had only allowed the club to finish last season, apparently, because the crowds had been so low.

I tried to enter into the spirit of it, too. I enjoyed doing a fans' forum where I got a rousing reception and outlined my hopes for the club, saying that we would play attacking football and that it would be an entertaining season. Ian gave them some daft phrase about "living the dream".

Even before a ball had been kicked, I entered into the spirit of it, too, on the field – quite literally. My dad knew a turf supplier – as opposed to me, who knew a lot of turf accountants – who could do the club a good deal, so we came down from Portsmouth in a van with a pile of turves and laid them in the penalty areas. I also got a bloke I knew in Portsmouth by the name of Terry Clarke, a mad-keen Pompey fan who was doing me a favour really, to sponsor the ground for £15,000 and Ian was delighted. I was pleased to be doing my bit.

I was also working hard just to get bodies in. We were starting from so far back. We had a core of players I thought I could work with, such as the goalkeeper Jason Matthews, once of Exeter City. He was a real West Countryman with a lovely nature and with no side to him and was definitely one of the good things about the club. He seemed to love the club and was very loyal. There was also a quick defender called Steve Tully, all bleached hair and white boots and who obviously fancied himself a bit.

Up front, there was a rough-and-ready striker in Lee Phillips who I thought I could bring on alongside me. He was a non-League player who had never really learned the game properly but who had the good raw materials of strength, pace and power. As soon I as saw him play I knew I had to get him on a proper long contract because he could be a saleable asset.

Then there was a nucleus of players who had been there for a while but who were coming to the end of their careers, such as club captain John Waldock, a decent centre-half but now injury prone, left-back Simon Browne, and midfield players Ian

Hutchinson and Mark Robinson, who were all good lads and good servants to the club.

Then there were local kids, like defenders Nathan Walker, Scott Dennis and Mark Kenway, and winger John Lamb. I would have to do the best I could with them, Ian said, and he wanted me to try and bring on the local talent that the crowd could identify with. I would try, but I would soon find out that the desire of some players in the area was not as strong as it should have been and too many fell by the wayside.

I did have some scope to bring in players and I hit the phones and put the word around about what I needed. Soon I would be getting faxes and calls from agents and players claiming to be top drawer, making you wonder why they hadn't made it at higher levels. In fact, I got tired of the excuses when they did come down for trials. I wished they had just stayed in my mind rather than seeing them in reality and spoiling the picture I had of them. Plenty of them thought they were Maradona. They must have meant the Maradona of now.

Part of the problem was I didn't quite know the level. The first couple of training sessions had told me we were not good enough, strong enough or deep enough and that I was on a very steep learning curve.

I had always been in contact with Lee Philpott, a left-winger from my Cambridge and Leicester days, who was a top player with a sharp left foot and a great bloke. He had been released by Hull City in League Two and had had injury problems, but I thought that he would do a good job in midfield and that, as a part-timer, would play plenty of games. How I persuaded him to drive down from Yorkshire twice a week for £500 a week I am not quite sure.

We got in a neat little midfield player called Martin Barlow who had been at Telford United and Lee Russell, a tough defender who was with me at Portsmouth. I was stealing favours on the money we were paying really, mostly between £200 and £400. Luke Nightingale, who had played up front with me at

Pompey, but was now out of contract there, came to the club for £300 a week.

We did splash out, in terms of wages at least, for a striker by the name of Scott Partridge. I had got Neil McNab, my former reserve-team coach at Portsmouth, in as my assistant for a month or so to work on pre-season alongside the coach who was already at the club, Gary Borthwick, someone else who had been a decent player for Weymouth in his day. Neil, who would soon be going to America to take up a coaching job there, recommended Scotty, who was out of contract at Rushden and Diamonds.

Ian and I met with him and his agent Clive Whitehead, who was quite a character himself. Now working for the PFA, Clive had been a left-winger with Bristol City in those heady days of the 1980s when City were in the top division and chucking money about.

In fact, he had a contract there – one that was in the *Guinness Book of Records* as the longest ever in football – for an amazing 11-and-a-half years, so I knew it would be a tough negotiation. In fact, though Clive had been retired quite a while I think he was still in the last year of his contract with Bristol City, probably now looking for a Bosman move.

Anyway, we got a result when we secured Scotty's services for three years at £550 a week, which was a lot for the club, but I convinced Ian he would be worth it. He trained brilliantly with us that very night, but I must admit I started to have the odd misgiving when he said he needed to go home and talk to his wife about the move before committing to us. He signed the next day.

I also had misgivings about a venture that Ian had got us involved in. Through his contacts in TV, he had got a production company following us for the season for a BBC2 documentary called *Football Diaries*. It would bring in good money for the club, £15,000 for the season, and for that reason I went along with it, but I know how the medium works and I was a bit worried about how I might come out of it.

Ian assured me, however, that we would have some control over the edited version. Hmm. Where had I heard that before? It's right up there on the list of reassurances with the one about the cheque being in the post.

We had inherited a very poor programme of pre-season friendlies, which included playing then Conference club Barnet, managed by Martin Allen – who didn't seem very happy to be sent to the stands by a woman referee – on a Friday night. Then, the following day in the afternoon, we played Chasetown, the Midlands club who would go on to achieve some fame with their FA Cup runs. The other highlight was a game against Stevenage Borough. No disrespect to these clubs, but we should have been attracting better opposition.

I was not particularly encouraged by what I saw. We had about half a dozen good players, another half a dozen who could mend and make do and another half a dozen who were just not going to be up to it. I was not optimistic.

Then we got a fax through from Aldershot Town, one of my former clubs before they went bust in 1992, after which they reformed as a non-League club. They had just been promoted from the Ryman League to the Conference and they wanted to play a friendly against us at their Recreation Ground. It would be a good match for us, I reckoned, and would provide a sign of where we were.

I played my first game of the pre-season and we won 2-0. It was very encouraging and, for the first time, after six weeks of pre-season slog trying to crowd in about a season's work on and off the pitch, I began to think this might actually work.

That night, I also got talking to Paul Buckle, an experienced midfield player in the Aldershot side, who had been with Colchester and Brentford among other clubs. He had not got the improved contract he was hoping for with them and lived down our way in Honiton in Devon.

Ian got on to the Aldershot chairman Karl Prentice the next day and they agreed to release him, with Bucks even taking a pay cut to play for us for £400. It was a great signing and, suddenly, we looked a lot better.

After all the aggro and grief, it was starting to happen. I would have liked to have been stronger and better prepared, but the season was upon us. We were about to find out if this mad adventure was going to work.

3.2 Expectations Grate

High expectation is both a gift and a curse in football. It means you have good support that is pushing you to achieve what you yourself want to achieve, but it can also be unrealistic. And if it gets out of hand, people think you should be doing better than the budget allows. My personal philosophy is that everyone should be optimistic but realistic. If it is not, the club itself can get crushed under the weight. Believe it or not for a Southern League club, Weymouth would turn out to be a very heavy club.

At first, we had the right combination. Anticipation was high but expectation was low. They had been served up some rubbish in recent years and were prepared to welcome me back and give me a chance. Ian was working on getting in more commercial income and livening up the whole place and people seemed to be pulling in the right direction.

In just a few weeks, he had put together a new board of directors, with a few local businessmen joining some he had brought in from outside, and it felt like the club was on the right track. I had got over some of my worries and was determined to stick this out and do it properly. We had even found a new groundsman who was making a difference.

In fact, I was starting to enjoy it. During my brief spell as Portsmouth manager I had seen how the game's finances worked – or didn't work – and could take some pleasure in doing things within budget and putting out the best available, of helping to build a club not just a squad. That was part of the art of management. We may have been poor but at this point we were happy.

Except that we weren't seen as poor. It was amazing to me having come from higher up football's food chain, but I kept reading articles in publications like the *Non-League Paper* or other teams' programmes describing us as "Moneybags Weymouth". If only they knew how we were scrimping and saving. The new directors may have put in a few bob to buy some shares, but that wasn't going very far, given the work on the ground that needed to be done and the old bills that needed to be paid. As I spoke to other managers as the season went on, I found out that our wage bill was somewhere around sixth to eighth in the league.

Perhaps it was something to do with me having persuaded Ian to let us stay in hotels on Friday nights, which was unusual at this level. He took some persuading again, not wanting to send out messages that we were throwing money about, but I saw it as part of good preparation. He agreed that if we were playing a match more than two hours drive away and if the players paid 30 per cent of the total cost – which they consented to – then he was happy for us to do so. I was pleased the players had agreed to help fund the arrangement. It showed they were sharing in my vision and wanted to be professional.

The opening day sent us to Hednesford in the West Midlands and their programme was full of all this big-time Weymouth stuff, but the game ended in a dull 0-0 draw. They celebrated it, mind, as if they had just held some top club at home in the FA Cup; it gave me an early inkling of how we were going to be viewed in this league, as well as an inkling of just how tricky a league this was going to be. I think Ian was hoping for a better result with this new team but I was realistic and knew it was about right.

Four days later, though, it came together better in our first home game. It was a bit of a close-run thing as we scraped through 2-1 over Newport County, with Lee Phillips scoring the winner. I was particularly pleased for Ian as the crowd was 1,454 – more than double the previous season's average and 250 up on the break-even figure. Actually, I was most pleased for myself, what with the win money and crowd bonus I was on.

There were warning signs in the game for me, though. It was very physical and I got a kicking that would be repeated several times throughout the season, notably our next home game against Bath City, which we drew 3-3, having to scramble a late penalty after being 2-0 up then 3-2 down.

It didn't help, I quickly realised, that the referees were very lenient at that level. It makes me laugh when you hear fans of Premier League clubs moaning on phone-ins about refs. They are geniuses up there by comparison. These fans should try watching some football at this level. The refs didn't understand the game and let defenders get away with murder. I also think there were some players who fancied their chances of being the man who sorted out Steve Claridge.

In contrast, we had a terrific game early on at Tiverton, whose manager Martyn Rogers had been a team-mate of mine during my first spell at Weymouth. He was a great lad and had really built "Tivvy" up into a decent side. In fact, he was one of those Ian phoned me up about to become manager before I took it and I said, "Yes, go and get him." Thanks to young John Lamb's brace of goals – and it gave me a lot of pleasure to play a part in helping him come through – we won 2-1 in a match where both teams wanted to pass and play the game properly.

We actually made a great start to the season, going ten games unbeaten, winning five and drawing five to go top of the table, although I was not getting carried away because I had also made a great start to management at Portsmouth and look what happened there. I was enjoying playing and scoring goals, two curled home from the edge of the penalty box in a 3-1 win at Chippenham, which were as good as anything I had scored for a while.

I was amazed, to be honest, that we were doing so well. I was picking decent sides, getting the best out of what we had, I reckoned, and the training was good, but we were relying on five or six key players and were filling in around them. Deep down, I knew we were over-achieving and papering over the cracks.

That much was seen when we went to Newport in an FA Cup second-qualifying round – the earliest I had ever been in the competition – and lost 3-2 after being 2-0 up. It is a horrible place to go, a wind tunnel with an athletics track round a bumpy, bone-hard pitch. They had been aggrieved to lose the league game at our place and it was a horribly physical game against a side managed by Peter Nicholas, the former Crystal Palace, Chelsea and Wales midfield player. Ian was particularly upset about the result, because he wanted the revenue and kudos from a cup run and he let me know it.

Still, he had to admit I was doing a good job. The Southern League recognised it and made me their manager of the month for August and September, though they certainly weren't going to for October and November.

The old curse of the Manager of the Month – the award being the signal well known in the game for results to go bad – saw our unbeaten league record go at home to Stafford Rangers. We followed it up with another miserable defeat at home to Havant and Waterlooville, when the crowd was a worryingly low 802, worryingly because it mucked up my bonus. As did the 1-0 reverse. Still, it would be the only time during the season our crowds dipped under 1,000 for a league game. I never know why they schedule non-League games on a Champions League night. It's bound to ruin the attendances.

Havant – who would later be tagged with all that romance-of-the-Cup stuff some seasons later when they went to Liverpool – were not in reality a particularly friendly or welcoming club and I had recently been refused access to their boardroom for a half-time cup of tea when scouting a player because I was wearing black jeans. And all this despite the fact that we had let one of their scouts into our boardroom pre-season who was wearing shorts. It was the sort of petty stuff that sometimes went on at this level and you could only laugh, though Ian, who was with me, didn't. I ended up having to quieten him down for a change.

It was a terrible autumn and I was driving miles and spending hours on the phone trying to get new players in to plug gaps. We did well to get Gary Johnson, the Yeovil manager who would go on to do so well with Bristol City, to agree to loan us his right-winger Andy Lindegaard, who came for a month and did well. I prevailed upon Dennis Wise to get Millwall to let us have a young defender called Tim Clancy for £50 a week and we had another good month.

One would go as well. Scott Partridge was a really nice lad, a very good trainer and player, but he was just not fitting into our side. I don't think he was strong enough mentally or physically and he was also going to be behind me and Lee Phillips in the pecking order up front. And so I got Ian to find him a new club. Scott went to Bath City, where he would do well – as you would expect at a club with less pressure – but we had to pay up part of his contract. He was a player I had taken on Neil McNab's advice; I decided that in the future I would only sign players if I had seen them myself.

The same happened with a young local lad called Mark Kenway. He always looked fantastic in training and was a centre-back who could pass the ball and play, but in games, worse than a chronic lack of pace was, I thought, a lack of mental toughness and determination. We let him go to Portland United of the Wessex League.

I was having problems with the local players. They either did not have what it takes or did not want it badly enough. They were used to playing in matches among local club sides and thought they were top players, but when it came to being matched against others from outside, they couldn't shape up. Maybe because it was a nice town, with its sweeping beach and esplanade, and a very insular little area, life was too cosy there.

For my part, I found it frustrating and I probably asked too much of some players who, to be honest, were not capable of giving it. Though we were playing some excellent stuff at times – and Lee Philpott said it was better than some of the football he had seen at Hull City the previous season – I was struggling to get used to the level and was perhaps expecting some of the players to be better and to give more than they were capable of.

For now, though, they were responding. I also have to admit, in a way that not many managers do, that every bit of luck was going with us. After the autumn wobble, I was pleased we got ourselves back on track and we went back to the top of the table one enjoyable afternoon in late November. The match was against Hinckley United in front of more than 1,500 spectators and we won 2-0.

One of the reasons we began to turn the corner was that I had now hit upon a system that suited the players. Steve Tully, for example, was quick and read the game well, so I turned him into a sweeper. No longer having great pace, tough Lee Russell was neither really a left-back nor a central defender, but because he was strong and good in the air, he fitted in well as the left-sided defender of a back three with Tully covering.

All the while, though, I did have reservations about how long we would keep it up with this squad. And I did have one regret, I have to admit. I had given up playing in front of 15,000 in what is now the Championship to perform in front of 1,500 – if we were lucky; away from home in the Southern League it was often just a few hundred. I knew I was still capable of playing at the higher level, too.

Instead, I was going to places like little Ryman League club Ashford in the FA Trophy. I had rested myself for the tie at home and we had played really badly to go 3-1 down until I came on for the last 15 minutes and we did enough to grab a replay. Ian was furious. He wanted the revenue from a Trophy run to finance new signings in January since there would be no FA Cup money. I think he was starting to worry about some of his board, who wouldn't put their hands into their pockets.

Now here we were a few days later on some mud heap at the end of a runway at Heathrow Airport. There was also a sewage farm nearby and a couple of the lads saw rats behind one of the goals as they were warming up.

The mood in the dressing room was sombre as Ian and I had exchanged strong words over the previous few days, with him saying that we really needed to win the game. Only very reluctantly did he agree to allow us to have a pre-match meal in a hotel, with me agreeing that the players would pay for it if we lost and that the club would pay for it if we won.

In fact, I used Ian's displeasure with the team as part of the motivation to the lads for the replay, saying that the chairman was seething at us for letting the club down and that it could have serious ramifications financially if we went out of the competition.

Then, all of a sudden, half an hour before kick-off, he comes into the dressing room all jolly Joe, asking "Everything all right lads?" before starting to crack lame jokes. I had got the lads in the mood, in the zone, and he had done this. I looked at him open-mouthed and thought, "If he doesn't leave soon he's going to get my boot up his arse." I was trying to instil a mood of determination and he was undermining it. I knew his intentions were honourable, but his timing was all wrong.

I asked him outside, told him how angry I was with what he was doing and said that he was ruining my pre-match talk. He accepted it and left and I got back to proper business. It was a rare moment of discord between us, but one we easily got over. Looking back, it seems almost comical, but it was not funny to me at the time.

Fortunately, we won the game 3-1 with me scoring a penalty for which I was strangely nervous, as edgy as that penalty for Millwall against Wolves that got us into the playoffs.

The victory came at a big cost, though. Lee Russell got injured in what seemed an innocuous tackle but which would sadly end his career at the age of 32. We would have to pay up the remainder of his contract to the end of the season, which totalled around £10,000. I would tell him that I wanted to settle for £5,000 as I thought that if I could save some money, I could get someone else in to replace him. Ian, though, was a softer touch, and he gave Lee £8,000. In hindsight, he was right. The injury – knee-ligament damage – came as a crushing blow for Lee and he needed something to soften it.

When you look back, there are many moments that you come to see as being significant and that was certainly one. Another potentially crucial moment would come on the first Saturday of the New Year.

In between, we had a very enjoyable Christmas. We were paired against local rivals Dorchester Town at home on Boxing Day, and a crowd of 3,734 showed our potential as a club, especially as Dorchester brought only a few hundred fans with them. We then went out and hammered them 8-0, with both me and Lee Phillips scoring hat-tricks. It was satisfying stuff and it meant a lot to the locals. It certainly made Ian's day as he came into the dressing room afterwards and planted a kiss on my forehead in front of all the lads. I could have done without that, but at least I didn't mind him coming into the dressing room on this occasion.

The return on New Year's Day was altogether less pleasurable. We took more than 3,000 of our fans up there, out of a crowd of just over 4,000, and worked ourselves into a 2-1 lead, but gave away a late penalty to draw after a controversial incident – one that saw me getting sent off. I got fed up with being kicked and after being tackled from behind by a clown called Jamie Brown, I reacted and kicked out at him while he was on the ground.

It was only the second red card of my career, the other coming when I was at Birmingham City against Watford and I retaliated by kicking David Holdsworth after he had taken me out. This was Brown's second red card in the two games against us, which tells you plenty about both his game and his attitude.

It showed the difference of playing down at that level. Full-time professionals are more cautious in their approach to tackling, because they know that if they get suspended, it might take them six months to get back in the team because their replacement is probably going to be good. At that level, they knew they would be back in after a three-game ban. It's not enough of a punishment.

Afterwards, Brown was being interviewed by a local newspaper reporter in the car park and I had words with him as I walked past, wondering if he was telling the real truth. He had words back and after another exchange we squared up before being separated. He was out of order. I was just getting sick of no-marks trying to make a name for themselves.

It was daft of me, but it was a day when everything had got on top of me. I never really let much work me up in the game, certainly once it was all over, but the combination of my players letting two points slip, the referee and the opposition really depressed me. Brown was typical of some of the people you faced at that level.

Two days later, we took on Crawley Town, who were emerging as our title rivals, at the Wessex Stadium. It was to become a big moment in the season, probably the biggest.

A good crowd of 2,016 turned out and saw a tough, attritional game that finally seemed to be going our way when they had their goalkeeper sent off and we got a penalty. But I didn't hit it well and their stand-in saved it. We lost 1-0.

All of a sudden, the pendulum of power at the top of the table had swung. We had Stafford Rangers and Nuneaton Borough behind us, but Crawley were coming up on the rails. Had we won the game, I feel sure we would have gone on to win the title. Crawley would have been eight points adrift of us. As it was, now they were just two behind. I am convinced it encouraged them to go out and spend money in a way they wouldn't have done had we won that day. A sponsor backed them and that January they got a lot of good players in, paying good wages.

I went to Ian and told him I could no longer make do without reinforcements. We had overachieved with local youngsters and veterans who had been with the club and who were now past their best, filling in around the core of six decent players. I had misjudged how good some were. They were simply not capable of playing how I wanted them to play and that was partly my fault. My demands of them were too high.

Ian said he would go back to his board, but I began to get vibes from him that all was not well in that department as he struggled to come up with the cash. There was a small increase to the wage bill, but not what I needed to compete with Crawley. We did buy one player, Shaun Wilkinson from Havant and Waterlooville, but the Supporters' Club paid the £5,000 fee. Shaun never really did it for me and, a couple of seasons later, would go back to Havant, where he played in their midfield in that FA Cup tie at Liverpool.

Otherwise, I got the odd player in on loan, a left-winger by the name of Lewis Cook from Wycombe Wanderers and a work experience striker from Plymouth called Stewart Yetton, who was very impressive and who I thought would go a long way, but who ended up scoring pots of goals beneath his level at Truro City in the Western League. These West Country boys do lack ambition sometimes.

Lewis was a strange case. One Saturday, we were about to leave the house that Ian had rented in Weymouth and which some of us from outside the area stayed in on a Friday night when Lewis suddenly appeared from upstairs, having overslept. I started with him but he played as if he was sleepwalking. At least the time I overslept when I had been playing for Millwall, I had the sense to make up for it and score twice.

He had not had a pre-match meal three hours before the game, as I insisted, for a start. It struck me as poor from a lad that was at a pro club. He should have known about his sleep patterns and how to prepare for a game. I asked him about it and he said he had never been taught, which surprised me. He would end up coming out of the Football League and signing for Maidenhead United.

Perhaps he thought at the time that non-League meant very little and that it would be easy. But I expected certain standards at Weymouth. It came as a shock to some players, I am sure. I have asked myself if I was too harsh on players who were part-time and who had other jobs, but I have always believed that even with semi-professionals, if you are going to play football for ten months a year, you need to be in the best shape you can.

I could be tough after games we had lost when my decibel level could go up the scale and once or twice I did keep them in the dressing room for an hour or more as we conducted inquests. It probably surprised some of them, but it wouldn't have surprised anyone at a pro club. Players like Lee Philpott and Paul Buckle were all right with it, and would give some of it back, but the lads who had played in non-League all their life probably found it overwhelming. I wanted to raise them up to my standards; and I certainly didn't want myself dropping to theirs.

Like Ian, I now wanted an FA Trophy run so that I might be given the money to get players in. We went to the Sussex club Lewes's quaint little Dripping Pan ground and won 8-5 in a ludicrous match. I had a defender giving it large and screaming in my face every time they scored, so I would give him some back when we scored. "Mate, you're shit," I said to him, and he was. The arrogance of some very poor players always amazed me at that level. Also, I had the courtesy to brush my teeth that day and I'm not sure he did.

After that, however, we lost 2-0 at home to Altrincham in the last 16 on a stinker of a day. Around 40 volunteers had worked through lashing rain all morning to get the game on and I wished they hadn't ... now there was going to be no financial windfall.

Despite our mend-and-make-do squad and the fact that we were doing better than we had any right to, expectations at the club were now huge. It's a funny place like that, Weymouth. You might think it is a little footballing backwater but, with little else in the way of entertainment in the place and with no big population centre for 30 miles until you get to Bournemouth, they really care about their club and let you know it.

It should all have been manageable, but I have rarely played at a club – believe it or not – where the pressure was higher, simply because that expectation was unrealistic. They thought they should be a Conference club at least, maybe even a Football League side, and that was fair enough. But it sometimes seemed as though they wanted it there and then. You don't get much patience in football these days, but in Weymouth's case it was daft at times.

I mean, expectation had been high at Millwall when we were going for the Premiership and that was fine because we had such a good side. The following season, when we lost certain players, they were much more understanding of the situation. That's all you ask for from fans, a bit of understanding. The other thing is that when a club is on the up, some people get left behind by the higher standards. To replace them you need money … and that was something we did not have.

I did get in a defender by the name of Robbie Pethick, who had been at Portsmouth with me, and he noticed straight away the increased expectation of a club he knew well. Robbie had been a right-winger at Weymouth as a kid before being sold to Bristol Rovers for £30,000 and who had then gone on to Brighton.

Now their manager – Mark McGhee, who had moved to the South Coast after his sacking by Millwall – had agreed to loan him to us and Robbie was taken aback by the unforgiving attitude that could prevail at Weymouth at the slightest setback. More than at Brighton, he said. There, he reckoned, after their ordeal in losing the Goldstone Ground, they were just grateful to still be in business. He reckoned that if the Brighton fans saw their side lose a game in the Football League, they were usually very philosophical about it.

But then Robbie could be a bit of a fibber. A group of us from the Pompey area would drive down for night training – the camaraderie reminded me of a time when I was at Birmingham City and a few of us living in the Luton area at the time would drive up

131

together – and arrived one night in Weymouth to find the dressing rooms still locked, so we changed in the car.

I had just bought an £80 Boss T-shirt that went missing after training, which annoyed me. The next week, Pethick turned up for his lift down to training wearing it and spun some story about where he got it. When I told him it was mine he seemed surprised but said I could have it back after training. I wasn't having that. I had it straight off his back and made him travel down to Weymouth naked from the waist up.

I tried to get other players in. I would go to reserve games at Portsmouth and Southampton, at places like Bishops Stortford to look for players, to Wycombe to see a big defender called Luke Oliver, but who to my mind didn't punch his weight, even though Ian liked him. I drove up to Coventry to speak to Terry Angus, the veteran Nuneaton Borough defender, but he couldn't leave them, he felt, while they still had an outside chance of the Southern League title themselves.

I did take a central defender from Exeter on loan called Gary Sawyer, but he lacked pace and when I played him at left-back he looked little better. He seemed a bag of nerves. It just showed how the crowd at Weymouth could get to some players. The last I saw and heard of him, he was playing for Plymouth Argyle in the Championship. So much for my judgement sometimes.

Then again, I later tried to sign an out-of-favour striker at Cheltenham Town called Kayode Odejayi, but they wouldn't let him go. He ended up going to Barnsley for £200,000 and scoring the winner that put Chelsea out of the FA Cup in that epic quarter-final at Oakwell. He may have then missed a sitter at Wembley in the semi against Cardiff, but he bagged two a few days later in a 3-0 win at Watford. At least my judgement was vindicated there. You win some ...

A peculiar issue that season was that it was the last before the formation of the new North and South divisions of the Conference, which would take the best 14 clubs from the Southern, Northern Premier and Isthmian Leagues. In other years, mid-table clubs would let you have players to get them off the wage bill. Not now, though, because they were desperate to qualify themselves. Tiverton, for example, rejected an approach for a big centre-half by the name of Nathan Rudge.

We were still clinging on to top spot, even though I knew the momentum was now with Crawley. We had some good character and characters in the side, proper men like Philpott, Buckle and Martin Barlow, who knew how to conduct themselves on and off the pitch, but I suspected that character alone was not going to be enough. We also had some who were more used to relegation battles and who were not comfortable with the pressure of a pro-motion push.

Robbie Pethick scored on his debut in a tense 2-0 home win over Hednesford, but narrow defeats in howling gales at Cambridge City and Eastbourne Borough – there were no big sta-diums to keep out the wind – were damaging. Eastbourne, par-ticularly, left a scar as I broke my nose in a collision for the third time in my career.

The first time was at Shrewsbury for Cambridge United when my nose was smeared all over my face. It was horrendous. I got the doctor to reset it quickly in the dressing room and it was hor-rendously painful. At least it saved my looks. Yeah right. The sec-ond time was at Birmingham City.

This time, I had to have an operation to shave the nasal bone to open up the air passages because I could not breathe and it left me with bruising on my face for weeks. I had always had a better face for radio than television, so for a while it was even harder getting bookings for the telly.

Anyway, by the time we got to Crawley on the first Saturday in March for a potentially epic game, the gap at the top of the table was down to just two points.

It was a good occasion I have to admit, even as someone who had seen a few higher up the scale. The crowd at their Broadfield Stadium of more than 4,500, with around 1,000 of them from Weymouth, was a reflection that they were on the up and fancied it. We had been hanging in there. After their win at the Wessex in the January, they had been encouraged to go on and spend money to strengthen their squad.

It was tense and intense stuff. We fell behind just before half-time and another arrived soon after. Steve Tully pulled one back. Then, with minutes to go, the ball arrived on my head a few yards out, but I put it wide. Crawley had won 2-1 and for the first time in five months, and at the wrong end of the season, we had been knocked off top spot. It was crushing.

I got in another goalkeeper by the name of Jimmy Glass because our No. 1 Jason Matthews had been making a few nervous errors. Jason always seemed to benefit from being rested for a few games anyway, always coming back stronger. People may remember Jimmy. Now living in the Bournemouth area, he was the keeper on loan from Swindon who scored that last-gasp goal for Carlisle – against Swindon, of all people – that kept Carlisle in the Football League on the last day of a season.

He did well for me, too, for a while and we hung in there for a few more games, eking out a win here and a draw there to cling on to Crawley's coat-tails.

Until, that was, we lost a titanic game at Nuneaton at the end of March 4-3 when we battered them only to let in silly goals, in which Jimmy played his part. Because he was so up and down, it would come as no surprise to me that Jimmy would come out later and talk about how he had been a gambling addict. Now I knew how Kevin Keegan must have felt that time Newcastle's title challenge faded as they lost that epic game by that same score of 4-3 at Liverpool.

That night, we also got a terrible, lame performance from the young Millwall defender I had had earlier in the season and who I had now brought back for another month, Tim Clancy. It saddened me. He had put on weight and was not giving it his all. I have seen too many kids like him who think they are going to make it and then stop working.

I was so furious I told him that, if he wasn't going to try for me,

I wasn't going to help him out, and that he would have to make his own way back to London. The chairman took him to Coventry station in the end. The player ended up at Fisher Athletic. Enough said.

In other seasons, we might have kept going better, instead of losing home games to the likes of Chippenham and Welling United, though we did manage a good win at Stafford, who would finish third. That came a few days after Ian had got in a sports psychologist he knew called Jamie Edwards, who had worked with England cricketers Michael Vaughan and Andrew Flintoff. It was a useful enough session – all filmed for *Football Diaries*, who weren't going to get the title-winning ending they wanted – but to be honest, our problems were as much physical as they were mental: we just weren't quite good enough.

When it came to being filmed that season, I knew what I was getting into because I know the way television works. They can edit things to make George Graham look like George Best. It is simply about portraying what they want to portray. I agreed to it because I knew it would bring in revenue. When it turned out we were the best story in it and taking up much of the air time, I told Ian to ring them up to get a bonus on top of the £15,000 fee. We did, but I think they got value and we should have got even more than the extra £2,500 they agreed to.

Both Weymouth and the TV company doing it got lucky, I think; the club with the money and the fact that they were quite kind to us in many ways, and them because they had the chance to film such a good rollercoaster season that saw us at the top of the table before ultimately finishing second. In addition, there was all the politics at the club.

I think we were there to provide the counterpoint to the Premiership and all the supposed glitz and glamour. I didn't think characters like Jermaine Pennant and Kieron Dyer emerged from it too well as they came across as being a bit superficial, while a lad called Courtney Pitt, who had been a young player when I was at Portsmouth after the club paid

Chelsea £200,000 for him, definitely showed himself up as he seemed to be more interested in cars than the game. He ended up at Cambridge United in the Conference. Only David James, a model professional, looked good.

I found the cameras a bit intrusive, even though the production company were nice people, but what concerned me most was that they had this idea that we were basically a tinpot outfit. It overlooked the professionalism we were trying to instil at the club and made us look a bit amateur at times. Yes, some parts of the club didn't work as well as they might have given more time, and there were also fun and light-hearted moments, but it was also very intense and we worked hard.

Ian allowed himself to be filmed on the beach at the end of the series as a postscript eating an ice cream and somehow managing to get the whole thing in his mouth. I knew he had a big gob, but that was ridiculous.

He shouldn't have allowed the camera crew to follow one of our directors, Tristan Murless, though. Tristan, not familiar with the ways of the media, played up to them as he took them on a tour of the town and his house, showing the nightclubs where he reckoned the players went and then the Jacuzzi at his home that "had seen some action". It was funny but it also came across as being a bit sad.

Anyway, as I contemplated where we were, I tried to stay optimistic, even if everything after Crawley became anti-climactic. The following season playoffs were introduced into Conference South, which meant two promotion places as opposed to this season when only the champions went up.

For now, it was a question of seeing out the season, making my mind up about who would be going and who would be staying. In the end, we finished runners-up 12 points behind Crawley. The double they had done over us made all the difference. It haunted me that if I had scored with those late chances in both games, we might still have made it, but I did take some solace in the role I had played in the club's huge progress.

Not that you would have known it with the attitude of some people. Thus far, everyone seemed to have been singing from the same song sheet for what people told me was the first time in ages at the Wessex Stadium. And the majority of the fans were great – with more than 1,100 turning out and applauding the players for a nothing game against relegated Grantham on the last day of the season. But now I saw how the club could turn and fall victim to the bitching and in-fighting that had plagued it for years.

Some seemed to ignore just what a good season it had been. I had scored 28 goals – with Lee Phillips contributing 24 on top – and we had gone from being 17th the previous season to second, with crowds up from 650 to an average of 1,490 in the league, the best in the division and one which put us in the top dozen or so non-League clubs in the country.

In reality, we had made a rod for our own backs. If we had produced a late run to finish second, we would have been heroes. Instead, having fallen off our perch, in some people's eyes we were villains. The best thing would have been to finish around an acceptable sixth without raising expectations.

According to some criticism I picked up around the place, I, apparently, was spending too much time on television and radio, even though I was doing nothing different to when we were clear at the top. The players were not training enough, I heard, even though we were playing twice a week through the last two months of the season. When we did train, once a week as opposed to the twice without midweek games, we trained hard and well.

I had also taken on Micky Jenkins as my assistant, paying him out of my own money. Micky had been co-manager with my old team-mate at Cambridge United Liam Daish at Havant and Waterlooville, but after he was sacked, he had come to Weymouth to help me out. I started to hear whispers that he was just my driver and that the club didn't need him.

Some of this stuff was coming from Ian's board. Men like

Tristan Murless and Jamie Lyones whom Ian had recruited from the local business community were harmless enough, in football terms at least. I could handle them and I never minded explaining my decisions. But I didn't like being questioned by Matthew McGowan, Ian's vice-chairman, who, having once played and managed the club but in a very different era, thought he knew it all. He, I sensed, was not in my corner and that worried me. When Ian questioned things, it was in a positive, supportive way, and he always accepted my answers if he felt they were valid; McGowan, on the other hand, always seemed to be unhelpful and working against me.

Despite all these concerns, I thought to hell with it and to them. I knew what a good job I had done and how much the club had come on. And I still felt encouraged. I knew Ian was working on things behind the scenes, notably in getting new investment while we waited for the Asda deal that we hoped would be lucrative for the club. He had a mate from London he had brought on the board called Charlie Lesser who was a top man, wealthy and who had got to enjoy his involvement with the club. But agreeing that a cash injection was needed if we were to kick on the next season, the board went instead for someone else – a bloke called Martyn Harrison, a Londoner who owned hotels in the town.

I didn't mind. As long as I had Ian on my side in the boardroom, and as long as there was money coming into the club to finance a tilt at promotion, I didn't care where it came from – provided it didn't bankrupt the club, that is. And the promise was certainly of money.

3.3 Fed Up, Paid Up

As I understood it from Ian, we either ran the club along strict business lines, which meant having a wage bill that was covered by gate receipts, Supporters' Club donations and the takings from the bars and sponsorship, or we had to raise money from shares, of which there were around £300,000 worth left unsold. That would more than finance a second push for the Conference. Having come this far, it would be a shame to stop now.

We could have done it the first way, breaking even for the season with a wage bill of around £6,000 a week, just above average for the new Confererence South. As well as the experience I had gained during my first year at Weymouth, I had learned much about budgets and the finances of football in my spell as Portsmouth manager when I was trying very hard to save the club money, so I knew a lot about getting the best out of what I had available. All you needed was for people – the fans and boards of directors – to understand the limitations and to cut you some slack.

I am not sure I would have got that at Weymouth, since our achievements of the previous season had seen the bar raised higher, and because of the ultimate disappointment around the place after we had narrowly missed out on promotion. Besides which, Martyn Harrison had agreed to buy up all the outstanding shares, and a load of other people's, to control a major share of the club.

Though I was glad we would have the money from him to advance Ian's five-year plan to reach the Football League, I wasn't that taken with Martyn when I first met him and I suspected he wasn't going to be my cup of tea.

He had very few teeth and sometimes I couldn't concentrate on what he was saying as I was fascinated by the way he fitted his cigarette in a gap between his teeth. He also seemed to surround himself with people who were beholden to him, like our coach Gary Borthwick, who did painting and decorating for him, and a director in Tristan Murless, an electrician who did work at his hotels. And his staff seemed to be on edge around him. It was a power trip for him, I thought, and that power base came from money.

Still, now that I had a much better shout at financing a tougher, more resilient squad, I wasn't going to worry too much about the personal element and I quickly got some players in.

We paid £12,500 for a decent left-winger in Adam Wilde from Worcester City, a position we had struggled with the previous season, and £10,000 for Chukki Eribenne, a striker from Havant and Waterlooville. These were decent sums at that level, I have to admit. If you are going to spend money, it should be on creative players and goalscorers.

Otherwise I picked up players who were out of contract elsewhere. In defence, I got in Nathan Bunce, a tough defender who had played for Farnborough against Arsenal in that famous FA Cup tie a few years previously. He had also once had to have 60-odd stitches in his arm after a gardening accident with a chainsaw, so I knew he was tough and resilient enough. So too was big Matty Bound, a centre-back with a good left foot who came from Oxford United along with Dave Waterman, an old team-mate of mine at Portsmouth.

A few drifted away, notably Luke Nightingale, who went to Bognor Regis Town, where he would enjoy his football more, I was sure, away from the pressure of the Wessex Stadium that he never quite adapted to. He also wanted to play up front, rather than wide on the right where I had been using him. Some of the younger players, too, went to local clubs as I pared down the squad.

I also missed out on a few players. I wanted a tough full-back called Dean Hooper from Aldershot, who had played against us in a pre-season friendly the previous year and who had been in my ear and my face the whole game. I thought at the time I wouldn't mind signing him. However, with all the holiday traffic, it took him six hours to travel down for a pre-season friendly and he decided against it.

That travelling, and the cost of it, was one of the reasons why you had to pay a bit more than some other clubs for players. Weymouth was a long way from anywhere and it took time to get to for players from our catchment areas – the London region, Portsmouth and Southampton, Bristol and the bigger towns of South Devon, Plymouth, Torquay and Exeter. The South Dorset area itself just did not produce a sufficient number of players who were good enough.

The main problem was that while it might have looked, particularly to our fans, that we were going for it, there were now other teams in this Conference South with money men backing them ready to spend much more than us. Chief among them was Hornchurch, under their manager Garry Hill, who had previously taken Dagenham to FA Cup third-round games against Charlton and to the brink of the Conference when they finished as runners-up to Boston.

Our wage bill had gone up from £6,500 a week to £8,000 a week – with Martyn saying I could go up to £10,000, although I wanted to keep money in reserve – but it was nothing compared with Hornchurch. I went after a striker called Kirk Jackson, who had been at Yeovil, but Hornchurch's wage offer was double what we could pay. Our top earner now was Matty Bound, who was on £650 a week.

In fact, the Hornchurch budget, having gone full time, was a reported £20,000, which was madness at this level, I thought.

141

There was talk of big signing-on fees, cars and flats. It would have been the envy of many a lower-division Football League club. Grays Athletic, too, were also investing heavily but, mainly because of our crowds and status, we were seen as favourites to win the league.

These clubs in Essex were attracting gates, if they were lucky, of around half of ours, but it was becoming a battle to see who had the sugar daddy with the deepest pockets. It was all a bit coincidental. Hornchurch had an owner called Karl Williams; at Grays they had Mick Woodward; we had Martyn Harrison. They were all going for the kudos of reaching the Conference and it became a battle of wills between them. It turned into a sort of bidding war and one which is unlikely to be seen again at that level.

In fact, I think non-League football would come to learn some lessons from it all. The Conference established some rules that clubs could only spend 65 per cent of their income on players' wages in an attempt to stop the overspending that was seeing too many clubs at that level going into administration or even going bust. It caught up with our old rivals Crawley Town, who went into administration, and Telford United even had to reform two leagues down. It's funny how even in the nether regions of the game, people chase what they see as riches – the Conference came to represent the non-League Premiership.

Our pre-season programme also gave people cause to believe we would do well. After the chaos of taking over the previous year, I had organised a proper training regime and fitness programme this time, with gym work and weights among it, so the squad was definitely fitter and better prepared.

Ian had also arranged a better set of friendlies, with games at home to Sheffield United, Neil Warnock agreeing to bring a strong side down, Bournemouth and Wycombe Wanderers, then managed by Tony Adams, and we acquitted ourselves well, losing the first two but drawing the third. Then, when we beat Exeter City 2-1, in what I thought would be a good gauge of our quality as a squad since they were in the Conference national division above us, I thought we were in good shape.

I felt as though I had addressed all the failings of the previous campaign and that we were now a stronger and more physical squad suited to this level. The pressure, I believed, would be less because this year there were now playoffs from which would come another promotion team to go up alongside the champions. It would keep us in the hunt all season, rather than it looking like the season was slipping away if you were out of the top two or three.

One of the problems quickly became apparent, though. Everyone who played Weymouth fancied it against, as they saw it, big-time Charlies with plenty of money. We had a bit of that with teams raising their game last year, but then we were a club that had just finished 17th so it was not so acute. This time we were going into the season as Southern League runners-up and started the season among the promotion favourites – we were definite targets.

Our opening match against Cambridge City was a case in point. Matty Bound, a free-kick specialist, gave us the lead but we got caught on the break twice and fell to a 2-1 defeat. It was seen locally as an anti-climax and almost a disaster, but we had lost to a decent side, one that would go on to be runners-up in Conference South. That, however, would not be taken into account.

A midweek 2-0 defeat at Newport County, a game in which we battered them, was then followed by a 2-2 draw at Bognor Regis where, wouldn't you know it, Luke Nightingale scored twice. Our luck was out. I felt particularly powerless as I was injured and had to watch it all from the dug-out. The defeat at Newport, where we were on top all game, was particularly painful to watch.

One point from the three games in the opening week and a place in the bottom three was not what we were expecting. After losing their first game, Hornchurch had won their next two so were already going well, as were Grays Athletic, who we actually did well to hold to a 1-1 draw the following week, seeing as they fielded Freddy Eastwood and Mitchell Cole, both of whom would go on to Southend for big money and Eastwood then on to Wolves.

It didn't help hearing what was going on off the field. I could sense Ian was trying not to add to my worries and that he was keeping most of it from me, but I gathered that he was being frozen out of decisions. This despite Harrison telling Ian and me that he wanted us to take all the football decisions.

Martyn had asked me to get rid of Micky Jenkins as my assistant, telling me that he was not popular with certain supporters, but when Ian heard about it he intervened, saying that it should be my decision, not the administration's or the supporters'. In the end, Martyn compromised and allowed Micky to be my scout, but it was a sign of conflict within a club that was losing the unity of the previous season.

It didn't have a great impact much on me directly, but it did become a distraction round the club when an open-air concert on the pitch was scheduled for mid-August featuring Girls Aloud as the headline act, along with other people like Peter Andre. It was not my thing and nor did it seem to be many others'. When I met Girls Aloud, I got the feeling that they didn't really want to be there and that this was beneath them.

It had been Ian's idea, as a way to get in revenue for the playing budget, but Martyn had taken it on and could not get it to work, with the whole thing losing money and causing more internal problems. Martyn virtually instructed me to be there for the Sunday concert and I went under sufferance. It did not go well, with only around 4,000 in the place when it needed around double that just to break even. With tickets at £23, I thought it was too expensive for Weymouth, but what did I, who was just a footballer, know? The happy, buzzy atmosphere around the Wessex Stadium was fast disappearing and rumblings of discontent were in the air.

August Bank Holiday Monday took us to Hornchurch and we

actually played very well. It hurt us, though, when we had Jason Matthews sent off after one of their strikers had been fouled when through on goal in what was a case of mistaken identity since it was Robbie Pethick who committed the offence. The referee was not for turning, though.

Even with ten men we battered them in the second half, despite going 2-1 down, and Lee Phillips should have equalised when clean through. They looked wobbly, with Garry Hill on the sideline not knowing how to turn the tide. The point-saver just would not come, though. With just one win from our opening six games, at home to Maidenhead United, we were still in the bottom half of the table.

Harrison seemed far from happy with me after the game at Hornchurch, particularly when I told him I was on my way to Sky Sports to do some work for them. He wondered why I was doing it and I wondered whether he expected me to go home and mope. I think he was worried – though he should have been above it – by a few fans he was close to who were complaining that I was doing too much media work and not concentrating on the job, though no one was more committed to the club than me. Besides, it had always been part of my deal for giving up my professional career, that I was free to make up the money I was missing out on by doing TV and radio work.

Ian also rang me that night. He said he had told Harrison he was going to resign as chairman, because he could no longer work with him and felt that the board were working behind his back. I had better watch mine, he said.

Initially I was stunned and felt angry with Ian. He had brought me to the club and I had only come for him. He had now left me on a limb and I was glad now that I had insisted on the protection of a long contract. Though I knew Ian would not have sacked me unless things got desperate, I always knew I would be vulnerable to the whims of a chairman who hadn't appointed me.

I began to get a sense of the beginning of the end, in fact. What Harrison had said to me after the Hornchurch game, rather than saying how unlucky we were, began to sound like the start of his search for reasons not to back me. Then, when we won 1-0 away to Margate the following week, his reaction was, "That wasn't very good, was it?", which really annoyed me. He had also told me that I was no longer allowed to get more players in, that the wage bill had to be pegged at £8,000 and not the £10,000 he had earmarked.

It seemed my allies on the board were also dwindling. Charlie Lesser had gone during the takeover and two others who seemed decent and who were on my side, in Nigel Winship and Andrew Brown, had also quit because they didn't like the new regime.

It left a bloke called Chris Pugsley, who I had the occasional dealing with as finance director but who didn't impress me much, and Tristan Murless, who struck me as something of a yes-man. With Matthew McGowan, who questioned everything from training to formations to selections as if he knew what he was talking about, it was, in my opinion, not a very knowledgeable or supportive line-up.

With Ian I had a relationship where we could question each other knowing it was going to be a constructive dialogue. It helped that he had a background of having written about the game for a long time and knew football people, which gave him some understanding of it, but I could not say the same of these people.

Harrison was difficult to fathom out. He was a strange man. I think Ian had thought he would be left alone to run the club as he had done the previous year, retaining all the powers of chairman, but with Harrison's money behind him. He was being naïve. People very rarely do that. Roman Abramovich's people at Chelsea clearly do what they are told.

Once, I was out with Harrison in a bar on Weymouth seafront, cursing Ian for not being there and leaving me with this bloke. At one point, a couple of fans asked me for my autograph and he asked them, "What about me?" It was only half in jest, I think.

He also asked me how wealthy I was and whether I had a lot

of cash. The alarm bells started to ring inside me. It was the question of a man who was thinking about sacking me. I wasn't going to make it easy for him, though, five-year contract or not. I knew I was a good manager, but I also knew that wouldn't mean anything if my face didn't fit. I would just have to win games.

And we did. Ian's last game was a 3-2 win at home over Bishops Stortford in which I scored a hat-trick. I don't think my celebrations, giving the thumbs-up to him in the directors' box, did me any favours with Harrison. I also signed the match ball and gave it to Ian. It was sad to see him go, though I told him it was good riddance.

Gradually I began to get the new team playing the way I wanted them to and they were coming to terms with the demands at the club. We won three and drew three in a good run of seven games to move into the top half of the table. The problem came with an FA Cup tie against Thame, a little Southern League regional division club from Oxfordshire.

We totally outplayed them at home, but they scrambled a 1-1 draw and took us back to their basic ground, which was an absolute mud heap. It was a nightmare worse than the previous worst place I had ever played at, Ashford the previous season. The reason it was worse was that we lost 2-1 and the Weymouth fans were not happy.

But it was only a cup game, I thought, and we were getting our act together in the league, which had to be the priority. I was convinced that we were a playoff team at least. Later in the season Hornchurch would go bust and, although Grays would go on and win the league comfortably by picking up a lot of their players, the lure of that second promotion place would have kept us going this time.

Fans do like the excitement of the FA Cup, though, and chairmen want the money that comes from a cup run. Managers, on the other hand, are more concerned with the bread and butter of the league, knowing that their jobs usually hinge on weekly results. I was not going to get the chance to reach those playoffs.

Tristan Murless came into the dressing room after the Thame match and informed me that the chairman would like to see me. I guessed what was coming, though I was a bit surprised to see my coach Gary Borthwick up at the back of the stand with Harrison, nipping away when I arrived. They were both smoking cigars.

"I think that will have to be it," Harrison said.

I was really taken aback. I couldn't believe it.

"You're sacking me?" I asked and he nodded.

As gutted as I was, as much as I knew I was doing a good job and that we were getting better, I was not going to beg for a job that had become increasingly less enjoyable under this man.

"OK," I said. "I'll expect a phone call to sort out the money I'm owed." I didn't need to remind him that my contract had around three-and-a-half years still to run. If last year's money, which in the end totalled £85,000, were to be repeated, that would be around £300,000 gross, but naturally I wouldn't be expecting that.

I went back to the dressing room to tell the lads, and to say how much I had enjoyed working with them. Most seemed more stunned than me. A few said that it was a joke, but then in my opinion the club had been a joke since Harrison had arrived. Basically he wanted me out, couldn't do it because of our league form and so took the opportunity to do so following a comparatively meaningless cup defeat.

Two days later, I found myself in the bar of the Hilton Hotel just outside Southampton with Harrison, Murless and McGowan. They offered me a drink. I told them that I was not here to socialise, that they didn't like me and I didn't like them, and that I just wanted the deal done and to get out.

Murless blurted out that they would not be offering any more than £200,000. I could barely contain my amusement. Had it been Ian – though I know he wouldn't have sacked me – I would have asked for no more than £50,000 because I knew the state of the club. But I thought Harrison was paying for everything and that he had treated me badly, so I was going to get as much as I could.

Later I found out that he was putting everything into the club as loans but, at that point, people thought it was money without strings because that's what he had told everyone. McGowan did let it slip that my pay-off would be coming out of any future Asda money when the stadium was developed, which struck me as a bit sharp given that Harrison had been saying he was bankrolling everything.

In the end, Harrison got out of the club a couple of years later soon after the Asda deal fell through. He tried to recoup all the money he reckoned he had put into the club – around £2.5 million as he threw good money after bad – from prospective new owners, but nobody would take over a club with all that to pay back.

Anyway, I thought £200,000 was a right touch. Being cheeky, I also asked for some expenses I was owed and for the loan I had put in the club to help tide it over at the end of the previous season to be paid back – it totalled around £38,000. They agreed to it immediately. It was done in about five minutes and the cheque arrived within a week. Fair play to them, but I couldn't help thinking it was all a bit odd and a bit amateur. They were just too much of a soft touch.

As had been the case when I was player-manager at Portsmouth, I had given it my all, mentally, physically and emotionally, and though I would like to have seen it through, because I knew I would have succeeded, I was relieved to be out of it, to be honest, especially when certain fans who used to chant my name and who had been nice to my face had turned and screamed for me to go. That saddened me.

And Harrison was very impressionable when it came to fans. He wanted rid of Micky Jenkins because a couple of his cronies thought Micky was rude. Asked by a couple of fans about my tactics, he would come to me and wonder why we weren't playing three up front or a man in the hole. At one point he asked whether we should be playing 4-4-3. I asked him what he meant and it was clear he didn't know what they were talking about. He certainly didn't. Perhaps he meant I should play without a goalkeeper.

He was a nightmare to deal with and to talk to. You knew when he talked to you that he was trying to find your weaknesses, to undermine you and to justify a decision to get rid of you. It wasn't the best recipe for getting the best out of people.

In hindsight, I should have gone when Ian went. I was never going to get a fair crack after that and now I understood why he had to go. These men were impossible to work with. One of the reasons Harrison didn't like me was that my profile was higher than his. I thought he wanted to be the hero, the saviour. Ian had not had a problem with my status, because he was in it for the club and, in my view, not for his own motives.

What saddened me was the aftermath. I might have known what the reaction to me down there was going to be when I tried ringing Gary Borthwick a couple of times, but he didn't return my calls. I had been thinking of grooming Paul Buckle as my coach – and Ian always said that he wanted Bucks as my successor if or when I left the club – so maybe Gary heard about that and got the hump.

Harrison also put it about how much I was earning, calling my contract ridiculous. I heard that he even showed it on a screen at the club's AGM. I reckon I was good value for the £85,000 I earned, which included basic and goals and crowd bonuses what with the doubling of revenue the club pulled in. Others obviously didn't and Harrison's campaign against me worked, because I got some serious grief when I went back to the club a while later.

The next season, Weymouth got to the first round of the FA Cup and earned a good result by drawing at Nottingham Forest. Sky were covering the replay at the Wessex Stadium and asked me to go down to be a studio guest in the portakabin structure they had built at one end.

Just walking to it from the car park was unpleasant as I took some nasty comments. They got worse when I was sitting watching the game. "Wanker," and "Money grabber," were among the kindest things said by a certain section who also chanted, "We want our money back."

I actually felt quite intimidated at one point and began to understand why some people want to get out of football in these harsh times. I had always been loved when I went back to previous clubs and had never been treated like this. In the end, I adopted the Catherine Tate approach – look at my face, am I bovvered?

What upset me most was the ignorance of it all. I gave up my Championship career, and the prospect of earning much more, when I went down there. I managed the team and the resources well, and scored goals on top. I know I would have got them into the Conference at the very least had I been allowed to finish the job.

What was strange was that, at the time, the club was paying more to the then manager Garry Hill and chucking fortunes at trying to get up into the Conference. But nobody cared about that then, until it all went pear-shaped a couple of years later when Harrison pulled out, as I warned it would.

It also angered me that Ian got dog's abuse, for voicing his concerns about the club into which he had sunk his heart. Without him having had a good go, the club would have just stagnated and without him later speaking out to alert everyone to the money issues, the club could have gone under as debt mounted. This was a bloke who gave up a lot for the club, including taking a pay cut in his job to devote more time to his role as chairman, as well as putting money into the club. It just showed what a fickle bunch they could be.

After I left, McGowan got what he wanted and got put in charge with Paul Buckle, who quite rightly said that he wanted a proper say, rather than be a puppet. Bucks, gent that he is, even rang me and asked if it was OK with me if he took on the role.

McGowan stood aside, but a week later Bucks was out of the club. Having been told he would get a crack at the job, McGowan recommended Steve Johnson instead, an Isthmian League manager who came cheap and via the reference of his brother, Gary Johnson at Yeovil.

But Steve Johnson proved a disaster as my side was dismantled. Astonishingly, they let Steve Tully and Lee Phillips go for nothing to Exeter and came to regret it. They also paid up Lee Philpott. As for Bucks, he got paid up too and went on to become assistant manager at Exeter, playing on for another couple of years as well, before getting the job as manager of Torquay United. What a loss to Weymouth he proved. It was just one of many bad judgements by McGowan and Harrison.

Johnson didn't last long, with Harrison ending the cost-cutting and then chasing expensive popularity by appointing Hill, following Hornchurch's slide into administration. Weymouth did get up into the Conference, but with a wage bill of £22,000 a week anyone could have achieved that.

Six months later, Harrison was tired of losing around £1 million a season and pulled the plug, paid up Hill and got out of it, to protect his worsening health. The bloke he sold it to then passed it on to a property developer a few months later. Ian asked me a couple of times if he should go back to try and help them out, but I told him not to get involved. People down there didn't appreciate it. If only they had continued to believe in me and Ian, I reckon we would have done a better job on much less money.

I just had to put it down to experience, but I could still hold my head up, because I know I worked hard to put together a decent side playing good football and that we had made progress at the club.

In the end, though, it all left a sour taste in my mouth. I get a rousing reception from people who appreciate what I did for them at every one of my former clubs I go back to. Weymouth proved the exception and now I feel no desire to go back. It is a real sadness to me, and a rare blot on my sentiments towards my former clubs.

4. *The Wanderer Returns*

It had been a stunning moment when Steve was sacked from Weymouth, one that would sadden me and colour my perception of the club and a certain element of its fans. I had been at the game and rang him to commiserate over the result about an hour later on my way home. When he told me of his dismissal, I had to pull the car over.

Paul Buckle was also shocked. "I was hurt that night," he recalls. "It was all so unprofessional. He was a good manager and would have succeeded if he had been left alone. I always thought Weymouth was a five-year plan."

For me, the sacking set in motion a bitter battle with Martyn Harrison over, as I perceived it, a fight for the soul of the club and, over the next couple of years, I continued a war of bitter words with him. It was the club of my youth, after all, and Steve had been abominably treated. It was something that angered me.

It rankled that Harrison would describe Steve's deal with the club as "the most ridiculous contract ever", before going on to offer more money to a successor who wouldn't be scoring 30 goals a season as well as managing the club. That distasteful reception at the Nottingham Forest FA Cup-tie from a group of fans who had been stoked up by such comments was the final straw for me and I sold my shareholding in the club to Harrison.

Steve did not deserve it. For me, he had been an exceptional figure and manager for the club. He had gone beyond what was asked of him and had helped build a club, not just a team.

Yes, there were moments when the two of us fell out, as Steve has, no doubt, detailed, perhaps over a difference of opinion about a player – naturally, he would get his way about the player, as managers should, if not about money matters – or something trivial.

Harrison used those moments on *Football Diaries* as another stick with which to beat Steve, as he claimed it made the club look stupid. In fact, Steve's profile took the club to new levels of consciousness in the game that Harrison could not understand. He was envious of Steve's profile.

And there was the irony. Steve, so often in the right place at the right time on the pitch, where he was in control, simply found himself in the wrong place at the wrong time off it, having no control when it came to a club owner acting precipitately. As he had found out at Portsmouth before and would have to find out again later in his story, such is football.

For now, he did what good men do when they have been knifed. He picked himself off the ground and pulled out the weapon from his wound. At that time, it was not too difficult to find another club to play for. There was still no shortage of takers. Whatever size of baggage people perceived came with Steve, managers always knew there was still more quality and value in him.

It is a pragmatic game. Steve's first phone call was to a manager with whom he had had his disagreements, first at Wolves and then at Millwall. Mark McGhee was now in charge at Brighton, just promoted from League One but struggling at the foot of the table, and in need of a striker. Steve knew as much – and also that it was a Championship club with a training ground 45 minutes from his home.

With McGhee unwilling to offer him more than a week-to-week deal, it was soon on to Brentford for another few weeks. There, Martin Allen wanted an experienced striker for his League One side but, after a couple of games, both he and Steve recognised a mistake had been made, given the direct style Allen and his Bees employed. No hard feelings but Steve was on the move again.

He was growing weary of moving from club to club, though, and just wanted somewhere to hang his hat for the rest of that 2004/05 season. John Gorman, former assistant to Glenn Hoddle with the England team and now manager at Wycombe Wanderers, needed a wily old striker to coax the best out of his young buck Nathan Tyson up front.

So Steve had four clubs in six months, from Conference South up to the Championship and back down to League Two via League One. It was yet another curious sort of record – and one that would be hard for anyone to beat.

Steve encountered an old mate at Adams Park who had been with him at Leicester City, Steve Guppy – another old favourite of Martin O'Neill – who had signed a pre-contract with DC United in America's Major Soccer League and who was keeping himself fit. Left-winger Guppy had started at Wycombe when O'Neill, who would turn out to be one of Britain's best managers in spells at Celtic and Aston Villa, was learning his trade.

"It was a short spell this time after I had five good years there as a young player, but it was good fun," says Guppy. Indeed, it helped Claridge rediscover some enjoyment in the game after some miserable times in the previous six months as he formed a good partnership with Tyson, who would go on to sign for Nottingham Forest for £750,000.

"Steve was still on the borderline of being late for training, and maybe not trying that hard when he was there," says Guppy. "He must have had many a manager tearing his hair out, but come the match, he would give you everything and that's why so many signed him.

"He hadn't changed all that much from Leicester. I remember him there reaching down into the pocket of his tracksuit trousers and pulling out biscuits to eat. He must have eaten a whole packet. But then, in the afternoons, he would be in the gym or on the treadmill. He did train hard. It was just on his own terms.

"He always has to be on the move. I think if he wasn't in football, he would be running four companies at the same time. But then, while he's got this image of being scatty, he is actually a very shrewd guy. When you see him on TV, he talks a lot of sense and I am sure a lot of people have had to change their perception of him."

Steve's TV work was increasing during his time at Wycombe. "I think he was struggling to juggle it all with playing," says Guppy. "At times it probably overtook him. But John Gorman was a nice guy and did his best to accommodate Steve."

Steve himself agrees, but grew frustrated by Gorman's reluctance to play with the width that he has always advocated. "John hated 4-4-2," says Guppy. "He preferred a 4-3-3 and that probably didn't suit Steve."

As a result, after a good start, Steve did not always fit in as the season came towards its finale. His frustration was growing; he was now thinking in two different ways. He saw himself as a player, and one who had the ability to keep playing for a long time yet, but he also saw himself as a manager who just wasn't in a job.

At the end of the campaign, Gorman made Steve a token offer for the following season probably knowing he wouldn't take it. He was out of contract and out of work again, even if the media was always an outlet for him.

Personally, I felt guilty. I had talked Steve into going to Weymouth and giving up his Championship career with Millwall at around a third of the money he could have got. And I had left him in the firing line after resigning as chairman, knowing that he would struggle to survive my trigger-happy successor. Not that I could have done much. Anyway, I would certainly have resigned when he was sacked.

He bore no grudge towards me, of course, and would get tickets for me and my son Jack for Brentford games – a home defeat by Torquay on Boxing Day, and at Wycombe a splendid victory over Scunthorpe United, who would go on to be promoted. But still, I felt I owed him.

Things were happening at his old club Millwall. Under Dennis Wise's player-management, they had reached an FA Cup final and had splashed money on players and their wages in an effort to reach the Premiership. It hadn't happened and the club had racked up considerable debt.

Theo Paphitis had had enough and stepped down as chairman. Another of the directors, Jeff Burnige, had taken over with a brief to cut costs massively. Dennis Wise decided against staying and was paid up by Paphitis. There was a vacancy for someone who could work wonders on a shoestring.

I had known Jeff for quite a while through my work and knew him as a decent man who loved the 'Wall. His father Herbert had been chairman before him and he was now achieving a lifetime ambition. I rang him and put Steve's name to him as a potential new manager. And I had no hesitation in recommending him based on his shrewdness of operating on a limited budget at Weymouth and his ability to galvanise a club that needed a lift.

The idea appealed to Jeff. Steve was a fans' favourite, he had good contacts and he wouldn't be too expensive. It added up.

I rang Steve, who was out in Germany at the Confederations Cup international tournament working for Channel 5, to tell him of my conversation and told him that he might be getting a call. Within a couple of days, Steve was flying back from Germany to talk over the job with Jeff. Within another couple of days he was Millwall manager and I was delighted, actually, more relieved for him. Little did I, or he, know what he was walking into.

Though Paphitis was ostensibly out of the picture, he was still holding the purse strings. The club had lost more than £4 million the previous year in its bid to reach the Premiership and though Burnige was able to make decisions, anything financial had to go through Paphitis, whose personal financial support would still be needed to underwrite the wage bill for a few more months yet. The club had sold Darren Ward to Crystal Palace for £1.1 million, but would not receive the first instalment of that payment until August.

Paphitis was known to be unhappy about Burnige's appointment of Steve. Though he had liked Steve as a player, he did not apparently consider him as management material, deeming him disorganised and chaotic. After that, Burnige and Paphitis would clash on several matters, including the buying and selling of players, and the new chairman felt he had no choice but to resign just a couple of weeks into Steve's management and allow Paphitis to take over the decision-making again, even if he would not be the named chairman.

Burnige stepped down as a director at the New Den in 2008 after various changes of ownership but, for a long time, those summer weeks of 2005 remained a sensitive subject. He is willing to talk about them, but reluctant to go into too much detail.

"There was another manager I wanted, but he was unavailable," he recalls. "Then Steve did really well at the interview and convinced us he understood the financial limitations. He knew the club and the players and could hit the ground running. He was also available immediately, so that's how he came to be appointed.

"The first wobble I had was over his appointment. Theo was not very positive about it. I presume he had an old image of him. That's when I thought, 'I am not even in charge here.' Soon my relationship with Theo collapsed, but that was not over Steve. In fact, I thought Steve's best chance of survival might be if I got out of the way and he had a relationship with Theo.

"It was an agonising couple of days," Burnige adds. "It was a role I wanted badly. Plus, Millwall had been in danger and I wanted to avert that. Now I was cut out. My choice was a slow death or a fast death. I chose a fast death."

Steve did indeed have a relationship with Paphitis for a few more weeks, but it was an unpleasant and uncomfortable one. It was all so sad. I caught up with Steve at a Millwall friendly against Southend United down at Root's Hall and, as was always his style, could see he was putting his heart and soul into the job. That afternoon, he had flown back from Norway, where he was overseeing others of the club's squad who were on a pre-season tour.

He was also determined to learn the lessons from his previous stint as a manager, and improve. "When Steve left Weymouth, he phoned me and asked, 'What did I do wrong?'" his old captain Paul Buckle recalls. "Then when he got the Millwall job, he rang again and asked, 'What was I good at?'"

He was good at plenty of things, according to Millwall's goalkeeping coach Tony Burns, who was around the club the whole time of Claridge's tenure, had been there for years indeed, and seen plenty come and go.

"He was massively professional," says Burns, one of those salt-of-the-earth, old-fashioned football men. "I was at the club when he was there as a player and he was the fittest man in the club then and still was this time, an example to all the young players."

Did he see the appointment as a risk for the club? "Not at all. He knew the club and the standard, knew the game, has a good brain and a good football brain. I thought Millwall was an ideal job for him. It must really have hurt to be the chairman's choice one minute and not the next."

One of Paphitis's gripes with Steve, it would turn out, was what he believed to be a chaotic summer programme that featured a pre-season training week at an army camp in Wiltshire.

"There was no problem with the training. It was fine," says Burns. "Players will always moan. If you take them to Dubai, some of them will complain it's too hot. It was his decision to organise the camp and the players had to accept that. The players worked hard and it was different. It should have had nothing to do with his time in charge.

"I do think that one of the problems was that Steve was so fit himself and his standards were so high that he got frustrated with people who were different from that.

"The simple problem was that he just wasn't given time. He didn't have time to get the club right. You couldn't judge if it was a good spell or a bad spell. I mean, how long was it? Just over a month?"

In the end, Steve lasted just 36 days before Paphitis sacked him. That came the night of a 2-2 draw in a friendly against Gillingham at the New Den, with Paphitis telling Steve that he should not be playing and that it was time he packed up.

"He was man of the match that night," Burns recalls. "He was the best player in the club. Remind me who Theo played for? He must have been a defender."

Steve believes that the sacking damaged his reputation enormously, unable as he has been to get another management job since.

"He may think it did him some harm, but I think one day he might look at it and see it as a good experience," says Burns. "Some people might see his character as a weakness, but it's his strength.

"I know at the end of the day he will make a manager. He gets stuck in to the job all right. It just needs someone to take him on and believe in him."

Following his dismissal – where he was succeeded by Colin Lee, whom he had just appointed as assistant manager – Steve was especially upset with Paphitis for a public statement that Millwall would have been relegated under him. Steve was not at that time allowed to have the right of reply due to the terms of his pay-off. No such restrictions hinder him in the next chapters, however.

Under those managers who took over from Steve, with Lee plunging them into trouble before being sacked and caretaker Dave Tuttle unable to rescue the situation, Millwall were relegated from the Championship anyway. The post of chair remained vacant for four months after Burnige's resignation, though Paphitis still held all the cards as majority shareholder.

The businessman and former America's Cup sailing entrepreneur Peter De Savary then arrived as chairman for a while promising to attract new investment and the club soon had new controllers. But Millwall struggled in League One.

Does Burnige think that Millwall would have stayed in the Championship under Claridge? "Yes, I do," he says. "It would have been tough, but as he said at his press conference when he was appointed, his objective was lower to middle of the table and I think he would have achieved that.

"I didn't expect him to be sacked because all the tough stuff had been done with a lot of money coming off the wage bill. The problem was he was never allowed to bring in the players he wanted and there were some good ones, like Marlon King, John Oster and Danny Cullip."

There are several theories about the demise of Burnige and Claridge. One says that Paphitis did not want to see his successor succeed, on the basis of "Après moi, le déluge", that he wanted to be seen as the saviour and not someone else.

Some say that he missed the limelight in these days before the *Dragons' Den* TV show would give him the profile he enjoyed. Some say that he just got the two to do all the unpopular dirty work of reducing the costs at the club before riding to the rescue as white knight again. Some say that he never went away in the first place, and was being fed information all the time from within the club.

Suffice it to say, Steve has his own views on all of the above.

4.1 One Season and Four Clubs

After my sacking at Weymouth, I did what I always do when I am down and when I don't know what to do next. I hit the roads and the gym to stay fit and lose myself in physical activity. And then I picked up the phone to find myself another club. As I did after losing the Portsmouth job, I just needed to play again without worrying about managing a team.

I knew I wasn't going to get another manager's job right now anyway. No matter how well you think you have done, you don't move from Conference South to the Football League to manage after you have been sacked. I needed a period of rehabilitation somewhere first.

There was probably another reason why no chairman would be ringing me up. *Football Diaries* had not long been aired on BBC2 and it hadn't done me too many favours, probably reinforcing the perception of me as being a bit knockabout. And I didn't need the publicity, as I was in the public eye through my own media work.

What I needed now was a club that would let me continue doing it while playing, and one not too far away from my home.

I rang Mark McGhee at Brighton and asked if he needed a striker – and I knew they did. They had been struggling in the Championship, having been bottom after the first four games, and even now in November they were in big trouble. Three defeats in a row, against Sunderland, Derby and Crewe, had put them right back in the relegation mix.

Yes I know I had previous with McGhee, having felt that he had not treated me the best at Wolves, where he never really let me do the job he bought me for, and Millwall, but I tried not to hold grudges in the game and to treat everything as a new situation. I had not said anything bad about him after my parting from Millwall and he was fine with me when I called him. There was never a problem in being polite and civil to each other away from the pitch or the training ground.

It's a bit like going back to an old flame, isn't it? You always hope and think it will be better this time around, though you do try to separate the personal and the professional. I remember being at a dinner with the former Nottingham Forest centre-half Larry Lloyd and he told me that if Brian Clough had walked into his local pub, he would have walked out because he disliked him so much. But, as a manager, Larry accepted that Cloughie was in charge and respected him.

With me and McGhee it was probably the other way round. I would have bought him a drink, but I couldn't accept he was a good manager, even if he did go on to do well in Scottish football.

At that time, McGhee and I both needed each other and in this game you have to be realistic. That much was clear when he took me on for a month, at £1,100 a week. It was the best he could do, he said, and that was all right by me. The training ground was just a 45-minute drive away and I was back where I felt I belonged, in the Championship.

Robbie Pethick was right, it was a very laid-back club and training was, shall we say, relaxed and the facilities basic. Not having proper goals, we used benches for five-a-side. And the mood around the club was always the same on Monday morning whether you had won or lost. They just looked to the next game. It felt a bit like Aldershot early on in my career.

That's not to say that football didn't matter to the place. You always felt that if they could build the new stadium that had been talked about for so long in these parts on the edge of town at Falmer, the area where we trained, they really could take off. They had the potential to pull in crowds and, yes, get up into the Premier League.

For the moment, though, they were having to make to do with the Withdean Stadium, an athletics track really, which was always full to its 6,000 capacity. The away fans were so far away from the pitch, I always thought, that it couldn't have been that much of a journey from their home town. At most grounds, the players look like dots to the fans. At the Withdean, the crowd looked like dots to the players. At least the big portakabins they used were decent dressing rooms.

After a week of proper training, McGhee put me straight in for the match away to West Ham, who were struggling under Alan Pardew at the time – well, comparatively anyway, at fifth in the table – but who would go on to win the playoffs and reach the Premiership.

It was a bit weird, as well. My last game just a couple of weeks earlier had been against Thame United in front of a few hundred fans on a miserable night and on a terrible pitch in an FA Cup qualifying round replay. Now I was turning out in front of just under 30,000 on a slick surface. I never felt intimidated or over-awed, though. Quite the opposite. I loved it. Where one was an alien experience to me, this felt natural and what I was used to. I was born for it.

From arriving in the coach through throngs of people to walking on carpets down the Upton Park hallways to a dressing room where you have room to move was all so much more a part of my comfort zone. And playing on a pitch where you knew that the ball would bounce properly. Even the quality of abuse I received from the West Ham fans was of a better quality, and I got plenty as a former Millwall player. There was even a grudging respect from people who recognised a player, I think. "Resign Claridge" was about the cleverest I heard at Thame from people who had short fuses and short memories.

And I played really well against West Ham and revelled in every minute. I played up front on my own, held the ball up and never gave it away, to ease the inevitable pressure we came under. I was on the field as we won the game with a goal by Guy Butters, who headed home from a corner to send our 3,000 travelling fans into raptures. It took us three places clear of the relegation zone.

McGhee seemed pleased and it was the start of five games in a row for me. We lost against Burnley and Ipswich by a single goal, but then beat Rotherham, to make it six points from four games, a better return than they had been getting and mid-table form.

I was barely getting a sniff of goal – just one decent chance against Ipswich that I missed but that was it – partly because we were a team set up to contain and not create many chances. In all honesty, I was probably not at my sharpest yet, either, having been in the part-time, non-League game for the previous year.

Although I was now 38, I still felt I had plenty left in my legs. You do go through a period at around 33 and 34 when people ask you regularly when you are going to retire. It does bring a certain insecurity and every time you go on a run and you don't feel great, you do wonder if it is age and whether your standards and capabilities are failing. For now, though, I didn't think my physical condition was a problem.

I was playing up front with Adam Virgo, who was more of a central defender, and it was hard work. Leon Knight, a player who is almost as well travelled as me, was also at the club, but he was in and out of favour with McGhee for not, as he saw it, working hard enough. Whatever else McGhee might have thought about me, he could never accuse me of that.

At the back, there was Danny Cullip, a clever bloke and a good player who played with his head, but someone who hated training. He never minded the weights but hated the running. Then in midfield was Charlie Oatway, who would end up at Havant and Waterlooville and who would play alongside Shaun Wilkinson, who I bought for Weymouth, against Liverpool at Anfield in the FA Cup.

I do remember in training one day, Charlie kicked a ball that hit one of the coaches, Bob Booker, who was a great bloke, on the head and he collapsed. It was one of those moments that you think are funny then realise the seriousness of it. We had to carry him into the dressing room. Fortunately he came round.

We also had Darren Currie on the wing, who I liked but who could be very frustrating as he did all his tricks as you were waiting in the box for a cross, then had to come back out to avoid being offside. Then had to go back in. Every time I played with him I felt like I'd had a drink. I'd fall over four times watching him. But he could play and just needed a good, strong manager to get hold of him. He went on to Ipswich and had his best spell there.

The fixture list took us back to Millwall in early December and I was up for it, getting a great reception off the fans. It was good seeing so many old friends again and I had a laugh with Dennis Wise, now player-manager. But we struggled as a team and lost 2-0. I felt frustrated at times just having to dine off scraps of possession.

Afterwards McGhee told the press that he didn't think I could hurt defenders any more, which I resented. I knew I could still hurt defences. Besides, my game was about holding the ball up and bringing others into play and in that I was very useful to Brighton, with the way they played in absorbing pressure and trying to hit teams on the break. Perhaps he was smarting from the fact that while the Millwall fans gave me a hero's reception, he took some stick off them.

My month was up and I asked McGhee about another deal, hoping that, having done well for him, I might even get a contract to the end of the season. He told me that he didn't have any money, that he couldn't even offer me another month, but that he could only keep me on a week-to-week basis. I didn't want fortunes but this was an insult, a real kick in the teeth. All I wanted was to be treated with respect.

Then I got a call from an agent on behalf of Martin Allen, the Brentford manager, who had seen me playing for Brighton and knew I was non-contract. He offered me £1,500 a week and £100 an appearance to the end of the season. It meant League One football, but someone wanted me, which was important. After all, I had been playing in Conference South a couple of months earlier.

And I had fond memories of Griffin Park. When I was an apprentice at Pompey, I was sent there with the reserves for a game to be kitboy. It was one of the first proper football stadiums I ever went to and sitting there impressed by the ground and the atmosphere of professional football stuck in my memory. Funny how life changes. Once one of the big grounds, now Griffin Park seemed quaint and outdated.

I was annoyed with McGhee. I think I could have done a good job for him for the rest of the season. And he wasn't completely open with me. A few weeks later, he signed Mark McCammon from Millwall on £1,800 a week. McGhee had also taken him to Millwall from Brentford and he had hardly played a game or scored a goal at the New Den. Mark was quick and strong, but wasn't as good as me, I believed. He would go on to score three goals for Brighton that season. Soon he and McGhee would fall out over something that ended up with the manager ordering him off the bus on an away trip up North and left him having to make his own way back.

I think McGhee can let personalities cloud his judgement. I have never had a problem with him when we meet outside of football but, within it, he seemed to enjoy picking me up and discarding me. It was almost funny in the end, as if he was thinking: "I'm feeling a bit low. I know how to cheer myself up. I'll sign Claridge short-term then get rid of him."

In the end, they were fortunate to survive that season. I went to their last game, at home to Ipswich, which they needed to draw to stay up. They did, 1-1, but Ipswich had a good shout for a penalty, which would have sent them down.

It was a bit of a culture shock going to Brentford. For a start, it was a tough drive to training at what always seemed a windswept training ground near Heathrow, as I had to go via the M27, M3, M25 and M4 during the rush hour. It meant leaving at 7am. Then there was the different intensity of Martin Allen, who was very domineering with his squad.

Now I knew a bit about Martin. He had been at Portsmouth as a player and I really liked him and wanted him in my team. He dug in and stood up to be counted. They used to call him "Mad Dog", a nickname he would come to hate as he tried to change his image when he went into management. My memories were of him always having a tear-up with Phil Parkinson, then at Reading and who would go on to be a successful manager of Colchester United.

The night before my first day of training, I stayed in a hotel at Heathrow – grey and grim and I feel sorry for any air travellers who have to spend too much time there – and Martin came the next morning to show me the way to the training ground. The training was all right. They seemed organised and well drilled during the two days I had before making my debut.

I knew within minutes of that, though, that I had made a mistake. It was at home to Colchester, which we won 1-0 thanks to John Salako's goal, but I spent the game watching the ball going over my head. Now I knew that Martin Allen liked direct football, but I didn't realise it would be as extreme as this. It was back to the John Beck era.

There was another element about Martin that I wasn't comfortable with and which also mirrored Beck. The previous season Brentford had got a good draw at Southampton, then in the Premier, in the FA Cup and a story emerged in the newspapers – which came from him – that he had thrown himself in the Solent the day before, as part of some superstition about swimming the day before a tie to keep the run going. It was as if they had only got the result because of his swim.

I bet some of the players weren't very happy about the focus of attention being taken away from their achievements, which was also the case at Cambridge United when Beck attracted all the attention with his antics, like forcing players to have cold showers before games and growing the grass long in the corners of the pitch so that the ball would hold up there when we pumped it forward.

I had no problems with what he had to say in the dressing room and there was not a lot wrong with his team talks, but the Bees had been going through a bad patch and were getting back to basics, based on free-kicks, corners and long throws. The problem was, they were drilled in it and I wasn't. It didn't suit my game anyway.

On one occasion, for example, John Salako had the ball in his hands for a throw-in and I showed, ready to receive it. I was yelling at him to throw it, as I was in space in the penalty area, but he just couldn't release the ball, even though as a player who had played to a good level, with Crystal Palace, even for England, you knew he wanted to.

It became comical. He looked like he was having a fit as he shaped to throw it to me then stopped himself. "I can't, I can't. He'll take me off," he was saying as 10 yards away on the touchline, Martin was shouting, "Don't you dare throw it short." John had to wait for two centre-backs to get themselves forward and for someone else to come and take the throw.

Sometimes when players are short of confidence, they will take the easy option and unload the ball early, rather than be patient, retain possession and wait for a better ball. That has nothing to do with a manager's instructions. What was happening at Brentford did, though.

They had some decent players as well, led by Jay Tabb, a busy midfield player who would go on to Coventry City. At the back, there was a real footballing centre-half in Michael Turner, who even had a spell on loan at Inter Milan during his time at Charlton Athletic since they had a tie-up with the Italian club at the time. There was also Stephen Hunt, who Martin didn't really

Socks still round the ankles at Pompey (*Action Images*).

Fratton Park characters . . . top, Tony Pulis (left) and Alan Ball (right); below, Guy Whittingham (*Action Images/ColorSport*).

Milan Mandaric liked to surround himself with local personalities – the more suntanned the better (*Action Images*).

Local TV presenter and fellow director, Fred Dineage (*ColorSport*).

100 UP

Pompey player-boss Steve Claridge today steps out against Blackburn Rovers at Fratton Park for his 100th league game in Pompey colours.

Ton up . . . My 100th game for Pompey, all the sweeter after my hat-trick against Wolves (*The News*).

Getting the point across as Portsmouth player-manager (*Action Images*).

Celebrating a goal for Millwall with Marc Bircham and Richard Sadlier.
I loved playing up front with 'Sads'.

Lions' boss Mark McGhee. I played
for him at three different clubs but it
is fair to say that our relationship
was somewhat up and down
(*Action Images*).

Tim Cahill – another outstanding
figure in an outstanding Millwall
side (*Action Images*).

In action for Weymouth against Altrincham. Ah, the beautiful game!
(*Idris Martin*).

Wessex Men . . . The Weymouth chairman who sacked me, Martyn Harrison, with fellow director Matthew McGowan (grey hair) next to him (*Idris Martin*).

Paul Buckle – my captain at the Wessex Stadium, who went on to manage Torquay United (*Action Images*).

With Ian at the Wessex in a promotional picture for the *Radio Times* ahead of the BBC 2 series *Football Stories* (*Finnbarr Webster*).

A rare sighting of me as Millwall manager. This was in the dug-out at
Southend for a friendly. I was soon in the doghouse (*Action Images*).

Theo Paphitis may have handed over the chairmanship of Millwall to Jeff Burnige, but to my mind there was no question over who was really in charge (*Action Images*).

Colin Lee, the man in the background takes centre stage . . . (*Action Images*).

Letting go of the game was tough, and for two seasons my wanderlust took me all over the country in search of a game, from the Championship down to the Ryman League (*Empics; Bucks Free Press/Newsquest; Steve Ellis; Kent Messenger Group; Action Images; Sam Bagnall/News Team International; Worthing Herald*).

Sheffield Wednesday

Gillingham

Bradford City

My one thousandth, and last, league game, at Dean Court (*Empics*).

A kick up the backside for
'Scummer', Matthew Le Tissier,
during my testimonial at Fratton
Park (*Empics*).

TV times and radio days: at the mike
with George Gavin for Sky and for
Radio 5 Live (*Action Images*).

The lights of my life these days – wife Mandy and baby Grace.

rate that much and who rarely played, but who would end up being a decent Premier League player for Reading.

It was good, also, to see an old friend in Jamie Lawrence, who had been at Leicester with me. He was a good character, Jamie. He once served a spell in prison when he was young, but he turned his life around and would go on to set up his own football academy for hard-up kids in London.

Not that he was a saint. I remember going back to his house with Steve Guppy after a night out when we were all at Leicester and we disturbed Jamie in the middle of some – what shall we call it – nocturnal activity. As he got up in shock at us intruding, he almost knocked the TV off the sideboard with a part of his anatomy. It was only an 18-inch, though. The TV, I mean.

Anyway, at home to Torquay on Boxing Day, we lost 3-1 to a hat-trick by Leo Constantine, a player who I had known at Millwall and never thought would make it, but who had improved a lot. After that we lost 3-0 at Swindon and I played really badly. The sun was in my eyes a lot of the time as the ball was lumped up towards me, but even so I was off the pace and got subbed after an hour. I had no complaints.

I went to see Martin but I needn't have because he was coming to see me and we virtually bumped into each other in our haste – me to get away and him to get me away. Sometimes you can be a bit worried about saying certain things to a manager about how it is going, and he can be reluctant to damage your confidence, but neither of us was reluctant to say what was on our mind here.

I said that I didn't think I was going to be much use to him the way the team played. My game was coming short, holding it up, and creating chances, and hopefully finishing some, with a bit of ingenuity around the penalty box, not dealing with bombs that dropped from the air. It didn't help that I was playing up front with Deon Burton, who had good ability, but who was not the busiest of players.

We both understood and Martin said that he was sorry, but he thought he had made a mistake with me. There was no animosity between us and a few years later we were doing a radio show together and got on very well, talking for ages about old times and a game we both have deep feelings for.

He would go on to manage Milton Keynes Dons and did well before getting the Leicester job, only to get Milan Mandaric-ed quite quickly, so we had plenty of notes to compare. I think Martin learned lessons from it all, mellowing a bit with age and accepting that he needed to show more flexibility with his teams.

Martin agreed to circulate my details to other clubs and, after one more outing, as a sub at Bournemouth, Wycombe Wanderers came in for me. It was another example of my career going around in circles. I met their manager John Gorman, a Scot who had been Glenn Hoddle's assistant at Swindon and with England, at the Marriott Hotel at Newbury. Twenty years earlier, I had spoken to Wycombe's chief executive after being out of contract at Weymouth the first time around before I moved to Crystal Palace. I think they were probably offering me more money back in those days.

I liked John, who seemed a very decent man, and I got a good feeling about Wycombe so decided to sign. Brentford were quite happy to come to an arrangement about the rest of my contract to save some money on the wage bill. I was getting paid up everywhere and, contrary to what people might think, was hating every minute of it. I would rather have stayed in the jobs, with some stability and a chance to prove myself. Wycombe were giving me £1,300 a week.

In the space of three months, I had gone from Conference South to Championship, then back down through League One to League Two. That was some graph. Not many players have done or will do that. I didn't mind too much being back down in the lower orders, though. I just wanted to play and play regularly and John Gorman assured me that I would. This was my fourth club in only three months and I just wanted to stay put somewhere for a while, at least for the rest of that season.

The team was below halfway in the table when I joined and I quickly saw why John wanted me there. He had a pacy young striker in Nathan Tyson and I became a good foil for him. I would come and get the ball short and lay it off or spread it wide. Nathan liked it over the top.

They had just lost three matches on the bounce when I got there, but Nathan and I began to gel quite quickly. A nice little run took us up to eighth and ready to challenge for the playoffs. Nathan and I both scored in a 2-1 win over Scunthorpe, who were then going well and who would go on to gain automatic promotion, and I grabbed another in a 1-1 draw with Darlington before netting a pair, one a penalty, the other slid in from a Gus Uhlenbeek cross, in a 4-1 win at Mansfield. That, on a snowy pitch, was some day. Tom Curtis, who had been at Portsmouth as a lad when I was there, tried to "do" me and I booted him back. I thought I was going to get sent off, but somehow got away with it.

Nathan also scored a hat-trick in a 3-2 win over Lincoln and two more as we beat Chester 4-2. We were flying and thought we had cracked it with John's 4-4-2 formation.

I was enjoying it. It was a lively, fun club with plenty of characters. My old mate Steve Guppy, who had been at Leicester with me, was there and it was always a laugh listening to him and defender Mike Williamson trying to give each other advice about life. Both were men with insecurities and it was a case of the blind leading the blind.

Steve, a single man, had strange domestic arrangements. He owned property abroad, but in this country only had a mobile home on a caravan park near Chichester in Sussex. He used to call it "The Love Shack". Tight? Steve would turn the gas off when he needed to turn the bacon over.

"Gupps" would later go to America to play and coach with Rochester in New York State, who were just below the Major Soccer League. In fact, he rang me when he got there having been a victim of Heathrow's new Terminal 5 and lost all his clothes. I told him that was the best thing that could have happened to them.

Then there was the club captain, centre-half Roger Johnson, who was a very good player and great in the air. He thought he was ready for bigger things than this club and this division and was probably right, eventually moving on to Cardiff. He might be remembered for that excellent diving header that gave Cardiff their second goal in an FA Cup quarter-final at Middlesbrough in 2008.

Roger always had to have the last word and was very chippy at times. At one point, John Gorman threatened to take the captaincy away from him over something and they fell out. That was difficult to do since John was such a nice man. In fact, I think Roger was the only man I ever knew who fell out with John.

Danny Senda, meanwhile, always seemed to be on the phone to his missus and didn't seem to mind everyone overhearing. On Friday nights at away games, we would sit around and try and sort out his marriage for him. We also had Stuart Nethercott, who had been with me at Millwall. He was known as "Trotters" because his touch was so bad he must have had feet like a pig.

Then there was Clint Easton, who epitomised the public's perception of a footballer. Brash and loud, he always thought he was the bee's knees with women and a great player too. Every day seemed to be a great day for him and you sensed he would be bubbly even if his dog had died. He never thought too deeply about life and was brilliant to have in the dressing room. Every club should have one. Brighton had one in Charlie Oatway. Robbie Pethick, a bit of a jack the lad and a nightmare at times, was the closest we had to it at Weymouth.

Sadly, a problem developed with the football at Adams Park. John had this thing he must have learned from Glenn Hoddle of not balancing sides properly. He liked, for example, only one wide player with three in midfield playing narrow. The times we played a proper 4-4-2 we did well and won, but then he would skimp on the width and we would struggle. When I went to see

Wolves play under Hoddle, they were exactly the same.

I didn't help myself sometimes, I have to be honest. My media career was taking off and Channel 5 hired me to be the summariser at UEFA Cup games. It meant flying out on a Thursday afternoon and back first thing for training on Friday mornings. On one occasion I didn't make it, though, and although John was not too angry with me, as he knew my situation and had agreed to it when I joined the club, he was not best pleased.

One time, I was going out to Alkmaar in Holland and we got delayed due to a faulty door on the plane. When I finally got out there, I ended up running the last two miles to the ground to make kick-off. It was not ideal preparation. Then again, another time, I flew back from Israel the day before a match against Rochdale and played well in a 1-1 draw.

I got dropped to the bench and things started to turn sour for me. In the Lincoln game, I had been brought on when we were 3-0 up and played in the centre of midfield, which didn't suit me and we conceded twice before clinging on. Things were slipping away, both for me and the team, and in the end we didn't have as many good players as we thought we did. In the last few games, Nathan dried up, I was in and out of the side, and we finished tenth when we really could have made the playoffs.

I was sorry I hadn't done a bit better for John. He was one of the good guys and was going through a lot with his wife, who was seriously ill from cancer. I often used to talk to him about it. I think he appreciated having someone a bit older around the place. Sadly, she would die from her illness the following year.

The club would also have to suffer more sadness. Mark Philo, a good young midfield player and a lovely lad, was killed in a car crash. It really did rip the heart out of the club for a while and it was sad to see. It was a good, friendly little club and the fans were very warm towards me.

John was really a coach rather than a manager. He has the right personality for the training ground every day, being very buoyant, which is how coaches have to be to transmit things to players. It was just that the shape of his sides didn't always work. Without wide players on both flanks, you had limited options as a striker and the opposition full-backs could play narrow, crowding the space around you and compressing the game when you wanted to stretch it instead.

John went on to work under George Burley's management at Southampton and then got the caretaker's job when George took over the Scottish national team. During his spell before Nigel Pearson arrived, Saints played just the same way as Wycombe and struggled against relegation.

We also had Rob Lee, once of Newcastle and England, to accommodate and though he was still a class player who could pass the ball and get his foot into tackles as well, his mobility was now limited and he had to play just in front of the back four. It restricted the balance of the side. I felt sorry for him after games. It was unbelievable how his knee would swell up.

The most disappointing thing for me was that at the end of the season John made me an offer for the following year that I couldn't really accept of £200 a week with £800 an appearance. If he had made it the other way round, I would have taken it. It was a sign, I think, that he was being polite, but that he didn't really want to keep me.

Once I would not have been too fussed. After all, though I had now turned 39, I was still playing to a good standard and reckoned I could still do a good job and score goals in the right environment.

The problem was that this season I had been brought in at clubs where they were firefighting, rather than being at clubs on the up. That situation was beginning to look as though it would increasingly be the norm for me. No longer would clubs who were flying be in for me and it was starting to look unlikely that I would find a place where I could play with good players to create chances for me.

In fact, a feeling that as a senior player I might struggle even to find a club, with certain insecure managers not wanting me around the place, was beginning to get to me. Martin Allen had been in a strong position at Brentford and had not feared that, and John Gorman never seemed worried. But I knew this might be a tricky summer.

It certainly would be. And a lot trickier than I imagined.

4.2 Back to the 'Wall

I never used to worry too much during the summer if I was out of contract anywhere. I just enjoyed the break and the time of year. Things often start to happen in late July and early August when a bit of desperation sets in among managers as they fail to sign their number one targets or they realise just how thin their squad is. Often the phone starts ringing then and it is a good time to negotiate, as you can sense the concern in their voices.

I realised that this year might be a bit different, though, given my age and status in the game, and I knew I may not get my first choice of club. I was a bit twitchy, in fact. Change was coming, I could feel it: this was a transition time. Insecurity and doubt about how long my playing days could last were starting to insinuate their way into my being. At this stage, I could still dismiss them because I believed and felt I still had enough in my legs.

For now, there was always the media work to supplement the income and, fortunately, I was getting more and more employment there. As I pondered my future and kept my options open, I took every bit of radio and television work offered to me.

It was mid-June and Channel 5 had asked me to work for them that summer of 2005 in Germany, co-commentating at the Confederations Cup, which would serve as a dress rehearsal for the following year's World Cup finals. I have never really liked flying, but I was generally all right with anything less than two hours, and didn't like being away from home for too long either, but it was an enjoyable experience, seeing favourites for the tournament like the host nation, along with Brazil and Argentina, as well as the new stadiums they were building.

I was in my hotel in Leipzig in the old East Germany one Friday night when my mobile rang. It was Jeff Burnige, who had taken over as chairman of Millwall at the end of the previous season. He wanted me to come back to England to be interviewed for the vacant managerial job at the club.

I had half expected the call. Ian had told me that he would be ringing Jeff to put my name in the frame and urge Jeff to talk to me, but I had been unsure and did not particularly encourage him. This was Millwall, this was the Championship and this was a chance to go back into management, I knew, but I was not that keen because I was aware of the background at the club, having remained in contact with figures there and stayed friendly with Dennis Wise, after taking a player on loan from him at Weymouth and speaking to him often. From what they were all telling me, it did not sound good.

Dennis had got them to the Cup final the previous season, against Manchester United in Cardiff. I was covering it for BBC Radio 5 Live and, on the Friday night before the game, found myself in a restaurant where the Millwall board and backroom staff were having a meal. I sat down with the then chairman Theo Paphitis, who had liked me as a player at the club, and we chatted amicably for a long time about how we were both doing and about how life at the club was these days. He seemed happy enough with things, had high hopes of promotion the next year, but this was to be his biggest moment. After that, it would be all downhill for him.

After the final, Theo decided to have a real tilt at reaching the Premiership and gave Dennis plenty of resources, paying big wages that their gates could not cover. But they could only finish tenth, seven points off the playoffs and never really challenging for them. And despite that Cup run, the accounts would show they had run up £4.5 million worth of debt.

Theo had had enough of running the club and of guaranteeing the debt with his personal fortune, I was told, and stepped down to let Jeff Burnige take over. When Jeff sat down at the end of the season to outline to Dennis how the club would now have to tighten its belt, Dennis did not want to stick around and, knowing that he would have little chance of having another go at reaching the Premiership, took the decision to resign. It would probably be the first time that a manager was richer than his chairman.

So when Jeff asked if I would be willing to fly back from Germany to London to talk it over I was very dubious. Not least because he wanted to see me the next day, but also because he said that he could only pay my air fare if I got the job. At least I couldn't say I didn't know in advance about the state of the club. I did like Jeff, though. He was a decent bloke, the sort I thought I could work with, and he did say I had a good chance of the job.

It would have to be a day trip as I was committed to covering Brazil v Greece for Channel 5 the next night and so I was up at 4am to get a flight 90 minutes later from Leipzig to Frankfurt, then to Heathrow to be at a 10am meeting at a country hotel near the airport. I spent most of the trip thinking that, having forked out nearly £600 for the fare, I had better get this job.

I think Jeff was checking how much I wanted it and what hoops I was willing to go through to get it. After meeting with him and one of his directors for a couple of hours, I decided that I did want it after all. From being a job that looked distinctly like a poisoned chalice, I realised that helping to stabilise a football club might well present an interesting and challenging management test.

We talked about what I had been doing, and what I hoped to do, and then moved on to the core business. Jeff was up front with me and told me that they had to cut the wage bill, which had been just under £5 million a season, a sum that just about gave you a chance to compete with the top clubs in the division, to around £800,000. That meant going from among the middle tier of payers in the Championship to around what the average club two divisions below were paying. His actual words were that for every £600,000 I saved on the wage bill by getting rid of players, I could keep £100,000 to build the squad.

It was a tough task, but what attracted me was the realism of Jeff and his board. This season, balancing the books was the prime object and success to them was simply keeping Millwall in the Championship as we rebuilt the club before any potential future promotion push. In those circumstances, with people being realistic and expectations manageable, I began to think that this might appeal to me as a rewarding job.

My last experience in management at Weymouth had told me how important it was to have a chairman who was aware of the difficulties and limitations of the job and the budget. Ian had been and Jeff certainly was, as they had been the ones setting it and were thus on my side. Martyn Harrison, on the other hand, could not grasp the issues and was never on my side.

Jeff told me he had one other bloke to interview the next morning and that he would be calling me. I enjoyed being inter-viewed and thought I came across well. It is always good to talk about football and your philosophy and I could do it all day long. In the end, I was reluctant to get my flight back. In my case, I do think people in football realise when they meet me that I have a depth they are not expecting.

I thought about it all on the flight back to Germany. In 24 hours, it had gone from being a bad job to a great one. The top earners at the club would have to go and there would not be much to attract replacements, but I would get the chance to use my knowledge of players and the market. And although some might point to Millwall having sunk from the top ten under Dennis to somewhere around lower mid-table under me – and I still reckoned I could do better than just avoid relegation – people within the game would know that I had done a good job given the circumstances. It is better to operate on a shoestring with a clear plan than to have millions and not know where you are going.

I felt sure the fans would see it that way. My playing record meant that they would give me a chance but, if they expected miracles, then I would still get torn apart, former Player of the Season or not. But I had been reading about some comings and goings at Millwall in the papers and, it did seem that expectation was coming down fast.

I had just gone through the airport at Leipzig and turned my mobile back on when it rang. Jeff told me that I had interviewed very well and he would let me know the next day. The call duly came. They had interviewed the other bloke but now wanted to offer me the job. Thank God for that, I thought, I'll get my air fare back now.

We talked about the club renting a flat for me and a salary and I said I wanted just to cover what I was earning from the media, as I would have to give most of that up for now. We agreed on £115,000 a year, for three years, which was a lot less than Dennis had been getting and even less than his assistant Ray Wilkins had got. Then there was Dave Bassett, director of football, on top of that. It had cost the club around £600,000 for the three of them, but I was glad they weren't on any less. By Geoff's figures, when they went, it meant I had an extra £100,000 on the wage bill.

My appointment was confirmed on 20 June and once I had finished my commitment with Channel 5 a few days later, I flew home and went straight to see Jeff, who lived near me at Bishop's Waltham in Hampshire. I had several things I needed to talk to him about – which players had to go, who I could keep – but one thing was bugging me, for some reason.

Jeff had assured me he was in charge and that he could make all the decisions, but I had known how powerful Theo had been around the place and found it hard to believe he was no longer involved or could just give it up. Jeff tried to reassure me. He dialled Theo's number and gave me the handset.

"Theo, it's Steve Claridge," I said.

"You can stop there, Steve," he replied. "I don't want to talk about football. I'm completely done with it."

Still I pressed him; twice more he gave the answer that he no longer wanted to be involved in the running of the club. It meant he had denied it three times.

We held the press conference to signal my arrival at a table on the pitch by the tunnel at the New Den and I was realistic with everybody about the club's prospects. I asked for people not to prejudge me on the basis of the past – except for the hard work I had put in as a player for the club and which I would now be repeating as manager – and to make up their own minds, rather than to believe some old myths.

I could do the job, I added, and I was ready for it having done my grounding in football at every level and in management spells at Portsmouth and Weymouth. Jeff sat alongside me and insisted he had confidence in me.

And so I got down to work. There was just a week to go before pre-season training, nothing for which had yet been arranged, and I also needed to find an assistant to help me organise it pronto. It was daunting, but I was relishing it.

The first priority was to look through the playing staff and see where I could save money. We had a Belgian called Bob Peters, a lanky striker – a smashing lad but not up to it – on £425,000 a year. He had been bought by Mark McGhee and had barely appeared under Dennis. Barry Hayles was on something similar and Jody Morris had been given a signing-on fee bigger than my salary. No wonder the club was losing fortunes. It was madness for a club with gates not much more than 10,000.

Ray Wilkins said he didn't want to stay and I was fine with that. He had about £60,000 after tax left on his contract and said he wanted to be paid up in full. Now, we were so strapped for cash that Jeff said I had around £30,000 for an assistant and it was going to be a struggle to find one for that. I had already spoken to Guy Whittingham, my old assistant at Portsmouth, and my coach there Neil McNab, now coaching in America, but both were earning double that these days.

I figured that if we could save a bit of money paying Ray off, I could get more for my assistant. I said to Jeff that he should offer £30,000 and that way I could get an assistant for £60,000. Or Ray could continue to keep working and I would find him things to do around the club, something I knew he wouldn't go for, which meant he would take the deal.

Two hours later, Jeff takes a phone call from the club's chief executive Ken Brown saying that Ray is in at the club collecting a cheque for £60,000. It has all been authorised by Theo and just a couple of days into the job I am starting to get that uncomfortable feeling of nagging doubt. Jeff looks embarrassed. He has been telling me that he makes all the decisions, that they just have to go through the board for rubber-stamping, and all of a sudden Theo has done this?

I rang Theo again. Don't worry, he said, it was just unfinished business. He felt duty bound to sort Ray out as he had brought him to the club. Just as he had been the one to sort Dennis out when he left. It was just Jeff and you working together, he repeated. All that was very well, but the money for Ray was coming out of the club and the budget, not from Theo's pocket and I was left trying to find an assistant for 30 grand a year in London.

Uneasy again, I went back to Jeff to ask where my contract was, and what was happening with renting the flat he said the club would arrange for me. It was on the board's agenda, he said, and would be sorted out. It struck me as strange that he could make decisions about cuts and saving money, but not about spending it.

I was getting calls from all sorts of agents and players, and was also on the phone to clubs to try and get rid of players. Jeff made it clear to me that if we didn't unload some of the playing staff soon, we would be going into administration and starting the season with a ten-point deduction. Then I read in the local paper, the *South London Press*, Theo saying that he would never let the club go into administration. It was all a bit odd.

I told everyone who rang that I would have a look at them on trial. We were bargain basement now and I couldn't afford to turn anyone down in case there was a nugget in there somewhere. I was trying to get players in on £1,000 a week and there had been first-year pros getting nearly double that previously. The staff in the offices weren't very happy with me trying to get work permits for overseas players. Funnily enough, I was OK with all of it, quite enjoying working it all through. This was proper management.

Darren Ward, a top defender, had already gone to Crystal Palace and Paul Ifill to Sheffield United. Kevin Muscat and Neil Harris had also departed. Danny Dichio was in the process of going to Preston for £160,000. I got the feeling when I spoke to the squad that most of them wanted to go now everything was being dismantled.

The goalkeeper Andy Marshall could hardly wait to get out and wasted no time in telling me so. In fact, now I think back, it felt like he was on the plane back to Germany with me. He thought he was too good for the club. I was getting the impression there would only be about half a dozen decent players who wanted to stay.

I knew, though, that I did have a 19-year-old gem in Marvin Elliot, a central midfield player who I really rated. In fact, I was ready to build the team around him, so good did I think he was. He was my type of player, because he really got about the field and did that little bit more than most players. When an opponent shoots, a lot of players give up. Marvin still tries to get there, to get his foot in or at the least to put the player off a true strike. Millwall would later let him go to Bristol City and suffered as a result. I really thought he was Premier League material.

I had persuaded Jason Brown, a goalkeeper from Gillingham, to sign for £1,000 a week – a pay cut for him of £250 – and I also took Sammy Igoe, who had been with me at Portsmouth, who came in for £850 a week from Swindon, where he was getting £1,200, just because he wanted to play in the Championship. Sammy would be a decent squad player.

I was also close to pulling off a coup that would have served the club really well for a few years to come. I was using my con-tacts in the game – agents, coaches and scouts who I had got to know well down the years – to the full. One came back to me say-ing that Marlon King was unhappy at Nottingham Forest and wanted to be back in the South-East nearer his family and since they were in Kent, we were the right side of London for him. He was ready to come to us for £4,500 a week with Forest also chip-ping in a bit and giving us an option to buy for £500,000. But again I struggled to get an answer out of Jeff.

On the credit side of getting players out, I did eventually man-age to offload Bob Peters to Twente Enschede in Holland. I was delighted for Bob, who was a really good guy but who had been a terrible buy, having hardly played and scoring just three goals in two years. It wasn't his fault and he was one of those you felt guilty about being nasty to if you needed to get him out of the club. He would never bite back or say bad things about you, so he was a tough nut to crack. Some players you don't care about because they don't care about you or the club, but I felt sorry for Bob. At least he got a decent club in the end.

I had had barely ten days to organise pre-season and we were now back in training, though we couldn't use the Bromley train-ing ground as it had just been reseeded. I thought a week of hard graft and bonding would do us good, so rang around a few places. I wanted to go to the Royal Marine base in Torpoint, Devon, where I had been with Leicester, but they were booked. Guy Whittingham, an ex-soldier, had recommended the army camp at Boscombe Down, near Salisbury, and they could take us.

I got the usual moans and groans from the players, but I knew that would happen, particularly from the senior ones. I also knew it would be a good fitness exercise that would bring us together as a squad and something they would come to look back on as being worthwhile. The facilities weren't the best, in dormitories without the luxury that some players were used to, but maybe that was a good thing and might make them count their blessings.

We had three good sessions a day from the army instructors, with me taking full part and even winning the running one day. It was a near one-and-a-half mile course and I did it in just over seven minutes, a few seconds quicker than a lad called Barry Conlan. He was a great runner, who had beaten Dennis Wise the previous season and Dennis was good too. Dennis was amazed when I rang him and told him I had won. Dave Tuttle, who had been chief scout and who was now serving as my assistant in the absence of me getting anyone in, was not surprised, having known me when I was at the club as a player. He won £100 backing me.

If it was all old hat for the senior pros, who naturally enough hate the fitness work of pre-season, it was interesting for me to see how the younger lads loved all this.

We were entertained on two of the evenings, with a boxing night and a trip out into the country to see a venue where the SAS trained before missions in Iraq or Afghanistan. It was a mini-town really where they practised going into occupied buildings. It was fascinating. We also kept the players amused in the evenings with visits to the cinema and bowling, the other nights early to bed.

I was still asking Jeff about that flat in London where my wife Mandy could come and stay, but the club still hadn't come up with one and I had been living in a hotel. And so, since Boscombe Down was not too far from Pompey and not having been home for a fortnight, I went home for five of the six nights, eating dinner with them then leaving the boys in the capable hands of Dave Tuttle, goalkeeping coach Tony Burns and our physio. The players probably also appreciated being able to talk about me behind my back. I was pleased with the week.

Things were starting to come together. I had an incredibly busy first couple of weeks in the job, wheeling and dealing with players, sorting out training and a fitness week and arranging some fixtures. We would be playing two non-League sides in Fisher Athletic and Crawley Town, to be followed by Southend and Gillingham for the first-team squad, with a week in Norway, to include three games, for all the triallists and fringe players. It wasn't the best of programmes, and we could have done with entertaining a Premier League club, but that was the best that could be done.

Then I got a call from Jeff. He was stepping down as chairman, he said, and handing the reins back to Theo. He had been undermined in a lot of the decision-making, he added, and could not do the job properly. He admitted that Theo was still in control of the finances of the club and that there was little he could do without his say so. It seemed that everybody in the club knew that Theo was really in charge except me, even if I had had my suspicions.

I was really disappointed with Jeff and felt let down, though he told me it might even benefit me with Theo back in the picture. Dave Tuttle also reckoned it was the best thing that could happen and that the purse strings would now be loosened. I wasn't so sure.

4.3 The Dragon's Den

Theo summoned me to the Ryman offices in central London for an afternoon meeting that would take place in a basement room. Now I know why when you watch horror films, you're shouting: "Don't go into the basement." The meeting lasted for six hours and I came out of there shell-shocked.

He put me through the mill. Why were we getting rid of players like Danny Dichio? Why was I asking for all these work permits for foreign triallists? What was going on with our pre-season?

Clearly he didn't fancy me as manager and all but asked me for reasons why he shouldn't sack me. I wasn't going to beg for the job, but I did want to keep it, partly to show him what I could do and also because I knew I could do it.

I went over the brief Jeff had given me, about the wage bill and the cuts. As for Danny Dichio, well, judgement was vindicated when he went on to make 33 appearances for Preston the next season without scoring a goal. Besides, Danny wanted to get away. He had also told me that his back was giving him trouble and he didn't think he would be going on for much longer anyway.

I explained about the virtually non-existent pre-season programme I had inherited and told him my thinking on the Boscombe Down week. He also asked why I was getting rid of a fitness coach at the club who had been on £800 a week. I told him it was because of the cost-cutting that Jeff had asked me to implement.

It seemed like the first time that Theo had heard it all or been aware of what was going on around the club. It seemed like he and Jeff had not been communicating and I got the impression that Theo didn't have much respect for Jeff anyway. But then, a secretary at the club had told me after I had only been there a week or so that she had heard Theo shouting at Jeff saying that he was doing things without referring to Theo. That should have told me that Theo had never gone away and that he was always in control.

Theo was obviously sceptical about what I was telling him. He asked why I was looking at all these players. Surely we were not that desperate, he said. I told him that Jeff had made it clear we were that desperate. There were two different agendas here. I could see he was reluctant but, for now, Theo agreed to let me get on with the job.

I think Theo had been getting earache from administration staff and I could see from their point of view how it might have been different from previous years. They were obviously getting fed up with me, but I reckoned they were used to working to Theo's agenda, when money had been less tight. I had been told to get in cheap players, and a lot of them needed registrations and work permits so that I could have a look at them. If I didn't get bodies in, we weren't going to have enough players to start the season.

Now he was back, though, I could talk to some of the higher earners again. I concentrated on Matt Lawrence, who I knew was a big influence within the squad and a defender I could rely on. He was part of the fabric of the club and I knew that if I could keep him, it would send out a statement that while we may be short of a few bob, we would be still be competitive. It would boost both the squad and fans.

Theo wanted to be in on the talks, because Matt was the club captain and he thought he could help, he said. I was not in a position to turn him down and, besides, I thought he could help. It would be a one-off, he added. After intervening in the Ray Wilkins pay-off, this would be a second one-off, then.

Actually, the negotiation showed what Theo and I could achieve together. The firm of agents representing Matt sent along two kids to do the deal for him, but Theo wouldn't have them in the talks. They had to sit outside and whenever Matt had a problem, he would ring them, with Theo putting in his two-penn'orth in the background.

I told Matt how much he was wanted at the club and what a hero he would be if he stayed. He had had better offers from Crystal Palace and Hull City than the deal I could offer him but, after five hours of talking, I convinced him that the New Den was his home. He took £205,000 a year, up only £10,000, and I was delighted not only that I had the player but also at my negotiating skills. He also agreed to take £155,000 if we were by some chance relegated. I hoped Theo would be impressed.

Matt was a big signing and now some other key figures, notably our midfield stalwart David Livermore, also then re-signed. We kept Barry Hayles too, mainly because no one else would take him on at his £8,500 a week wages and we would have had to pay him to go. I sat down with Jody Morris, once a Chelsea prodigy but whose career had lost its way with him developing a reputation as being difficult, and I told him to take his earrings out and he could play a part for me. He knuckled down and respected that and fair play to him. I also took Don Hutchison, the former Liverpool midfield player on a month's loan and he also got his head down.

Then Theo took over the transfer of Danny Dichio to Preston, to be fair getting all of £15,000 more than the £160,000 I had negotiated. He also told me I had two weeks to evaluate every player left in the club and that I would be reporting to him, in meetings like this, every week to discuss who should go.

The goalposts had certainly moved and I did think about my position, but I wasn't ready to walk away yet. I had already given a lot to this and I really thought I could make a go of it, even with all the restrictions, and just wanted a chance. Theo's attitude had just made me more determined and I didn't want him to win. I could tell, though, how I was viewed. The Ryman staff as I came and went were now stand-offish with me, whereas they had always been friendly with me when I had been at the club previously.

The pre-season had been meagre and the problem with the games arranged in Norway was that they coincided with the week of the Southend friendly. I decided first that I would use the domestic games for the first-team squad, at 14 players such as it was at the moment, and the Scandinavian trip for the triallists and peripheral players.

And I decided that I was going to have to be in two places at once. I would fly to and from Norway in between preparing for Southend because I wanted to see everyone playing in a match, as training was not necessarily representative of a game and did not necessarily reveal a player's pedigree. If people only looked at me in training, they probably wouldn't take me on, but I came alive in matches. I was going to be deciding players' futures here, so I owed it to them to give them every chance.

After the Fisher and Crawley games, both of which were drawn, I ended up flying out to Norway and back twice that week, coming back to oversee the Southend game, which we lost 2-0. I also played in a couple of games in Norway. They weren't the best results, but seeing what was going on at the club at the time, they weren't too bad either. I wasn't too upset because I was just assessing what we had really.

I knew we had some injuries and shortages in certain areas, but I was now negotiating for some decent players like Marlon King and that goalkeeper from Gillingham, Jason Brown, so I knew reinforcements were on the way. I also reckoned I could get the talented midfield player John Oster, who was out of favour at Reading and who I had on loan, and Danny Cullip, a more than decent defender, from Brighton.

I was also close to appointing a full-time assistant, which I needed to ease the burden on Dave Tuttle as first-team coach and chief scout. Given the budget of £30,000 – with a couple of candidates laughing when I mentioned the figure – it had proved difficult until my agent Phil Morrison told me he had heard Colin Lee might be interested. I had known Colin as a decent bloke at Wolves, where he was assistant to Mark McGhee, before eventually taking over from him and getting two years in the top job. McGhee had not spoken highly of him since, but I had not got on with McGhee either and anyway, as I had not had any problems with Colin at Molineux, I could only speak as I found.

Since leaving Wolves, Colin had been working in property around the West Midlands and doing the odd scouting job. He also had a home in Devon and I agreed to meet him one Friday night at Wycombe, where I was going to watch a pre-season friendly to see if there were any players worth recruiting as he was on his way to the West Country.

After finishing taking training at 1pm, I did my own training that replicated the session the lads had just done, then nipped into Bromley town centre to go to the bank to transfer some funds concerning a house in Portsmouth I was buying as an investment. I was done by 2.30pm and thought I had plenty of time to get round the M25 for the 7pm meet.

It was a nightmare. There were three separate crashes around the motorway and I rang Colin at around 6.30 to say that it could take me another hour given the traffic. He said he couldn't wait, that he needed to be getting on so would call it a day. I was a bit surprised but we arranged another time. In the end, the traffic eased as it can do all of a sudden after you've been stuck in it and I arrived in Wycombe at 7pm, going straight to the game.

Next thing I know, Theo is on the phone to me having a go at me for missing the meeting. He asked why I hadn't left straight after training at 1pm. I told him four-and-a-half hours ought to have been enough to get to Wycombe.

Then I started to wonder about things … He knew when

training had finished and also knew that I hadn't made the meeting. Was someone inside the club acting as his "mole" to get stuff against me? Was he building up reasons and excuses to get rid of me?

Anyway, I met with Colin a few days later, at Toddington Services on the M1, and we spoke for more than two hours. I wanted to get his ideas on formations and shapes and balances of teams and I soon realised that he would make a reasonable coach for me, particularly given the pittance the club was offering, although in my view he was not a manager. He was solid, but not thrilling. He said he just wanted to come and help and I was happy to take him on. You have to be careful who you trust in football and I felt I could trust him. Besides, we couldn't afford to be too choosy.

Now perhaps I wouldn't be so isolated at the club any more. Dave Tuttle was a good man and had stepped up well to fill in as my coach but, other than that, I felt pretty much exposed to Theo's moods. I did speak to Jeff, but he was more concerned with his own situation than mine, I felt. He had decided to stay on the board, when many men might have resigned on a matter of principle, which said to me that he loved the club more than he loved himself. But then, I couldn't really speak, given what I was putting up with.

Theo had not assumed the role of chairman again and officially the club was without one, but I continued to have to report to him in these regular marathon meetings and, given the tone of his voice in phone calls, I usually went into them thinking I was going to get sacked.

It was tiring having to legitimise myself all the time. Of course, you expect to report to your employer and discuss things with him, but this was not the way to foster any relationship – probably the most crucial one in any football club – between chairman and manager and it went way beyond normal communication.

I would explain why I was recruiting certain players and getting rid of others. Why I was picking this team and not that one and, after a while, he couldn't pick holes in me any more. He even agreed before the Southend game that I had picked the team he would have done. Thanks a lot for the endorsement. In fact, he grudgingly came to see the logic of what was going on at the club. Unless he was going to put fortunes in, it was the only way. And he wasn't going to put fortunes in.

I had also been wrangling with him about my contract and would receive a new draft every few days, faxed to where I was staying, the Hilton at Surrey Quays. The first one that arrived contained a 30-day release clause in it. He must have thought I was born yesterday.

Then came one with the agreed £1,000 a month for a rented flat taken out of it. And another cut from three to two years, with just a six-month compensation clause after the first year.

Perhaps he thought I was just some stupid footballer, who wouldn't read any of them and just give in and sign. I said to him at one point: "You must think I am daft, Theo. I've done as many of these contracts as you have." I asked him why we were even talking about this, that it should have been done. I just wanted the deal that I had arranged with Jeff – three years at £115,000 a year – no more, no less and that he should just talk to Jeff to confirm the figures.

Through the contractual stuff, it was plain that he wanted rid of me with all these derisory offers. He was just trying to get away with the least amount of pay-off. I was not going to make it that easy for him, though. And, anyway, now I was getting stuck into the job.

After assessing the squad, through the friendlies and the Norway trip, and meeting with Colin Lee, I had another session with Theo at the Ryman office where he was finding other things to nit-pick, having had no luck getting the better of me through the contract talks.

He told me that by rights he should be sacking me and he had four reasons:

- I had been gambling, he reckoned. Except that I hadn't – unless he was talking about that silly bet on the running at the army camp.
- Pre-season was a mess and I had only fixed up the training camp for Boscombe Down so I could get home every night. This even though more distant Devon had been my first choice and what little else there was of pre-season had been dumped on me.
- I had been out of order telling the local paper that we were struggling financially and having to tighten our belt. But it was a bland quote and a simple fact.
- My missing the meeting with Colin Lee showed up my lack of organisation and time-keeping. I had been on time in the end, though, and it had all worked out.

It was all pathetic, I thought. I told him that he might take a look at things from my side of the fence. I had not received a penny yet, in wages or expenses and had even been paying my own hotel bill. I still hadn't even had the plane fare back from Germany for the interview reimbursed. I didn't have a contract, but we had sorted out Matt Lawrence's all right. I added that if the club had rented the flat they promised, so that my wife could come and stay, I wouldn't have to be going home to catch up with her when I got the chance because I was within driving distance.

I think he was hoping that I would walk, but by now I was digging my heels in, knowing that I wanted to do this job. Perhaps if I just took the abuse, he would give up and come to see that I could do it and let me get on with it. I was fooling myself.

Theo backed off – or a least I thought he had until I got a phone call the next day. It was from a local journalist who said he had heard I was going to get the sack after the Gillingham game the following Friday. I joked that he didn't even know the result yet. There was no joking in his voice, though, when he said the result wouldn't matter.

It just showed what a carve-up it all was and just how

premeditated Theo's actions were. To this day I am baffled by his antagonism towards me. He never seemed to underestimate me as a person, as so many had, when I was a player at the club, but now he clearly believed I was not capable, that I was not management material, despite the growing evidence to the contrary.

And so it arrived, the day of the night friendly against our old bogey team Gillingham. I got there early in the afternoon. Theo had asked me for a run-down on every member of the squad, so I was determined I was going to provide him with it. We met in an office at the New Den and I read him the report I had compiled, going through each player's strengths and weaknesses, saying who we should keep and who should go. He seemed uninterested and distracted. I wasn't surprised by either state. It was just an exercise and he obviously had other things on his mind.

We were short of players, what with all the comings and goings and usual pre-season strains, and I decided to have a run-out myself that night to keep my eye in just in case I might be needed, though I didn't expect to be as I was due to meet Marlon King to finalise a deal the next day and I saw him and Barry Hayles as my first-choice pairing.

With no left-backs fit, and just one right-back, I decided to go for a 3-5-2 formation. I was going to bounce it off Colin Lee, but he had rung to say he would be late. I wondered if Theo would be bollocking him for missing a meeting. He would certainly have every opportunity. As I looked up at the directors' box just before we kicked off, there was Colin sitting next to Theo. Funny.

We were 2-0 down in half an hour. The shape wasn't working and so I switched back to 4-4-2, even though we had no proper full-backs. After that, things got better, we clawed it back to 2-2 with Barry Hayles scoring twice and ended the game on a high with the fans getting right behind us. I was pleased with my own performance – getting a standing ovation when I came off with ten minutes to go – but above all with the character of the team. There were plenty of things to encourage us for the campaign ahead. With Jason Brown also there watching that night ready to sign along with Marlon King the next day, it was promising.

I went up into the directors' lounge afterwards and there was Theo with my agent Phil Morrison, which struck me as strange – just as it had struck me as odd when someone had told me earlier that the two of them, along with Colin Lee, had been in the manager's office while I was warming up the team before the match, a job I was hoping Colin would be doing. Next I saw Colin doing a hasty disappearing act from the lounge.

I could tell the moment I walked in what was going on. The atmosphere was distinctly frosty. There were a few of Theo's Ryman minions there and a couple from the Bank of Cyprus who were involved in the club somehow and I got the impression he had been talking to them about it all.

Theo started at me. He wasn't shouting or swearing, but he listed his gripes. That performance was not good enough, he said, and if I thought it was I was dreaming. His body language wasn't convincing, though. I don't think he believed what he was saying and was just trying to convince himself.

He added that I was not good enough as a player any more and that I should hang up my boots.

That was the final straw. I could take so many things, but not being told when my playing career was over. That was my decision. I was willing to stop playing to manage, and I did have a strike partnership lined up, but I knew I was still good enough if required. Besides, I had agreed with Jeff that I would be saving the club money if I was a back-up striker.

I had taken enough and I told Theo so. I told him that this was nothing to do with football, this was about him wanting rid of me and not being willing to give me a chance. I had been a dead man walking from the time he came back into the club. The exchanges became curt and sharp. There was little to be said.

He said he would like me to leave immediately. I asked him if he was sacking me. He said, yes, he was. I wanted him to say it, as I had with Martyn Harrison at Weymouth, to avoid any confusion about me walking away of my own accord and thus giving up any pay-off.

I told Theo that I would expect him to pay me up. He said I didn't have a contract. I said that I would see him in court then.

In the mood I was in, I knew that if I had to bankrupt myself to do it, I would have gone to court to fight this. Theo must have sensed how determined I was. And I would have called Jeff Burnige as a witness about what was said and what happened. Theo would not have wanted all that aired in a courtroom. I may not have had a paper contract, but I still had a verbal one, and that counted for something.

I felt sickened and empty as I drove back to Portsmouth that night mulling everything over. It was 27 July and I had been in the job for 36 days. Except that I hadn't been in the job. There never really was a job for me. I was angry with myself for allowing myself to have been treated as I was and to have compromised my self-respect, but then I had really wanted to make a success of the job.

Things began to click. Theo had stepped down from the club and Jeff had been made chairman. Jeff got me in as manager. Between us, new chairman and manager, we did the dirty work, it seemed to me. We got rid of players, we cut the wage bill. We were the fall guys.

Theo was out of the limelight for all that, but he missed that limelight, I reckon. His ego was not being fed. He was just a businessman now, not a football club chairman. And so he took up the job again, if not the title, and got back to the business of being centre of attention and back in the papers.

I also began to think that I was doing a good job and getting the club sorted, but the more Theo and I got to know each other, and the more he agreed with what I was doing, he realised I might make a success of it. And he couldn't have that. He got rid of me because I could have done the job, not because I couldn't. If I had started the season, and started it well as I expected to, he wouldn't have been able to sack me.

I was not his appointment. If I did well, it would reflect on Jeff, not Theo. And Theo did not respect Jeff either. I don't think he disliked him, because Jeff is almost impossible to dislike, but he didn't have much belief in his judgement.

I could also see that Theo had been making my life very difficult with these meetings in the middle of London sometimes twice a week, with all the hassle it involved going from training to there then back to a hotel near the club or on to Portsmouth at 7 or 8 at night.

There was something fishy about the fact that Colin had been sitting with Theo but had not appeared in the dressing room. Why had Theo limited me to £30,000 for an assistant, but had no trouble finding £60,000 for Ray Wilkins?

I rang Colin and asked him if he had been offered the job. He said he had, but that he was unsure about taking it.

"I'll tell you what Colin," I said. "I bet you do."

If I could have found a bookie's open, I would have staked my mortgage on it. And guess what? He did take the job. If he was that desperate for a job he was welcome to it. Finally I had something in common with Mark McGhee, who had spoken about being disappointed in Colin after being succeeded by him at Wolves.

I wanted answers from my agent Phil Morrison, too. What was he doing with Theo and Colin in my office while I was out with the team? Why wasn't he sticking up for me?

He was close to Theo and admitted when I rang that he was taking a risk losing me as a client, but that Theo wanted Colin, who had become another of his clients, and that he had to take the practical view. He was right. He had lost me as a client. I have not spoken to him from that day to this.

The whole episode that night disgusted me, but I should have expected it. I only ever used agents to gauge interest in me, not to do contracts and I always knew my worth. They always do the deal that will bring them the best return. Same with players sometimes, I suppose. They will go with whatever agent promises them the best deal.

My main beef with agents is that they take so much out of football and put so little in. OK, so I have bargained hard and been well paid, but I played professionally for more than 20 years and gave everything in every game. I suspected that he thought he might be able to place players more easily at Millwall now.

As a manager, I only ever took decisions based on a player's ability, not because of any closeness I may have with their agents, but I am aware that there are some managers who have relationships with agents and take on those agents' players. Yes, it could be for a kickback sometimes for all I know, but often it is just a case of having a supply of players.

I had told the squad before the Gillingham game that I wanted them in the next day for a warm-down and that I wanted to keep the appointment, so I drove back up from Portsmouth to the Bromley training ground the next morning.

Often players don't want to speak out in front of their teammates, so I saw them one by one at 20-minute intervals, seeing the ones who lived furthest away first. Most said they were saddened by my departure and I asked them if they were unhappy with anything about me, had any complaints or if they had been speaking to the chairman about me. They said they were on my side and had not gone behind my back and I believed them.

I asked for honesty and David Livermore pointed out a few times I hadn't been at training. I told him I had been in Norway and he said they hadn't realised that. Otherwise nobody seemed to have a problem. Someone had it in for me, though, and had been supplying Theo with one-sided facts.

A lot got distorted, though, and things were said that became twisted and exaggerated by the time they appeared in the press. The hardest thing to handle was all the rumours about my sacking and the gossip that came back to me in football. I hated the thought of being considered unreliable. Apart from the Colin Lee episode, and despite all the travelling I was doing, I was never late for, or missed, anything.

After I left, the goalkeeper Andy Marshall had a few things to say about me, mainly that I had not been around enough. I couldn't understand that and why he was so interested all of a sudden. He hadn't been interested in staying at the club after I took over, although he trained well enough and I thought he might have been coming round. In fact, he had been desperate to find another club. After I left, he was on his way to Coventry City. I wish I had sent him to Coventry sooner.

As I spoke with Theo over the next day or two during discussions about my pay-off, he went over the old ground and said he was hearing more and more about how poor pre-season training had been. I reminded him that this was Steve Claridge, who was one of the fittest footballers around and who expected his players to be as well. Some of them had said it had been the hardest pre-season they had known.

What about not being at training in the build-up to the Southend game, he asked? It was because I was in Norway, assessing the fringe players, as he had asked me to do. It was straw-clutching.

I had had no money, no support and no players, but I was still proud of what I had done. I didn't deserve it. I had put in 20-hour days sometimes and had put everything in my life on the back burner. And all for no wages.

Gradually we came to an agreement over money. I would get £90,000 after tax, payable in three six-monthly instalments. Fair play to Theo, he always stuck to his word about money when he had made a decision. All of a sudden he found some for Colin Lee, too, and allowed him to get a few players in. I knew Colin wouldn't spend it right, mind.

I was asked by Sky to be a studio guest for coverage of 'Wall's first league game, away at Leeds United, and agreed. There was so much I wanted to say and couldn't due to an agreement as part of my pay-off that I would not talk in detail about the sacking. I watched them lose 2-1 and was as diplomatic as possible and when we were off-air the presenter George Gavin said: "That must have been difficult to watch." "Yes it was," I said.

It's funny. I had a real attachment to Millwall. After leaving Portsmouth – which has my heart and my home – at a time when I seriously thought about packing up playing, 'Wall had picked me up off the ground and given my career new impetus a few years earlier. And their fans had taken me to their hearts. They were a proper club. When the New Den rocks, there may only be 14,000 in there, but they sound like 40,000. Even now fans there tell me how good I was for them, but they were good for me, too.

That day, though, I was pleased they lost at Leeds, I can't deny it. They, or rather Theo, had treated me disgracefully and I didn't want him to get away with it. It's funny, 36 days is a ludicrously short time to judge anyone's managerial capabilities, but it can feel like a long time when you are suffering abuse.

I was keeping my part of the bargain in not bad-mouthing Theo or the club in public, but when he made a statement that he thought we would get relegated if he had kept me, I thought about suing. I knew that comment would damage my reputation, but I decided to wait and see how things panned out with my next career move.

I could see from that Leeds game that they were going to struggle badly. In fact, after 17 points from 24 games, Colin Lee got the sack and found a job as director of football at Torquay. I felt a bit uneasy for my old mate from Weymouth Paul Buckle when he took the manager's job at the Conference club after they had been relegated from the Football League, moving from being assistant at Exeter, but I thought he should be OK. As director of football, Lee had enough hands-on interest in the club without getting any of the grief that comes a manager's way and he was back home, so he should have been happy.

Lee was replaced at the New Den by Dave Tuttle, who had little chance of keeping the club up. Poor old Dave then got the push when 'Wall got relegated as a result of all the turmoil that had preceded him. And it is actually quite some achievement to go down from the Championship, given that it is the most level league in the country and one that sees some very average sides stay up.

After Dave, Nigel Spackman took over and they spent more money – with Phil Morrison getting a load of sub-standard players in for him, so I could see his strategy – before Spackman also got the bullet. Willie Donachie then steadied the ship for a while, doing OK, but when he started a season badly, off he went, with Kenny Jackett coming in.

By now the ownership of the club had changed hands, with Theo getting rid to some business concern. When Spackman went, I did show some tentative interest in coming back as manager and got a third party to ring the club's new head honcho, but the message came back from the new people that they weren't interested in me.

Once that would have worried me, but after the initial anger and sadness at my sacking, I reconciled myself to the fact that a view of me had gained credence within the game. For a while, though, I was upset that some apparently saw me as unemployable. I wanted to know why.

And so, in the summer of 2006, a year after my departure, I rang Theo. I wanted to talk about my sacking now that the heat had gone out of the situation. He agreed.

This time we met at the Ryman headquarters at Hayes in Middlesex. I wasn't going to go back into that Central London basement. It was nice seeing his old PA, Jane. Now she knew how to handle Theo and I think he respected her for her unwillingness to be bullied.

The main problem with me, Theo said, was that I was high maintenance and that he didn't have the energy to deal with me … all those work permits, all those players coming and going. And he had had "a number" of players ringing him with their concerns, he said.

But it had to be like that, I told him, that's what Jeff had wanted, unbeknown to Theo. Dennis Wise was fortunate, he could buy players and put them on big money and the chairman could sit back and light a cigar. I had to wheel and deal and any chairman is going to be twitchy about that.

As for that number of players concerned, there may have been one or two, but one or two who wanted to get away anyway. When I reminded him I had all but signed Marlon King – who would go to Watford instead, then on to Wigan for £5 million – he raised his eyebrows. He knew that was one, and one whole bundle of money, that got away.

Theo did concede that he thought I was one of the most streetwise and switched-on footballers he had ever met and that maybe he had been hasty in getting rid of me, and that perhaps he should have done it differently. It helped to hear that.

One of the problems was that by then Theo had lost his appetite for the club and the game. It happens to a lot of people with responsibility in the game and is understandable. It is draining and demanding. A few months after I left the club, he began his withdrawal and was hardly seen at the New Den again. I think he wanted to be the one making the final decisions. Had I been his manager five years earlier, when he still had a lot of enthusiasm, I think we could have been a formidable operating partnership – just as we had shown when we did the Matt Lawrence deal together.

It was a good meeting for me, one that lasted about two-and-a-half hours, and I walked out of there having got a lot off my chest and feeling a whole lot better. And I had received the closest to an apology I was going to get from Theo.

I saw him again about six months later at an FA Cup tie between Horsham and Swansea, he being a keen non-League watcher with his company sponsoring the Isthmian League. He was a lot more relaxed now he was out of the firing line and we exchanged handshakes. He smiled at me as if nothing had happened and I thought to myself that he probably did not have a clue about what he had done and the effect of it on my career.

Not that I was relaxed about being out of the firing line, I would have happily been back in it. Yes, I am intense and enthusiastic about football and doing a job well and I was sorry that Theo didn't want those qualities and that he couldn't admire someone who worked hard. I am also sorry he bought into the old myths about me being tardy and chaotic.

I know that 'Wall wouldn't have got relegated if I had stayed in charge and, to be honest, I think they paid the price for sacking me for a long time afterwards. Just recruiting Marlon King – whose goals would certainly have kept us up as he went on to be the top scorer in the division and got Watford promoted to the Premiership – would have brought a pot of money into a club that has haemorrhaged it instead.

In my opinion, Theo missed the spotlight when he stepped down and so came back to Millwall to raise his profile again and be at the centre of publicity. It is why I blame the BBC. If only they had put on *Dragons' Den* sooner, then Theo would have been back on centre stage with his ego being fed ... and well away from me and Millwall.

5. *Grand Finale*

Life was taking on a familiar pattern for Steve. After the unhappy and premature ending to his management of Millwall – the job that never was – it was back to the drawing board and to the phones to try and find another club.

But while he may have been physically in A1 shape and had done a pre-season with Millwall, playing in a few friendlies as well as doing the training, he was now doubly dangerous to any manager – or at least those not secure in their position or personality – who might be contemplating taking him on. Senior pros can be more critical and questioning; they are also on the spot if a chairman is looking to make a change of manager. By and large, managers prefer young players because they are more impressionable and obedient.

Steve needed to be at a club with a similar intensity to Millwall and Sheffield Wednesday sprang to his mind as he thought he could do a job for a squad lacking strikers. And so he rang Paul Sturrock, who gave him one reserve outing as the 2005/06 season was kicking off, but no contract.

After that, it was to Gillingham, so often Millwall's nemesis and certainly Steve's that night of the drawn friendly – and the drawn knives – when he was sacked by Theo Paphitis.

After just a couple of games, though, he took up an offer from Bradford City. Their manager Colin Todd, the former Derby and England defender, had seen him play well in that reserve game for Sheffield Wednesday and gave him a call.

Feeling wanted, and with the money being right, Steve signed on the dotted line, though it became a decision that he would have a long time over the winter to question as he found himself at odds with Todd.

"Colin brought him in to help us," says Dean Windass, the Bradford City legend with a personality close to rivalling that of Steve Claridge, and who went on to have a tilt at the Premier League with Hull City, his other great love, at the age of 39. In fact, having scored the Wembley playoff-winning goal against Bristol City that echoed Steve's for Leicester City, he probably is the Northern Steve Claridge.

Adds Windass: "I think he saw Steve as more of a sub. Whatever went off was between him and Colin, but I think Colin did him a favour by bringing him in.

"What I will say is that he was brilliant in the dressing room and when we played together five or six times I really enjoyed it. We must have been the oldest partnership in football." And how was Steve's timekeeping? "He was always on time, as far I know," he says. "But then he was staying in a hotel locally.

"He was a colourful character, but a bit of a fucking tramp," adds the blunt Windass, who is a colourful character with language to match and a nice line in the pot and the kettle comparisons. "He had a kitbag like a Sunday League player, with all those boots and dirty socks in it.

"But he didn't play like a Sunday League player and his record speaks for itself. He's had a great career. It's gone on a long, long time," says Windass, whose career has also gone on a long, long time. "He's certainly the fittest lad I ever worked with. If we went on a long-distance run, he would be first and I would be second.

"If you keep fit, you should play as long as you can. Too many players retire early, not because they can't play any more, but because they don't enjoy training. I don't think Steve enjoyed the training that much, but he did enjoy his running." Sadly, a lot of it was up and down the touchline at Valley Parade.

Windass remembers a couple of episodes that tell us much about Steve. The pair, along with three other City players, had a night out at a Ricky Hatton fight at Manchester City's Eastlands Stadium.

"We went out afterwards and got pissed, went to a club and the silly old bastard is dancing on his own," Windass recalls. "To all that hip-hop rubbish. I wanted a bit of Elvis on, but he wouldn't have it."

Windass was also sitting in a lobby of a Bradford hotel with Claridge one Saturday morning, only to find the Bournemouth squad also staying in the hotel. As they checked out, Windass recognised Marcus Browning, the pair's paths having crossed in a game between the two clubs earlier in the season, and Windass began berating the Bournemouth player.

"He came out and said I had bitten him on the arm," says Windass by way of explanation. And had he? "Had I 'eck. He's stuck an elbow in me. He came out and said some stuff about me that I remembered and I wanted to smack him. Fortunately, Steve stopped me."

As at most places he had been, Steve enjoyed a good rapport with the City fans and felt for them after all they had endured, with the club reaching the Premier League and enjoying a couple of seasons there, but then paying the price for overspending and gradually slipping back down the divisions.

He believes that with a bit better guidance they would have reached the playoffs that season. He himself would not see it out with Bradford, who eventually finished just above mid-table, however. He finished the season on loan at Walsall, but it left him having played 999 professional games.

Steve thought little more about it as he got on with his expanding media career until a local journalist in Hampshire, Alex Crook, rang him up about that 1,000th game, wondering if he had retired. He hadn't – and he probably never will officially – and the Bournemouth manager Kevin Bond read the article in a local paper.

To his credit, Bond set aside any grievances he felt against Steve from comments Steve had made about him when the pair were together at Portsmouth, when Bond was assistant to Alan Ball, and offered him a month at Dean Court.

Sadly, the 1,000th game was a disappointment, but it did give him the taste for more and he even turned out in the Ryman League, first for Worthing, along the Sussex coast from his home, then for Harrow Borough. There was some irony in the fact that he was playing in a competition sponsored by a Theo Paphitis company.

The Harrow manager was David Howell, one of Barry Fry's coaches at Birmingham City during Steve's spell at the club in the mid-1990s.

"I saw that he had been playing at Worthing and rang him up," says Howell. "I didn't know he was willing to play at that level, so I told him that if he was going to do it, he should do it for me as a favour for a friend. I think he felt a bit guilty and when his time at Worthing was ending, I put in a seven-day notice of approach." It is a system that happens a lot at non-League level with non-contract players.

"He came and made an amazing impact," says Howell. "Whatever people's views of Steve, he loves playing football. He is one of the ultimate pros who gives everything, a great example to some young players.

"With a lot of older pros, they come to that level for a bit of pin money at the end of their careers and they either bring a bit of exposure to the club or something to the team. With Steve you got both. He will always be value, no matter what money he is on."

Howell recalls his first spell working with Claridge at Birmingham. "He lived in Luton and I lived in St Albans, so I used to pick him up at Toddington Services. My introduction to horse racing came from him. 'Just stop here,' he used to say as we went past a bookie."

Claridge has his own stories about Howell, mind, notably how he acquired his nickname of "The Claw" – to do with his, shall we say, protective ability to envelop a young lady in his considerable wingspan.

"He told you about that, did he?" Howell asks. "I thought it came more from the time I was a DJ in Ayia Napa. All the footballers used to come over on holiday and were always asking about the young ladies locally. I knew all the ins and outs there. I just used to put a protective arm around the girls. But the lads knew that when The Claw comes out, it's all over." Among Howell's other interests these days is being the after-awards party organiser at the Café de Paris for the Professional Footballers' Association following their annual April bash.

Back to Claridge. "I don't know how he ever became a professional footballer," Howell adds. "He was the worst trainer in the world, was always getting the yellow jersey for it at Birmingham. He hated all the drills, the keep-ball, but loved the running. I suppose he was like those horses he used to back. He just kept ploughing through.

"And he certainly applied himself come match days. He came alive then. Steve Claridge will never cheat once he crosses that white line."

Howell recalls Claridge's debut for Harrow. "A local bookie was offering good odds on him scoring and taking off his shirt. Of course Steve noticed that and everybody got on it. A few of the lads did well that day and Steve took the yellow card."

Was he management material? "I would have said no at Birmingham," he says. "The next time I saw him was at Weymouth, when I took Harrow down for a pre-season friendly. It was early for him and it's a difficult transition to make when you want to be one of the lads as a player, but have a wider job to do.

"I think I realised he could definitely be management material by the way he spoke to the lads when he was in the dressing room here at Harrow. He had a good effect on them."

Howell cites a young attacker by the name of Albert Adomah and affords Steve some credit for the 20-year-old's move to Barnet for an undisclosed fee. "He responded to Steve, linked up well with him and got a good move in the January." The then Barnet manager Paul Fairclough, indeed, talked of Adomah being Premier League material.

"I don't know what happened at Millwall, and there were a lot of stories flying about, but in some ways it might prove a good experience for Steve if he gets back into management," adds Howell. "I think he would have the respect of players. I think he was enjoying himself in the media, though, and wanted a break for a while due to his indifferent experiences in management. It can be a risky business and he wanted an environment that was stable and secure. But he's biding his time. He'll be back."

In the end, Steve played four games for Harrow, finishing on a total of 1,008 matches, his last game against Bromley yielding him a goal with an overhead kick.

He reminds me of the Tony Hancock character in the comedian's spoof of *The Archers*, called *The Bowmans*. Hancock plays a local yokel who is being written out of the series, but refuses to go quietly, shouting in the background during the recording: "I'm not dead yet." They had to carry him off kicking and screaming.

5.1 Damaged Goods

A strange thing happens, a strange feeling comes over you, after you have lost a management job. It happened to me at Portsmouth, at Weymouth as well, and now it was happening to me after Millwall as I spent the days after my sacking thinking it all over.

At first, there is almost a relief. It has been a struggle, you have given it your all, and it has taken over your life, so a part of you is just glad to relax and you can feel the tenseness draining away from your body. Then a huge emptiness sets in. How are you going to fill that void that seems so deep because the activity of being a manager is so intense?

I phoned the Professional Footballers' Association and the League Managers' Association for some advice about my position and what I could reasonably expect by way of settlement from Millwall. I phoned Theo Paphitis, briefly, and he said he would be fair with me. I spoke to Jeff Burnige, but again it was a short call. I think he was embarrassed about the whole situation. There was not much he could say and I think he knew it was coming. He may still have been a director, but he was now in a weak position.

Inevitably you analyse your own role in things: where did I go wrong? What could I have done differently? People told me I shouldn't have sold players, but that was the state of the club I inherited and what I was told to do. It was just that I was being told it by someone who didn't have the authority to back me. When you are told one thing and another thing happens, you haven't got much chance.

When it came to Theo, I reckoned it was a bit like facing a fast bowler. It's all calm enough when he's 50 yards away at the start of his run-up but, as he runs in, you know what's coming and that it's going to be a bouncer. My problem had been that I came in to bat when the slow bowler was on and the fast bowler was off the field having a drink.

The familiar, "Where do I go from here?" thoughts started to cross my mind. It was too close to the season to get another management job. Everyone was sorted and settled. Besides, I knew now that people in the game would be wondering about me, thinking that I had got the sack for a reason. And I was stone-cold certain that Theo's statement about me getting Millwall relegated would seriously damage my chances of working as a manager again.

I was torn, though. I wanted to speak out and give my side of the story and I did do an interview with Ian for the *Mail on Sunday*, but spoke only in general terms about my sadness and the difficulty of the situation. I could not go into detail because Theo was holding all the cards. Any word out of place, and he could and would withhold my pay-off. Looking back, I wish I had taken the risk and spoken out because any potential employer would have seen the mud that Theo hurled and watched it stick.

Friends reassured me, said that I would get hired come the inevitable annual cull of managers in the autumn in all the divisions when the optimism of late summer was gone and the harsh reality of an oncoming winter was dawning. I knew differently. Within this game, perception is nine-tenths of the law and I knew how I would be perceived. The Millwall episode only reinforced it. It didn't matter that I had found myself in the middle of boardroom politics at a club in painful transition.

Fortunately I had lost only a couple of media jobs over the summer and quickly got my work back with Radio 5 Live and Sky, who phoned me immediately. Actually, it was not really as if I had been away, was it? It had been just over a month of the close season when there wasn't much football about anyway, since it was an odd-numbered year which means no major international tournament. It was just like I had been away on a holiday. The worst holiday of my life.

I was down and I had to admit it. The media work was reassuring, but I didn't feel finished with this game just yet. I wanted to play again. Football had always been my therapy, helping me to get over things and through things.

When I first became a manager at Portsmouth, I was a player 60 per cent and a manager 40 per cent. At Weymouth, those percentages swapped. At Millwall, I had even been willing to give it up and told Theo that I would, as soon as I had got a better striker in place, which was quite something for someone who loved playing as much as me. I just resented someone else telling me to give up.

Also, I may have been only eight months away from my 40th birthday, but was still fit and hungry and knew I could do a job for a decent club. They say a new life may begin at 40, but my old one wasn't over yet.

I thought about what I had been through and where I wanted to go. I needed another club with a passionate support. Knowing their roster – being well clued-up about these things – and knowing that they were short of a striker, I thought about Sheffield Wednesday, a big club who had been going through hard times, but who were now back in the Championship. I had always enjoyed playing at Hillsborough in front of knowledgeable fans and had even played against them in the Premiership for Leicester. That goal to win City the Coca-Cola Cup against Middlesbrough in the final replay had been at Hillsborough.

And so I rang Paul Sturrock, their manager, who had been at Southampton briefly after four years doing well to get Plymouth Argyle promoted from the bottom two divisions, and asked if I could come up for a week's trial. He agreed immediately and I went up and trained well. The distance from my home of about 240 miles didn't bother me; I just had a real hunger to play. I enjoyed it, even if they did put me up in a £40-a-night hotel.

I even had BBC's *Football Focus* taking an interest in me and was being interviewed by Mark Bright one day when some of the players started taking the mickey out of my Millwall experience – which was a good sign as it showed that they were beginning to see me as one of them. They interrupted the interview to present me with a bottle of champagne bearing the words "Manager of the Month". "It should say manager for a month," I said.

At the end of the week, Sturrock said he wanted to put me on the bench for the home Championship game against Southampton the following day but, although I was physically fit, I still didn't feel quite sharp and didn't want to let the team or myself down. I asked him to let me have another week of training and then I would be ready. He agreed, and asked me to play for the reserves at home to Walsall the following Monday.

I did and loved it, setting up both goals in a 2-0 win. There were more than 3,000 fans there, which showed Wednesday's size as a club, and I got a standing ovation. Plenty even stayed behind until after the warm-down to applaud. I got a real buzz again. This was the level I was known at and the higher you go the more knowledgeable the fans are. They appreciate good players. I had encountered it during my week of training when, just walking around the city, people were coming up to me and welcoming me to the club.

Sturrock said that he knew I would be good, but that his hands were tied for the moment and that he needed to have a word with the chairman. I had had a doubt before the game when all the other players had tracksuits and when I asked for one, he said I wouldn't be needing it. He wasn't to know that I col-lect training gear from all the clubs I have been with and would wangle one out of the kitman.

Now I feared the worst. I didn't like the look in his eyes. I felt gutted on the drive home – it had taken me six hours on the way up on the Sunday, five back now after the game – as I could have done no more in the game.

My instincts were right. When he called the next day, he said he had spoken to the chairman and they couldn't afford me. They hadn't even made me an offer. A couple of days later it made sense when they signed a boy from Wigan called David Graham for £300,000. The lad played half a season, scoring twice in the league and once in the Carling Cup. At one point they got a very raw kid from Aston Villa in on loan called Gabriel Agbonlahor. I would go up later in the season to cover a Wednesday game and saw him. He was poor at that time.

I thought I deserved better than that. I had not asked for any expenses and had put my heart into it for ten days only to get dumped. One minute I am good enough to go on the bench when he is struggling for players, the next not good enough to sign.

I thought Sturrock lacked class for doing that to me. It was small-time, lower-division behaviour. Within a month, in mid-September, Wednesday would be bottom of the table and, although they narrowly avoided relegation, he didn't last much longer before getting the sack. After that he went to Swindon before Plymouth took him back.

I went back to my media work and got talking to Chris Kamara at Sky, who had played the game with Stoke and Bradford City and who was now a presenter, about wanting to play again. He asked if I fancied Gillingham, where the chairman Paul Scally was a contact of his, and I did. It made a lot of sense. I could travel from home and given my experiences against them with Millwall, I figured that if you couldn't beat them, join them.

I went down to talk to the manager Neale Cooper, who seemed a decent bloke. Gillingham had taken him on from Hartlepool after he had got them promoted from the bottom division, and he rated me. And so he signed me on a week-to-week deal for £1,000 a week, which I took initially knowing that I would be sure to prove myself and get a deal to the end of the season.

It was a bonus for me that an old mate, Iwan Roberts, who had been at Leicester with me, was there. I also got on well with the chairman, who I had met before when covering a playoff final for Sky. I know a lot of people in the game seem to think Paul Scally is a very controversial character but he was straight with me.

I made my debut at Bournemouth – another of those clubs who keep popping up in my story – and we won 1-0 courtesy of an own-goal by Marcus Browning, a player I had always liked and who would go on to be assistant manager at Weymouth. Small world, this game.

My only other game was to be a 1-0 Carling Cup win over Oxford United. The club were proving reluctant to give me a contract to the end of the season – they would offer one month, two months, then three – and I was getting frustrated. They knew what I could do, surely. I was starting to feel like a washing machine on a hire-purchase agreement.

Then I got a call from Colin Todd at Bradford City, wondering if I fancied Valley Parade. It was an interesting thought. I'm not sure why, but I told him that he needn't worry that I would be after his job. I think I was concerned that managers were getting reluctant to sign me for more than a few weeks as they might be thinking I had ulterior motives.

Colin was offering a basic wage of £500 a week more than Gillingham, plus appearance money and travelling expenses, and with a contract right through to July rather than the May that was now on offer at Priestfield. It was a very good offer, but provided me with an agonising decision. I liked Gills, thought they knew how to play me properly, and I quite fancied it there.

Bradford asked me to come up and talk it over and so I went up to meet Todd and his chairman Julian Rhodes, who was also the chief executive. He was a nice bloke, very approachable, and was obviously working hard to get the club on the move again after they had reached the Premiership, paid fortunes to the likes of Stan Collymore and Benito Carbone and then got relegated and gone bust.

When I went up to watch them beat Bournemouth on August Bank Holiday Saturday, I liked the stadium and the fans. They were an earthy lot, like I was used to, and though they seemed to be struggling a bit commercially, they still had a lot of potential and a decent fan base.

With all these factors, on top of Colin Todd ringing me, which I appreciated, and Bradford being a bigger club than Gillingham, I decided to sign. It also helped that Colin did not expect me at training every day – he knew I would keep myself fit – but would only need me for games and training the days before games.

Need me? I spent the first five games on the bench without even getting on. I couldn't understand it. It was only September, but my feet were getting frozen – what was it going to be like up here in the middle of winter. What am I here for? Does he know I am here? It's not like this was Brazil and I was being left out for Kaka. It was obvious they weren't good enough. They were mid-table.

I accepted that Dean Windass, a club legend, was always going to play and I had no problem with that, though it was almost funny how untouchable he was, in Colin Todd's eyes. Take the time when Dean was brought off with a minute to go in one match.

Now, my spell at Bradford would prove to be a case of in and out of the team, on and off the field as a substitute or being substituted, but I just kept my head down, and said nothing. When Dean was taken off, all hell broke loose as he took off his shirt and threw a bottle down. I was the one sent on to replace him and said to him afterwards in the dressing room that he wanted to look at it from my point of view. I also said that I felt like throwing down my shirt in disgust at just being given one minute. It could have been the only time that two players threw the shirt down in anger at the same time.

Some of the lads were unhappy with Dean's influence around the club because he was Colin Todd's favourite and he had such a strong personality. I was all right with him, as a senior player who had pretty much seen everything, and I liked him, but I could understand a few getting fed up with him because he was a blunt sort of bloke.

Actually, Dean's relationship with Colin reminded me of that old sitcom *It Ain't Half Hot Mum* when the sergeant major thinks one of the squaddies is his long-lost son and treats him better than everyone else. It was a situation I don't think the manager should have allowed to develop.

Perhaps Colin was reluctant to play us together because he would get stick for our combined ages being around 75 but we were the best pair since the other strikers, Danny Cadamarteri and Andy Cooke, were just too inconsistent. Dean and I would take some getting used to as a partnership, I could see that. My game was about movement and his about standing in areas and battling defenders, which could have been a good blend, but we needed playing time together.

When we did get it, things happened. In my fifth game, as a sub against Swindon, the score was 1-1 after Dean had equalised. Todd turned to me and sent me on and I replied by scoring twice in eight minutes as we won the game 3-2.

It earned me a run in the side of seven games, but I was often taken off just when I was getting up a head of steam. Later in the season, I would even be taken off before half-time, which is humiliating for any player. You're tempted to feign an injury to ease the embarrassment, but I'm not like that.

It was against Tranmere and came after only 20-odd minutes when we were already two down. In fact, there was a double substitution with Owen Morrison also "hooked". It was deeply embarrassing. I was playing badly, I have to admit, but I think Todd had the choice of several others. What made it galling was that he himself was struggling really badly, but you can't sub a manager during a game, can you?

Still, during that seven-game run I managed to score twice, in a draw at Doncaster and a win at Port Vale, as we climbed up to sixth in the table. Then, to my shock, I was dropped, apparently the victim of two games without us scoring. Not that it helped as they went another two without a goal and then slipped down to 14th, at which point I was brought back into the squad, even though I was on the bench.

I went in to see Colin and asked him why I was being left out. He said that he thought I did not play well at home. That was a new one on me. I pointed out that I had just scored four goals in six games, but it cut no ice. It was true that my goals were coming away from home, but there were reasons for it.

Colin, I am afraid, may have been a great player for Derby County and England, a cultured but hard centre-back, but I was coming to the conclusion that he was one of the worst managers I ever played under.

He was old school, with his teams playing the game in straight lines. We were just too predictable, our tempo was slow and none of our players broke past another player. We just didn't do enough work on team shape or pattern, as I would find out when I trained with the team on the days before matches. Colin just could not see that it was movement that won you football matches. At Valley Parade, teams would just sit in their shapes and we struggled to break them down. Away, when home teams were more adventurous and left gaps you could exploit, it was easier for me to get chances and score.

We had full-backs who never overlapped, which is all right if you have got Cristiano Ronaldo in your side and you don't want anyone going past him taking the space he wants to run into, just a full-back who backs him up to offer him an out. But we didn't really have wingers who could go past players, so we needed full-backs to bomb on. Colin couldn't work that out. He also had central midfield players playing wide. And no movement.

He did have players with some decent ability, but they were never used properly. Bobby Petta, the Dutch winger, was a case in point. He had talent but would play with his head down. He needed someone to get hold of him and work on him. There were others who would go on to do well – Lewis Emmanuel went to

Luton when they were in the Championship and Mark Bridge-Wilkinson was in on Carlisle's promotion tilt at the Championship.

I never really talked to Colin about my views. As a player I would have been stepping over the line. The problem again was that as a senior player, who had also been a manager, I now had a picture of how to get teams playing and succeeding and was becoming frustrated when it didn't happen.

Also, I had to think of the repercussions if I spoke out. I didn't want to upset him because he had the power to have me in every day, rather than just two days a week when there were matches. To be fair to him, he was sticking to his word about cutting me a bit of slack, so I just decided to keep my counsel and do what was asked. Even though I knew I was pretty much finished at the club.

In weeks when it was just a Saturday game, I would drive up on a Thursday, stay at the Cedar Court Hotel just outside the city, train on the Friday and be available for the match. Over Christmas, though, I decided to stay up for four games in 12 days, home and away. It was my professionalism, I suppose, and if I did get a chance I wanted to be in the best shape possible. It is the best time of year for football and I loved it.

It was a strange 12 days and training with them only increased my frustration at the way we were doing things. The food at the hotel was not great and it felt like I spent a lot of time watching old movies, including *Bedknobs and Broomsticks*, which took me back, in between using the gym and being out running. I did have some company in Andy Taylor, a decent young lad and a left-back who was on loan from Middlesbrough. He was sweating on a contract there. He would eventually get it and made the first team.

I also remember Bournemouth staying at the Cedar Court one night ahead of a match at Huddersfield. Dean Windass was also staying at the hotel as he was in the process of moving house and, in the morning, I was sitting with him in the lobby as the Bournemouth boys were checking out. Apparently, earlier in the season – at that game at Valley Parade I had come up to watch – Dean had had a run-in with Marcus and had been accused of biting his arm.

He spotted Marcus across the lobby and started on him. "Oi, Browning, you big fucking girl," he shouted. It was funny but a bit embarrassing and Andy Taylor and I were trying to get him to stop. "You tart," he went on. You could see Marcus thinking, 'What the hell …?' Fortunately he just looked over and glared and it passed off without any bother as we persuaded Dean to calm down.

Dean could be like that, shooting from the lip and being boisterous. He once gave a referee the benefit of his accumulated wisdom in the game in the car park at Valley Parade after a match and got a three-game ban for it.

He was also good fun. I remember going to a Ricky Hatton fight at the City of Manchester Stadium with him and three of the other lads, Owen Morrison, Lee Crooks and Steve Schumacher. I got recognised by a few people and asked for autographs, and Dean started telling people, "I'm here with Steve Claridge." What made it funny was that Dean ignored the other lads, who naturally gave him an earful, as did I.

He would also get grief off the boys for having to be home early because his wife said so. I don't know what she would have thought when he came in following a night out with the boys that ended up with him doing a forward roll through a puddle.

I've kept in touch with him since. I suppose in some ways I see a kindred spirit as he kept on playing into his late thirties and playing well in the Championship, too, with Hull City. Even before that great winning volley in the playoff final against Bristol City that took me back to mine with Leicester, he had earned himself a new one-year contract that would take him past 40.

He used to call me a "soft Southern bastard". So after he scored that goal in the playoff final for Hull and I saw him on the telly blubbing, I rang him up and said, "Who's the soft bastard now?" Cue a tirade of abuse back down the phone.

He may have thought I was a bit of a scruff, but those who know me are aware how I spend money on clothes. Anyway, he's got some front. A Southerner versus a Northern Millets' Man? Actually, it's nice to have someone other than myself to share stories about.

Anyway, needless to say I was on the bench for the four Christmas games. Results were patchy and Todd did give me a run of four starts in January, though he always seemed to take me off. I began to forget what it was like to play 90 minutes or that games lasted that long. He should have known that I get stronger as games go on and opposition defenders weaken because I keep working when others give up.

After that it was back to the bench, although we took five points from three of those games after I had taken the first game, against Chesterfield, to find my feet again. It was soul-destroying and I was just serving time now. It was something that went completely against the grain for me and I could not allow that to go on.

I asked to go out on loan somewhere, but Colin said he still needed me. He then gave me a run of three games in late February/early March, but although I scored in a 2-1 defeat at Milton Keynes Dons, I was out of the side again. This time, he said he would let me go. To be fair to him, he always kept his word off the field and never stitched me up.

We were a much better team than Colin made us. In the end, City finished 11th, even though we were good enough to make the playoffs. It was a shame. Colin would lose his job the following season and ended up managing in Norway.

At that time, the club was picking up the tab for its indulgence of overpaying during its stint in the Premier League. Had we gone up, or at least made the playoffs, it would have given the place a lift. As it was, it would not recover for a long while and would actually go down to the depths of League Two.

The club was better than that. The Valley Parade ground had been rebuilt, first after the tragic fire of 1985 and then upgraded

221

again during the Premier League days, but whoever did it didn't know much about football. The dressing rooms were among the worst in the League. It was a good club with likeable fans who gave me a good reception, very decent for League One and potentially the Championship. But it was going downhill and the fans had had to put up with more than most.

It was a big stadium that struggled for atmosphere and which needed a spark. And every time we got one going, it seemed that Colin Todd would pour a bucket of cold water on it with his selection and tactics. Towards the end of that season he was losing the support of both the fans and the players.

At one away game, against Kidderminster in the Football League Trophy, he dug out our midfield player Lee Crooks, apparently about not doing his job properly, but Colin had it wrong and Lee took exception. A fight developed, that ended up with Colin head-butting Lee, who had blood pouring out of a cut above his eye. Soon after, Lee was on his way to Northampton, even though he had been one of Colin's favourites until then.

Once upon a time I had been involved personally in something similar with John Beck at Cambridge United, when I gave him a black eye. Now I just sat there shaking my head in disbelief and thinking that this was typical of the club right now. Everybody was frustrated and fed up with Colin's dourness, which was reflected in the team.

I was thinking of signing for Oxford United but Darren Patterson, then the manager, was about to be replaced by Jim Smith and it fell through. I got a call from Kevan Broadhurst, who had been the youth-team coach at Birmingham City when I was at the club and with whom I had also crossed paths when he did some work for the radio station BRMB. He had been promoted from being in charge of the youth academy at Walsall to caretaker manager following the departure of Paul Merson.

I did have other offers – notably from Yeovil, which would have upset the Weymouth fans, not that I would have cared – but in the end I just wanted to go where I knew the manager and where I would be sure of playing, as Kevan had told me I would. In other words, after all the lack of it for the past year I wanted some certainty and, on top of that, they were offering another year's contract if they avoided relegation down to League Two. Walsall it was, then, and I became one of 46 players used by the Saddlers that season. It felt just like old times just down the road from the Bescot Stadium under Barry Fry at Birmingham.

Unlike then, though, when I was at a club on the way back up, this time, following the Paul Merson era, the club smelt of decline. The training facilities were poor and the dressing rooms were smashed up. It was another place to add to the list of those who were now hiring me as a firefighter. I should have been travelling round the country in a red engine with a bell ringing.

The attitude among the players, who frankly were a bit of a joke, was shocking. It upset me that there was a total lack of discipline, which some people around the club said had crept in under Merson, who had even been sharing a flat with one of his players, Darren Wrack, which didn't strike me as the best arrangement for a manager. In fact, Paul Devlin, who was a talented player at Sheffield United and Wolves, simply quit before the end of the season because he was so fed up with the environment and the attitude.

I felt a bit sorry for Kevan. This was a side on its way to relegation to League Two and he was powerless to halt the drop, as was I. I played seven games and scored once as we took just four points. That goal was the only one in our only win, over Gillingham in what would prove my final game of the season. The irony was immense. I had played against the Gills preseason and lost my job at Millwall. Then I had played for them. Finally I had got a win over them. I got a good reception from their fans. I should have stayed there for the season.

I played up front for Walsall with James Constable, who they had paid around £50,000 for to Chippenham of the Southern League. His touch was poor, along with his anticipation – he always seemed to be where the ball wasn't – and he was not the best on the ball, either. But he had something, the raw material of being tall and strong, and I would have liked longer to have helped him learn the game properly. He ended up at Kidderminster in the Conference then Oxford United and went on to do well at that level.

I hope and think I am still quite fondly remembered there for my short spell, which came to an end with one game of the season left.

I had trained all week for the game at home to Barnsley, which was meaningless since we were already down. It meant that Kevan Broadhurst would not be getting the job, which went to Richard Money. I got a call from him on the Friday to say I would not be required. Along with other senior players Simon Osborne and Mark Kinsella, I was being left out because he wanted to look at younger players. It was fair enough, but he could have told me face to face, man to man, earlier in the week rather than getting me to stay up and train all week. It seemed strange to me, incidentally, when the following season he recruited another veteran striker in Tommy Mooney.

Kevan out and Money in, Walsall were not going to hire me for the next season, which was a shame because I felt I had done well and would have liked to have come back. Neither were Bradford going to keep me on. I went back up to Valley Parade for one last day to pick up my cheque for my last couple of months' salary.

I was a free agent again, one who had just reached his 40th birthday. What had made being left out by Money for the last game of the season worse was that I had played 999 professional games and was left high and dry, short of what would have been a notable landmark and a good note to go out on.

The media work was plentiful, covering games for Radio 5 Live mainly on Sundays and in midweek evenings, and a phone-in on Sky Sports on Monday nights, but the sands of my playing time were running out.

Age seemed to be a big factor to some managers, if not to me. They would only have to check the fitness performance data to see what I had left in my legs. And my status as an ex-manager probably worried many, outweighing the value I might have been to them as a player.

I was even willing to sign a piece of paper saying that I would not take their job if they were sacked, but I still knew that would not encourage anybody of an insecure disposition. It was only ever going to be people I knew, and who knew me well enough to know that I wouldn't tuck them up, who were going to take me on. And the most I could expect now was £1,000 a week, much less than I could earn in full-time media work.

On top of that, I was running out of clubs. I had now played for 16 in the League alone. There was no getting away from it. My playing career might finally be over, just one game short of the magic 1,000.

5.2 Game Over

For the first time I could remember, I felt disillusioned with football during the summer of 2006. The last two years, going from club to club and twice getting the sack as a manager, had been tough and enough to dent anyone's self-confidence.

I had enjoyed Walsall and had a really good spell of seven games in just over a month, so I had showed I could still do it and play twice a week. I was fitter than anyone inside the club and felt I could play for at least another three years. The problem was that it now looked as if it was going to be based on age not ability and I was not going to get another shot.

Too much had happened over the previous two seasons. I had taken plenty of knocks in the game and had always rolled with the punches, but now they were coming thick and fast. I suppose it is true that as a player's body ages, he takes longer to recover from injuries. It is also true emotionally. While you may have experience to guide you, you also wonder how many setbacks you can take.

I just couldn't get a foothold anywhere, and the bad times were outweighing the good. I had played well enough when I did get the chance to play in the right system with decent players, but those moments were becoming infrequent.

It is the dilemma of the ageing pro nearing the end of his career. He desperately wants to keep playing, not just because of the old adage that you are a long time retired, but also because of a reluctance to let the game go. It is in your heart and soul and it is hard to picture a life without it.

But equally, you want to do yourself justice and not have people remembering you as some bit-part player who used to be somebody. I had also lost a bit of faith in people within the game. I knew a lot of people and I would call old team-mates, some of whom were now managers, along with people in the media and scouts and agents, but it was now becoming hard to find many who believed strongly enough in you.

I was in a position, given how I was feeling about the game having had the stuffing knocked out of me, of not actively looking too hard for a new club, but if someone did ring, then fine. It was a bit sad for someone who had always been a great enthusiast. And for the first time my phone did not ring over the summer. It was a strange feeling knowing that I was no longer in demand, but that I could still do a job for someone. I mean, your legs aren't going to go over the summer, are they?

I was, officially it seemed, a has-been and it felt like I had become someone who was being found guilty until proved innocent. There were preconceptions of me because of my age.

As for management, people's memories still seemed to be fresh with my Millwall experience. I did apply for the Exeter City job, but lost out to Paul Tisdale, who had been the coach at the university team, Team Bath of the Southern League.

Later in the season, when Exeter were in the Conference play-offs against Oxford City and lost the first leg – though they would win the second before being beaten by Morecambe in the final – I heard him say that they deserved to lose the game because the ball had gone more towards the Exeter goal than towards Oxford's. It was a bit depressing. I'm better with excuses than that, surely.

It was World Cup year and although I was asked to go out to Germany for Radio 5 Live, I had committed to working three nights a week for Sky on their phone-in, *You're on Sky Sports,* which gave me a chance to vent my anger about England under Sven-Goran Eriksson. I had never been a big fan of his and

227

thought that he sent out very dull sides that lacked width and balance.

It was so frustrating as the players took the flak for going out on penalties in the quarter-finals to Portugal and some of them did not perform to their best in a heat wave at the end of a long, hard season. But I maintain that we had a great squad and could have won the tournament. I mean, nobody is going to tell me that we couldn't have won Euro 2004 either. If the Greeks were good enough, then so were we. It came down to a management team that was short of ideas and inspiration. I didn't think it could happen, but then it got worse under Steve McClaren. Anyway, rant over. For now.

Gradually a lot of other work began to arrive, co-commentating on Sky and Radio 5 Live, as well as private work like doing voiceovers on football footage for mobile phones and the odd after-dinner speaking engagement. The *Guardian* newspaper also hired me to do a scouting report once a week on a lower-division player, which meant getting out and about at games, which I always enjoy.

I was in my element going around grounds and seeing fans who appreciated me having played for their clubs. At Walsall later in the season, it was really nice to have a lot of supporters coming up to me and thanking me for playing for them.

Before I knew it, pre-season had come and gone, and the start of the season too. I hadn't thought too much about playing, or missing it, or getting back into the game. Now I didn't have the time, what with media commitments at least four days a week. Clearly it wasn't out of my system yet, though.

My old room-mate at Bournemouth when I was a teenager playing there, Sean O'Driscoll – we used to call him "Noisy" because he was so quiet and the then manager Harry Redknapp deputed him to look after me as a supposed calming influence – was now manager of the club, had been for six years, and had done a great job on a limited budget, getting them up into League One via the playoffs.

Come early autumn, he had taken them up to eighth place when Doncaster Rovers came calling. He decided the time was right to move on, that he would have a bigger budget at Doncaster and a better chance of getting a club into the Championship. Who could blame him? He duly achieved it when they beat Leeds United in the playoff final at the end of the 2007/08 season.

I fancied the Bournemouth job, despite the limitations, because it was a club I knew well having played there and because it was near to my home. I sent in my cv to the chairman, but was told that I would not be considered. It was really disappointing. At the very least I thought I was worthy of an interview and I always believed that if a board just spent half an hour with me, they would be impressed. I knew what the perception of me was – encompassing the old stereotypes about timekeeping and gambling – but if anyone talked to me, they would see there was much more to me than that.

I remember going to a game at Dean Court around that time to watch a player for my article in the *Guardian* and word must have got out at the club that I had applied for the job. A knot of fans spotted me and started chanting: "We want Claridge out!" I think it dated back to a misquote from me in a local paper when I was alleged to have said that Weymouth were the biggest club in Dorset. As if I would have said that about a club I had a lot of respect for against a non-League one I had little respect for these days. Anyway, chanting to get me out was strange when I wasn't even in.

I mused that the sack was getting quicker and quicker these days. Thirty-six days? A lifetime. Now I was getting it before I even had the job.

The position eventually went to Kevin Bond, who had been Harry Redknapp's assistant at Portsmouth before taking up a similar job at Newcastle. When that *Panorama* programme named Kevin in connection with transfer irregularities at Pompey, he lost his job at St James's Park.

Now I knew that Harry still had influence at Dean Court from his time as manager there and living on millionaire's row in nearby Sandbanks, so I am sure he recommended Kevin to Bournemouth. It struck me as odd, though, because I had not rated Kevin as an assistant to Alan Ball when I was a player at Pompey and had said so forcibly in *Tales from the Boot Camps*.

And so I got on with my new day job. Then one day around that time a call came from a local journalist. He asked me if I had packed in playing. I said that I hadn't, but that playing might have packed me in. He knew I was on 999 games and wondered what I would do about it. I had not really thought about it, what with everything else over the last few months, along with my disillusionment, but I found myself saying that I would love to get that 1,000th professional game for someone at some point. Bournemouth were struggling for strikers, he said. Would I like to play there? I would love to, I said, but I didn't think it would happen given my previous experiences with Kevin Bond.

The article duly appeared in the Bournemouth evening paper and the next thing I know, I am getting a phone call from Kevin Bond. He asked if I would be interested in coming down and training with them with a view to helping them out. They were slipping down the table and were short of bodies. Would I like to come down and talk it over?

I drove down the next day and sat in the dressing room at the training ground and discussed it with Kevin. The subject of me being less than complimentary about him in the past did crop up. I said that I had only called it as I saw it back then, that I had not always been impressed with the training under him. He accepted what I had to say and said it was water under the bridge. I thought it was big of him to see it that way and ring me up. That's what football management can be like sometimes – you have to do what is necessary.

He offered me a month's contract and I was happy to take it. I would be getting the basic minimum of £100 a week plus £700 an appearance, so it was hardly for the money. The training ground at Canford School near Poole was convenient enough for me, though, and it was a beautiful place, far better than the old days when we trained on King's Park.

I hadn't kicked a ball for six months, but after training on the Thursday and Friday, Kevin said he would like to play me on the Saturday at home to Port Vale. He needed to rest players, he said, because they had an important FA Cup game at home to Bristol Rovers the following Tuesday. Their big striker, Steve Fletcher, was coming to the end of his career and couldn't play two games in four days.

I wasn't ready, and really needed ten days to get myself sorted, but I remembered that after turning down the chance to play at Sheffield Wednesday, Paul Sturrock let me go. And so I told Kevin that I would give it a go, but that he needed to understand I wouldn't be at my best. I was worried about doing myself justice but it was, after all, the chance to play my 1,000th game at the club where it had all really begun back in 1984, so I could hardly turn it down.

When we lined up, I quickly got the impression nobody was going to do themselves justice. Kevin put out a sort of 1-3-4-2, which was innovative, I have to admit. Never before had I played, or seen, a side with a sweeper with three defenders in front of him.

In central midfield we had Darren Anderton, whose illustrious career – that had seen him play for Pompey, Spurs and England – was winding down and great player that he may have been on the right side, he could hardly get about the pitch much any more. While he was good on the ball, he was not able to give much defensively. On the left-wing, Kevin played the right-footed Lionel Ainsworth, who was really a wide-right player. Played out of position, he was more like Lionel Blair.

Lionel was typical of the mess. He was getting the ball and smashing crosses in, yet he was an excellent player, just being played out of position. He went on to Hereford, where he did well, before being picked up by Watford. I told him that if I ever became a manager again I would get hold of him and play him in his right position. Elsewhere, people didn't know whether they were coming or going. We were getting run ragged and being done two on one all around the pitch.

Kevin did change it, to get Eddie Howe into central midfield to shore things up, but we were 2-0 down at half-time. We improved early in the second half, but I was just getting into it, my legs and lungs finally getting going, on the hour mark when he took me off. We ended up losing 4-0 with Leon Constantine scoring a hat-trick. He had done that against Brentford for Torquay while I was with the Bees before he moved on to Vale. I guess you could say he did as much as anyone to end my career.

And it was to be just about the end. I was ineligible for the FA Cuptie against Bristol Rovers, as I had not been signed in time for FA clearance, and the following Saturday, when everyone was fit, I was left out. To be fair, Kevin was probably right when he said there was no point putting me on the bench because to get fit I needed to be starting and I was not going to make too much of an impact coming on late. Plus, I was associated with the Port Vale débâcle. He obviously thought I had "gone", even though he had hardly given me a chance.

The problem is that as you get older, people judge you according to your age, both inside the game and spectators. If you make a mistake or have a bad game, you can almost hear the comment that "he's gone". They don't look at the other circumstances of the game.

I was signed up for a month and dutifully kept coming to training every day over Christmas. Without any appearance money, just getting the £100 a week left me out of pocket in petrol money. It seemed that every time I was at Bournemouth I lost money. All it needed was Harry Redknapp to come back and sell me a dodgy car, just as he had done in my first spell there.

As a bloke Kevin Bond was fine, seeming sincere and genuine.

I never had a run-in with him and never went to see him about not figuring in his plans, because I had stopped fighting the system these days. The month just ebbed away and nothing was said. Towards the end of the last week, I asked if I should come in again the following day and he agreed, there being no acrimony between us, that it wasn't worth it.

Nothing more was said and there was no offer of a contract. It was just another of those frustrating experiences, but twofold on my part. I still felt I could have played well for them, and I also thought I could have managed the club better. Kevin was struggling with the team and, I reckoned, struggling to be a No. 1 having been a No. 2 for so long.

He would come to blame a lack of money, and the Cherries would go into administration for the second time in a decade a couple of years later, but Kevin inherited some good players from Sean O'Driscoll, who had managed to get them up to eighth in the table before leaving. Kevin just staved off relegation in his first season but succumbed the next year when the 10-point deduction for administration did for them, despite a late rally.

I still reckon they shouldn't have gone down with the squad he inherited, mind. There was, for example, James Hayter, a very decent striker at that level, quick and lively – and I thought I would have played well alongside him by slipping him through – with two other young ones in Brett Pitman and Sam Vokes, who were not bad, coming through.

In fact, I was there when Sam started training with the first team – I don't think Kevin knew what he had coming through in his squad at that time – and his delight and enthusiasm reminded me of how I was when I was a teenager. He would come in and do well to the point where he got a move to Wolves and made his debut for Wales.

On top of that, Kevin thought Steve Fletcher and Marcus Browning were also past it and got rid of them, but I thought they could still do a good job, along with right-back Stephen Purches, who went to Leyton Orient and played well for them. Eventually

Kevin was sacked, ending up back as Harry Redknapp's assistant at Tottenham after he had left Portsmouth for Spurs.

The experience just added to my gloom about playing during the last couple of years under some poor managers. I got back to the full-time media work, but then came another call early in the New Year, and I just can't resist the call to arms. Or should that be boots.

It came from a lad called Danny Bloor, who was the chairman at Worthing of the Ryman League. Playing for him was Jamie Lawrence, my old team-mate at Leicester and Brentford, and he had recommended me. Send for the firefighter. This time I was willing because it would be just a fun experience with no expectation and no pressure. The level of the club really didn't matter; when someone values you and wants you to play for them, you respond. Or I do, anyway.

Worthing were struggling at the bottom of the table and needed some experienced reinforcements for a month. Danny was a bookmaker in Brighton, a nice lad and a bit younger than me, and he offered me horse-racing tips instead of being paid. I told him I wasn't into that any more and settled for £600 a game and £300 for a win. It was good money for that level – better than Bournemouth.

I played four games and did all right. We won two, by 3-1 against Folkestone Invicta and the same score against Ashford Town. Yes that Ashford Town in Middlesex, where I had gone with Weymouth for that notorious FA Trophy tie. I was glad this was a home game.

One of the two draws was against AFC Wimbledon, who were flying and I was just driving out of town when my mobile rang, with Danny on the line saying: "I've got something for you." I went back and he handed me £100. I hadn't realised he was paying for a draw as well. It was good of him to stump up. I think I was quite good for them, too. My little spell helped them get out of the relegation zone, though sadly they would later fall back into it.

In fact, I enjoyed it and went on to become friends with

Danny. I left, I guess, because he couldn't afford me any more. As for the standard, let's just say I was glad I was being well paid. What the spell also did, for which I was grateful to Danny, was to give me back a bit of enthusiasm.

I got a call from an old mate who had been a coach at Birmingham City, David Howell, who was now manager of Harrow Borough in the same league. He asked me why I hadn't told him I was willing to play in the Ryman. If he had known, he would have snapped me up.

He said he needed a player who would show his lads how the game should be played, to illustrate some dedication and professionalism. He knew how to appeal to the right side of me. And so I got flattered into it. Not that flattered, mind. I managed to get £500 an appearance and £100 a point out of him.

The football in the Ryman League, though only just below what I had played in with Weymouth, was much less intense and friendlier. People didn't have chips on their shoulders, it was much more relaxed and jokey, with no players really wanting to make a name for themselves by cutting me down to size – literally. And I wasn't coming in with any great fanfare.

Besides, I had always got on well with David, who had one of the best nicknames in football. We used to call him "The Claw". It was because whenever we all went out to a club, you would see him put his hand around a girl's shoulder and know she was never going to escape.

Funnily enough, I was watching a holiday programme a few years after leaving Birmingham and there was a shot of a woman in a thong and a huge black hand massaging sun tan lotion into her backside. I thought, "That's The Claw. I'd recognise that hand anywhere." Sure enough it was. When the camera panned away, he had a big cheesy grin on his face. I think he must have been out there with his disc jockeying, which he used to do around the Mediterranean holiday islands.

Once again, I enjoyed the one-month spell with Harrow, though it was not easy, I have to admit. By now the pitches were getting bobbly as they were drying out with the onset of spring and, to be honest, the players in that league are not that great. They were decent lads trying hard, though, and I did my best to work hard for them. I just played home games, trying to put a few more on the gate for the club. It worked. I think Harrow's average went up by 34.

I particularly enjoyed a game against Margate, who were top of the league, which we drew 4-4. When I turned up at the ground, one of the lads told me that the local Paddy Power bookmakers in the High Street was offering a novelty bet of me scoring a goal and taking my shirt off to celebrate. At 5-1 it sounded like value to me and I told the lads to have some of it. I naturally scored in the first few minutes and even more naturally took off my shirt to celebrate, the booking being well worth it. Nobody outside of the squad could quite work out why we were celebrating like we had won the FA Cup.

I finished off scoring a good goal against Bromley, who were near the top of the table, with an overhead kick from a flicked-on header. And that was that. It was not a bad way to go out. Harrow couldn't afford me any more, I don't think, and by now I was doing too much media work to commit to it properly. I hate not preparing as best I can, even for a semi-professional game in front of a few hundred. One Saturday, I did a guest spot on *Football Focus* on BBC 1 then dashed up through North-West London, not getting there till 2pm. I wasn't happy about arriving just an hour before kick-off.

I thought that, at 1,008 professional games, that would be that, but I still struggled to get it though my head that I might be finished, even at the age of 42. I always kept myself fit after all

I was in a bar, in fact, one Saturday and one bloke had had too much to drink and offered me his place in the Great South Run around Portsmouth the following morning. I took him up on it and ran the ten miles in just over 55 minutes – a couple of minutes faster than I had done it a few years earlier – even though it was blowing a gale.

Mind you, I will probably think I can still play in the Premier League at the age of 72 and I was still thinking that Rafael Benitez needs a good partner for that young lad Fernando Torres at Liverpool.

6. *New Games*

When it comes to people on radio and television, one man's meat is another man's poison. No matter what you say, how you look or how you sound, people are going to bring their own tastes and prejudices to their view of a media personality. Somebody is going to take against you. And someone else is going to like you.

Steve Claridge is fortunate that more seem to like him than have taken against him. Yes, I have met some who are not big fans. They think Steve can get over-excited, that the pitch of his voice rises with the intensity of his feeling. To them, it is worse because he does appear on a lot of outlets, which actually shows just how much in demand he is these days.

More, though, seem to appreciate his candour and humour on Radio 5 Live, both on co-commentary and the 6-0-6 phone-in show. There were also regular appearances at one point on the Friday night football preview programme where his relationship with fellow guest Gabriele Marcotti, an Italian/American football journalist, was best described as creatively tense and which kept the presenter Mark Pougatch on his toes.

Then there was the insight he offered in his Scouting Report feature for the *Guardian*, in which he he analysed a lower-division player each week, and his appearances on Sky and Setanta Sports, where his ability to think on his feet was much in demand before the recession and the demise of Setanta curtailed some of his work.

Perhaps Steve's popularity lies in the sheer number of clubs he has played for and whose fans came to admire his wholeheartedness. There are even those whose hearts he broke sometimes by scoring big goals in big games against their team who seem to have a grudging respect for him.

Most probably, he is hired and retained by radio, television and newspapers because he has a rare ability to relate to the fan. He has often said that if he wasn't getting paid to watch the game, he would be paying to watch it. Now he can bring around 25 years of playing experience, along with an ability to express that knowledge gleaned from inside the game, with wit and down-to-earth communication skills to a wide audience outside it.

"I love him on TV," says David Howell, his old coach at Birmingham City. "He can't really be fake. His emotions all come out.

"I do think he identifies with the normal supporter. He is not just going to say the politically correct thing but is going to be honest. It's that underlying passion he has for the game that people like as well. He gets worked up, even if he has nothing to do with either team. They like that. That endears him to football fans."

Adds his old Portsmouth playing colleague and then chief scout Andy Awford: "He's no mug. I see him on the telly and he knows his stuff, he's got a good eye. He speaks his mind and can be controversial."

It is also, according to BBC commentator Ian Dennis, who has worked with Steve extensively, down to that identification with his audience.

"He has got a natural rapport with the fans," says Dennis. "You see it when we are sitting in commentary positions. They will always talk to him and they show him a lot of respect."

Dennis first worked with Claridge back in 2002. "I had just joined Radio 5 and wasn't selected to go out to the World Cup in Japan and South Korea that summer," he recalls. "So they put me and Steve together in a little studio for BBC Interactive. The idea was that we would watch the games and commentate, and people would text in with their analysis and we would read them out and discuss them.

"It was just like two blokes in a bar talking about football and the next thing you know we have got a bit of a cult following. A lot of people texted in. There was a nice chemistry between us, him from the South and me from the North. You know how quick-witted and sharp he is, so the banter was really good. I think he backed Brazil to win the tournament so he was in a good mood most of the time.

"I remember they gave us some of this new technology at the time where you could draw lines on the screen to illustrate a point. Steve left a lot of arrows and white lines everywhere so you could hardly see the game. But he was a joy to work with. We really hit it off. I think the world of him. He calls me 'Ee' now as an abbreviation of Ian and only my family call me that."

I point out to Dennis that Steve also uses the abbreviation for me but that rather than a sign of affection, it is more probably a sign of laziness as he can't be bothered to say the whole word.

And the timekeeping? "Well, some of the matches kicked off at 6am so he would arrive sometimes with the teams on the field and with 30 seconds to spare. It did keep the producer on his toes. I think around that time it may also have been the first time I saw him in a suit. I thought he was going on to court. I have to say his timekeeping has improved these days, though. Now, he's one of the first to arrive and he's still smart."

From my own point of view, Steve was always there in plenty of time when needed, when the real work had to be done, come match day for example. And as the media work now provides his full-time source of income, rather than being the sideline it was in the past, he now accords it the same professionalism that he did with his football.

Claridge and Dennis are now paired quite regularly in co-commentary and they form an entertaining duo.

"The good thing is that if you're on with him and it's a dull game, there will still be some unpredictability," says Dennis. "He will always bowl you a googly, come up with some random question, like, 'When was the last time so and so scored four goals on a Tuesday at Preston?' You may have done your research, but he still catches you out.

"I remember once doing a Conference playoff game at Dagenham and Redbridge with him and, just before half-time, they brought us some food, among which was a huge blueberry muffin. I was thinking, 'Right, I'm having that when my commentary finishes.' When the whistle went and I handed over to him for his comments before going back to the studio, I tucked into the muffin, only for him to try and involve me in the conversation again, knowing that I had a mouth full of muffin. He can be wicked like that.

"Then he will say, 'Who do you think is on top in this game? What do you think of it so far?' and you will think, 'Hang on, that's your job to tell us and I'm the one answering?' But it's good. It means that he's doing something different."

Dennis also enjoys the repartee they spark in each other. "I remember saying during a game, Charlton against Fulham it was, that he was on the thinnest of thin ice. He came back quick as you like with, 'It's a good job you're not.' He despairs of my eating habits. He's always eating fruit. I'm more of a burger-and-chips man." And blueberry muffins.

"I did worry once that I had overstepped the mark with him in something I said on air," adds Dennis. "It may have been about his hair thinning or taking the mickey out of his laugh sounding like Blakey out of On The Buses and I had to check it out with him afterwards. He said, 'Don't worry Ian, you'd never upset me.' It was nice of him. It showed what little ego he has."

And for all the humour, there is a serious side. "He reads the game exceptionally well," adds Dennis. "That's why he's on the show every Friday night. He has good, strong opinions."

It could once have been more serious in a different way, Dennis recalls. "We were out in Zagreb doing Dinamo v Arsenal," he says, "and I wandered into what I thought was a shop, but which turned out to be the headquarters of the Dinamo Ultras, the Bad Blue Boys.

"They were all wearing Burberry, smoking dope and drinking beer. Now I have got a shaved head and so had Steve at the time, so I was glad I had lost him temporarily. I think if he had been with me and we had opened our mouths, two shaven-headed Englishmen, we would have been in trouble."

Many of Dennis's experiences with, and views on, Steve mirror my own.

Technically, I was his employer as chairman to his manager at Weymouth, but I never thought of it like that, more that we were a partnership in a project. It may be that in there is the mistake that some make in trying to control him. It is like trying to nail a blancmange to a wall.

When I departed Weymouth, I said as much to the incoming chairman. "If you give Steve the freedom and time," I said, "he will do a fantastic job for you." But I sensed they were words that would fall on deaf ears. Martyn Harrison gave him neither freedom nor time.

Steve's eccentricities were worth it. He was always prepared in-depth for the most important thing – the match. And his depth of knowledge of the game, players and people, his shrewdness, frequently astonished me. There was a fierce professionalism in him. We were paying him what for him was a pittance, but he could not have given more hours or attention to the job.

As for the scruffiness of legend, with people supposedly imagining that he must be as unkempt off the field as he appears on it, all I can say is that he is the only Weymouth manager I ever knew who wore Armani suits and Hugo Boss shirts and ties.

Then again, whenever you visit him at his home and he is relaxing, he will be in a sweatshirt, tracksuit bottoms and trainers. Each time there will be a different piece of kit carrying the club crest of the various clubs he played for.

It emphasises the two sides of Steve. There is the guy who looks as if he is sloppy and laid-back. But it is just a guy in standby mode for the time when he needs to be dressed properly, ready for action, should someone turn on the remote.

I would hear later that, as his boss at Millwall, Theo Paphitis found him hard work and high-maintenance. I know how he felt. It was my experience, too.

But, unlike Theo, I saw it as an experience that was worth all the work and maintenance. Steve is a maverick who rewards someone who allows him to get on and do the job by delivering results. He has that spark and touch of ingenuity that requires the indulgence the talented need. In return, he brings a liveliness and vibrancy to the place and to your existence.

He also needs a degree of patience, as does any manager, and has never really received that quality from others. His departures at Portsmouth, Weymouth and Millwall talked, to me at least, of what was wrong with the people over him and the lack of strength they showed when confronted by the inevitable pressures of the game.

"You have to understand what you are going to get with him," says Guy Whittingham, his assistant manager at Portsmouth. "He's not that difficult, he's just very dogmatic about football and has his own ideas. He won't change a lot of the time, but he doesn't like yes men and appreciates people who are willing to argue the point with him."

It was a great sadness to me that no football club chairman would take an immediate chance with Steve since the Millwall experience because I believed he would make some club a very fine manager.

These days, he understands club budgets and what is achievable. Add to that a copious contacts book – and I am constantly staggered by his mental database of players – of people he has known and played with in the game these past 25 years. It, he, represents a potentially excellent investment.

As his old Leicester and Wycombe team-mate Steve Guppy sums up perfectly: "There's never a dull moment. He's very passionate and works very hard. If anyone does have the courage to take him on, they will be in for an enjoyable time."

Ours has been a, er, challenging relationship ever since collaborating on *Tales from the Boot Camps* and in the decade since, but it has never been less than worthwhile and more frequently life-enhancing. It is what Steve Claridge does. He can frustrate and even anger – though as Guy Whittingham perceptively noted: "You can't stay angry with him" – but, generous of spirit, he ends up enhancing the lives of those he comes into contact with. Many of us can do the former; fewer achieve the latter.

It was why I had no hesitation in agreeing to be a character witness for him when he had to appear before Coventry Crown Court on a dangerous driving charge. It was serious, as he acknowledged, and very worrying for him as he even faced a jail sentence.

Two examples that tell of the rewards of knowing him, which out-weigh the debits:

I happened to mention one day that I was in need of a new sofa. A day later, he phoned to say that his mother-in-law was getting rid of hers and it was mine for £100, plus £50 for petrol to deliver it.

"What colour?" I asked him.

"It's very comfortable," was his answer and his way of deflecting the fact that I might not like the colour.

A few weeks later, he arrives at my doorstep in a white van with his sister Ruth as help and a sofa in the back. Strictly cash, 150 quid. He had gone out of his way to do a friend a favour, as he does with many people. The sofa was a curious pea-green, though he was right about it being comfortable. Buying throws to cover the thing cost more than the sofa.

Sometimes he tries too hard to do favours. During work on this book, he agreed to meet me at the BBC, where we could talk in a canteen, one Sunday morning before he covered a Queens Park Rangers game in the afternoon. He was trying to do me a favour, to save me a trip down to his home, but because of a Radio 5 Live interview being put back; he was late. It is sometimes how he causes problems for himself – seeking too hard to accommodate other people. I was growing tense as our deadline was nearing.

There we stood in the car park of the BBC having a stand-up row, bellowing abuse at each other.

"We are never going to finish this bloody book," I warned him.

"Course we will," he said with that annoying, disarming grin.

6.1 Radio and TV Times

I thought my first experience of television might be my last. It was on a Sunday afternoon highlights programme on Anglia TV, the regional station in the East of England, when I was a studio guest while at Cambridge United.

As we got to the end of the show, I saw the producer revving an arm up faster and faster in a windmill motion, similar to Mick Channon's goal celebration at Southampton, for those old enough to remember it – and I've just been told about it. Anyway, she panicked me and apparently I looked terrified when the camera fixed on me. How was I to know this was her way of signalling that it was time to wind up the show? If this was TV, I wasn't sure I wanted to go through all that again.

Thankfully, it got easier, though never as good again as doing a "Goals on Sunday" programme for Central TV when I was at Birmingham City. It was literally five minutes work, just short, sharp comments on the games, and I got £750. It was with Gary Newbon, who used to do the ITV Champions League interviews in the days of Ron Atkinson, and I asked him if I could come every week.

Media work, to be honest, is second best to playing or managing, but it is a very good second best. If you go into radio and television from normal life or another job, it is a fantastic living, watching and commenting on football. But I am coming from playing the game and managing teams. To be honest, anywhere after that is a downward step, if not in profile because I am probably better known now than I have ever been. The good thing about the work, though, is that I remain close to football, the game that makes life worth living.

I first got on to the radio in the late 1990s when someone from Radio 5 Live rang me up and asked if I would co-commentate a game, as someone had pulled out. I didn't really know what it involved, but agreed to give it a go. It was a match at Ipswich kicking off at lunchtime and I soon understood why someone had pulled out. I think, what with getting there and back, I did a 14-hour day for £200.

I did enjoy it, though, just calling the game as I saw it when the commentator asked for my opinion, and they seemed to like me and asked me back. Gradually the work has built up, as it did down the years with Sky and then Setanta. You start to get a name for yourself and if you are reliable, people turn to you. It's strange; this reputation of being late for things has followed me around just because I had a habit of turning up for training with five minutes to go till it started – though I never cut it fine when it came to actual games – but now I get everywhere hours early ready to work. In fact, several times I have covered for people who have turned up late due to bad traffic or something. And you don't keep getting hired if you don't show up on time.

I love it all, being on the airwaves or in vision, and I am very fortunate to have outlets for my views on the game. I am an opinionated bloke and do like to get a good argument going, which is probably why I started to get asked to host the Radio 5 Live phone-in show *6-0-6*.

Radio is the more enjoyable discipline for me, I suppose. You get more time to develop themes, to express yourself in an off-the-cuff, even an off-the-wall, type of way. It is about painting pictures and having fun. Imagination can be a wonderful thing. I think it was Bryon Butler, the late and great BBC radio commentator, who said that a child had once told him he preferred radio to TV because the pictures were better.

You can be in a little cubicle of a radio studio round a table with just a microphone in front of you and sometimes you forget people are listening because you are just having fun with some mates. Perhaps that is half the art. You need to be relaxed so that you can think on your feet, which has never been a problem for me. It is, in reality, a huge audience and I know from going round the country and speaking to fans that they listen to the show. They are not slow to pick you up on any daft things you may have said in the heat of the moment.

I remember doing one phone-in after England had beaten Switzerland 2-1 at Wembley in Fabio Capello's first match in charge and had been unimpressed that he had played five across the midfield – it was something that Steve McClaren would have got pilloried for.

"I think it was a case of too many cocks spoiling the broth," I said, and there was a brief moment of silence before I corrected myself.

I could see the producer and sound engineer behind the glass in the "gallery", from where the show is controlled, with a mix of horror and amusement on their faces.

Then a bloke comes on the line. "I think you were right first time, Steve, the way we played tonight," he said.

Apart from that, I am fortunate that I have not sworn on air – yet, touch wood. I suppose I am lucky I have an inbuilt censorship, like a lot of us in football. When I am in a football environment, my language can be a bit rich, but I never swear around my mum or family.

You are always vulnerable, though, to the commentator's curse, where you talk about someone having a nightmare game – just before they go and score. I did also manage to invent a word – saying symptomonious instead of symptomatic. I was quite proud of it. It should be a word. I look forward to the day when something I say finds its way into the dictionary.

There is also the risk of saying something that sounds silly if it is taken out of context. *Private Eye* magazine has a column devoted to commentating gaffes and I have found myself in it a few times for saying things like: "They are losing because they haven't scored enough goals." You try and avoid it, and sometimes people know what you mean but, in the heat of the moment, it is bound to happen now and then. It's better for that to happen than to freeze or panic on air, something that fortunately has never happened to me. In fact, I think I come alive with a microphone in my hand. It's a bit like talking to a woman. If I am talking to a man, I am in first gear, but if it's a nice-looking woman, I go into fifth gear – like Tim Lovejoy used to in that "Soccerette" feature on Sky's *Soccer AM*. It's like getting a sniff of goal.

With radio, you can get a lot of banter going. When you work with people for a while, you get to know their personality and character. On 5 Live, I seemed to have developed a bit of a double act with Gabriele Marcotti on the Friday night weekend preview show and the producers liked the edge between us. Fans also said to me that they enjoyed the conflict.

Gab is an Italian-American sports journalist who comes at the game from a different angle to me, having never been involved professionally, and we can be abrasive as we argue about issues and personalities, most of the time in complete disagreement. Fortunately, we seem to be as thick-skinned as each other. For me it is quite simple. In the end, I am right and he is wrong.

Mind you, I can get chippy with anyone on air if I disagree with them. During the 2006 World Cup, when England's players were getting hammered for their performances, some MP called Roger Godsiff, who was clearly in need of some extra publicity, tabled some motion in Parliament criticising them. I wasn't having that and had what Mrs Merton would have called a heated debate live on Radio 5 with him. It caused a bit of a stir at the time. My point was that the players were top quality and that they just weren't being managed well. He may be good in the House of Commons, but he was on my turf here and I reckon I saw him off.

Outside of the studio in the press box or on a windy gantry high above the pitch, I do like the double-acts you can develop at live games with commentators and you can stretch them without crossing a line. The same with me – they've been known to lob me the odd grenade now and then. I like working with most of the commentators on 5 Live. Mike Ingham is a class act and Ian Dennis and I can get a bit of a rapport going, but I get on well with all of them.

Working in the media has also opened some interesting doors to me, like the summer of 2007 when I was away from home for almost three months.

As well as radio and television work, I was recruited by the *Guardian* a couple of years ago to do scouting reports on young, lower-division players. It was something I really enjoyed, travelling around the grounds, picking out promising kids and analysing their games. After I had made my notes, I used to get a call from one of the paper's sports journalists on a Monday morning, give him my views and he would write it up into a column.

Anyway, first stop during the summer of 2007 was Holland for the European Under-21 Championship finals, in which England reached the semi-finals. The *Guardian* wanted some scouting reports of international youngsters, including the Dutchman Ryan Babel, shortly before he joined Liverpool. It was a good experience, even if I did get stopped for speeding, which had me sweating as I was already on nine points. Fortunately, when the ticket arrived through the post it was only a fine.

After that, I was invited by a TV production company to go to China to help make a "search for a star"-type programme for seven weeks. Yes, China. For seven weeks.

Now it really should not have been my scene. For a start there was the initial long flight to Shanghai via Paris, then a load of two- and three-hour internal flights. On top of that, there was the heat and the humidity, something that does not suit my constitution.

But I went up to London to meet the producers, Steve

Cartwright and Steve Bellis, who had been a commercial director at Stockport County, and they seemed like good lads. I was also at a loose end for the second half of the summer, the money was good and I thought it might be an experience. It was.

That started at the airport in Paris, where I teamed up with Paul Jones, who would be working with me on the show. Paul had been Sam Allardyce's partner at centre-back during their playing days at Bolton Wanderers and I hit it off with him straight away. Within two minutes he was talking about his divorce and I thought I would be fine with someone who was so open.

The programme was a reality show for Chinese television about finding three promising young players who were good enough to take up academy places that were being offered by Everton, Bolton Wanderers and Nottingham Forest. It meant travelling around eight different cities and provinces where 1,000 boys would be whittled down to three by a series of drills and skills and games that I was judging. There would be a grand final of 24 boys from which the three would be chosen.

We travelled from Shanghai to Beijing to Guangzhou, taking in other cities I can't spell or pronounce, and the enthusiasm of the kids for football at each centre was staggering. As was the bureaucracy of just getting these days to go ahead, what with all the wrangling between local associations and the Chinese national FA, not to mention between me and a local television producer out there.

At each venue, Paul and I would put the kids through their paces with FA-approved drills, like keeping the ball up, passing, shooting and speed tests. Then we would have six-a-side and 11-a-side games to whittle down the candidates. It was like *Pop Idol* really: there was a lot of rubbish on offer, but there were also one or two gems. It was good for me. It showed I could lay on sessions and bring the best out of the players I was given.

I got the hump with the Chinese producer, though, because we were supposed to film for eight hours and I would get 45 minutes with each of the final 11-a-side teams to prepare them for set-pieces and the like. He was trying to rush me into 15 minutes and, as you may have already gathered, I am someone who likes to do my job properly. It was just so he could get done and have a kickabout. He also started trying to tell us who we should pick for TV purposes because of their stories or looks, rather than on ability, and I wasn't having that.

After my seven weeks out there to get to the last 24, Kenny Sansom, the old Arsenal and England left-back, who had had the easy shift in Beijing while we carried our own luggage and TV equipment all over the country, took over for the eight shows that found the final three to come to England. I have never seen the series, which was aired out there, but I have the feeling I may be the Simon Cowell of China. I just wish I had his money.

It was certainly a fascinating country. To be honest, I found a lot of people very rude and ignorant with their refusal to queue, notably at the airports when there was just a free-for-all whenever a flight was called. When you saw the general mayhem of people pushing each other around, the idea that China has a culture where people have a lot of respect for each other seemed a little far-fetched to me.

Against that, though, it always felt very safe. There were no young lads hanging about on street corners and once when I was out walking I got lost and went through what was clearly a very poor area without ever feeling threatened, even if I did get a few strange looks. Then again, I've been used to those in a few areas in England. With the police around the place looking menacing, though, you sensed that you were in for serious trouble if you did anything they considered unacceptable.

One thing that did shock me was the pollution level everywhere. I remember walking around the Forbidden City in Beijing in 100-degree heat and almost 100 per cent humidity and not getting burnt because there was so much smog screening the sun. I hated people spitting in public, something I will never get used to, but I could see why it happened – the pollution had caused problems with the chest and lungs. Those paper bags on

251

aeroplanes in China are not for people being sick, they are to spit in. The authorities try to do something about it, such as limiting cars coming into the cities by odd and even number plates on certain days, but with so much building and development going on, it is an uphill task.

The reality show was good fun, but really I am all about live football. I love being out watching matches and would do even if I wasn't getting paid. I would rather get out and watch, say, Fareham Town live than a Premier League match on the telly. Only when you are watching a match live do you get a real understanding of what the players are trying to do.

Mind you, going to a live match can present some unseen problems sometimes – and on a couple of occasions for me they have involved Southampton fans.

There was once when I was travelling to London to do some work at the BBC and I was in the back carriage of a train into Waterloo. When I got off, I had to walk all the way to the ticket barrier past carriages full of Saints' supporters who were coming up to town to see them play Queens Park Rangers.

Naturally they couldn't resist having a go at a Portsmouth fan. Once I had been spotted someone started up a chant of 'Claridge is a wanker' and it spread down the platform like a Mexican wave.

Much worse, though, was the time I was covering a Southampton home game for Radio 5 Live and parked my car at a pub away from St Mary's Stadium at Shamrock Quay. As I walked to the ground, I was spotted by a group of about a dozen lads who looked as it they had had a few drinks.

At first, I responded with just a smile when one or two started at me but soon I was surrounded and got a bit worried. They were trying to tell me that Matthew Le Tissier would get a hard time around Portsmouth and so I was going to get it in Southampton. Playing for time, I tried to say that I knew Matt well and admired him.

Then one of them threw a punch at me but fortunately

another had given me a push just as he did so it missed. It was my signal to leg it and I ran as fast as I could – which was just about quickly enough even though I might have lost half a yard of pace. Out of breath, I just made it into the reception area at the stadium while outside they gathered to shout more abuse at me.

Occupational hazards, I guess, but back to the more obvious part of the job …

I am not big on statistics. I like to go to a game with an open mind and with no preconceived ideas. I know players and formations, so beyond that I think I will be able to talk without worrying about needing stuff to fill the airtime. The stations often provide you with statistics if you want them, but I prefer a blank canvas. If I am the studio guest, I might look at the stats as a backup. It is always important to have a good host as well – and I have enjoyed working with George Gavin at Sky – who will ask the right questions to draw out your expertise.

Actually, I think I get too technical at times because I am very into the tactics and strategy of the game, which you need to be as an expert summariser, both on radio and TV. I like to explain why certain formations work for certain teams, why this player is good in such a role, what his strengths and weaknesses are. I think what people like, or at least they say to me they do, is that when I say something, I give an explanation for it. If something is wrong, I say why. People also like a bit of humour, a bit of lightness amid the lesson if you like, and I think I can deliver that. That goes for both radio and TV, even if TV is the straighter medium.

The more I have done, the more I have taken notice of the shape and balance of sides, analysing games and teams. I have learned a lot just through watching, thinking and noting games, because you have to concentrate all the time and pay attention. If I am going to host 6-0-6 or a TV phone-in show and people are ringing in wondering why Liverpool played so badly, I have got to know why.

To be honest, I don't think there are too many who do know

more than me. Tactically, I think I am right on the button. I can tell you after ten or 20 minutes what is wrong with your team. I just see a picture. I know why a team is doing well or struggling and, hopefully, I can convey that.

Who do I like in the media? All the boys on Radio 5 Live go out of their way to be friendly with me. And I like Andy Gray on Sky. He understands the game. There are too many who have played the game but who don't know it.

Having played the game at every level, from Premier League down to Ryman League, I think I can appreciate all the ins and outs of the English game, its culture and what clubs mean to their communities. Because I have been both, I can identify with both players and fans.

And while some friends tell me that I sound like a cynical old professional sometimes – and I will agree with them about certain characters and personalities in it – I am certainly not cynical about the game.

6.2 Best of Times, Worst of Times

People often ask me if I look out for all my old teams' results. The answer is, of course. The problem is that it takes me about half an hour to check them all. Then, when I've been through all their league standings, I can find that hours have elapsed. I suppose I take most notice of, in order, Portsmouth, Leicester City, Millwall and Birmingham City. They have been the big four of my career, but I retain varying degrees of fondness for, and interest in, them all.

And I suppose I like the Championship best. It is almost becoming the real English game, the top level for English players – apart from the very elite – with so many overseas players in the Premier League these days. With the Premier League, you know everybody's budget from the start and you can pretty much predict the top four and the bottom four, with those in between merely jostling for position. In the Championship, anybody can beat anybody else on any given day and any club has the potential to reach the top of the table.

My concern is that the Championship has the potential to become predictable too, mainly due to the growing amount of parachute money relegated clubs from the Premier League will be getting. It was good, though, to see the cities of Stoke, Bristol and Hull having a crack at the Premier League, for example, during a recent season but you knew that West Bromwich Albion, with their ability to pay £3 million for Chris Brunt, a left-winger who didn't play regularly, were going to be the team to beat. So it proved, just as you know Colchester and Scunthorpe would be the ones to go down. In the end, it was fair play to Stoke and Hull for getting promoted.

I hoped they wouldn't go the way of other teams who in recent years have got up into the Premier League just for the money and hoarded it, rather than invested it, accepting their fate of a quick relegation. Derby County seemed a case in point. They did very badly and really should have done better. And Watford seemed to know straight away when they went up a couple of seasons back that they would get relegated, so looked as if they were just regrouping to prepare themselves for another push that this time they hoped would be permanent.

With all the money coming into the game, these are the best of times in many ways, though it does worry me that, despite the television boom, fans are having to fork out more and more. We need to be careful we don't kill the golden goose.

With the latest TV deal, the parachute payment is a huge £13 million a season for two years for the relegated clubs. That gives them a major headstart over other clubs in the Championship. I think the money should be more evenly distributed through the division, and also through Leagues One and Two as well, so we have a more level playing field.

In the end, a club's fan base comes into it and the bigger it is, quite simply, the more likely that club is to progress. Otherwise, you rely on a sugar daddy, who will come and go and who can leave you in the mire. You may have a season or two when you over-achieve thanks to a good manager or crop of players but in the end you will find your level and there is nothing wrong with that, as long as you appreciate your team, enjoy the good times and keep perspective through the bad, savouring the experience of football at a decent level along the way.

Some fans need to get real. A lot of clubs are only going to have one good year in four but instead of recognising that and enjoying it, some supporters think over-achieving should be the norm and they then get angry if it isn't repeated.

We should always take into account the circumstances of clubs. It is all very well, for example, to say that West Brom were the best footballing side in the Championship in 2007/08, but just look at their budget. In my view, my old team-mate at Leicester City, Simon Grayson, did the best management job in that division because, having got Blackpool up on limited funds, he kept them there and made them very competitive. It earned him the job at his home-town club Leeds United, where he began to restore their reputation and to get them promoted from League Two.

I remember driving home from a match once, for example, and hearing Yeovil fans talking on the radio about their manager Gary Johnson – a man I rate and who had been John Beck's assistant at Cambridge United. The Somerset club were going through a patchy spell at the time and the fans were saying that he had taken them as far as he could.

Now, Gary had got them up from the Conference before they were promoted again through League Two, and he had just turned down the Derby County job to stay at Huish Park. I was thinking that if he was listening to this, he must be regretting his decision. Very soon after that, he took the Bristol City job. He could see which way the wind was blowing. Yeovil were lucky to have had him, but some fans had turned and although Russell Slade took them on to a playoff final, you sensed that League One was an over-achievement for such a club, and Gary knew it too. They should have been grateful to him.

I have never been one of those to talk about what the game was like, how it was better in my day, or to pit generation against generation. It is just as difficult to become a professional foot-baller nowadays, even if scouting networks are wider meaning that anyone with talent is going to get pick up very young, rather than being missed until later.

I still think this is my day, anyway. And if you are to retain your enthusiasm for it, you have to stay modern and keep up with trends. I have, though, seen plenty in my 25-year playing career

– and there aren't too many around who have played for that long. By and large, I believe the game has changed for the better in so many ways.

For a start, because attacking play has been encouraged more over the past 15-odd years due to things like cutting out the tackle from behind, there are more players who can play, but I do believe there is too much money going to some very ordinary players in the Premier League. Too many are getting £50,000 a week for sitting in the stand. It's almost as if they are saying, "Thanks very much, you can't hurt me, I've got a contract and I'll pick up my money without even playing."

I never begrudge the top players earning the big money, but it should be more incentive-based. I think there should be a salary cap of £20,000 a player and after that a club is free to award – and a player and/or his agent free to negotiate – win bonuses, appearance money, merchandising and the rest. That way, players will be busting a gut to get out there and play to boost their income.

You'll never take away the drive of the top players at every level, and that applies from Weymouth to Manchester United. You admire them for it. I particularly like Steven Gerrard because of the way he plays the game, with drive, determination and his heart on his sleeve.

But I also believe there are some who are cheating the system, who don't go the extra yard. Too many kids who haven't done enough in the game are getting too much. If you made it, say, £25,000 an appearance and £20,000 a win, you might see more determination from players. And if they don't get in the side and aren't earning enough, they might then take a move to a lower club and play every week rather than just pick up money for doing nothing.

The game now is definitely quicker than it used to be and, thank goodness, forwards are getting better protection. Occasionally I do some after-dinner speaking, which I enjoy, and was doing a function with Ron Harris, old "Chopper", the Chelsea defender of the 1960s and '70s, and he told me that managers used to tell him to take certain opposing players out of the game. It doesn't happen now, fortunately. How forwards survived in Chopper's day I don't know.

In recent times, you may have had Sir Alex Ferguson claiming that Cristiano Ronaldo was being targeted and getting tackled badly, but he was a lot better protected in English football than George Best ever was, and quite rightly so. That was more about Fergie getting into referees ahead of games than a genuine fear that Ronaldo would go to Real Madrid. That move became about the timing and money – all £80 million of it – being right, not because he would get kicked less in Spain. They are just more subtle, less open, about it over there and in Italy.

People always used to think I invited a kicking by just using cut-off shin pads on the lower leg and baring the rest of my shin. To them it seemed like a red rag to a bull to defenders. You can point to the horrific broken leg Eduardo suffered at Birmingham after being tackled by Martin Taylor and say that players should wear protection, but how is a shinpad going to stop that? It didn't for Eduardo, did it?

I like to think that I was clever and knew how to avoid the worst. Most of the time, I was getting kicked from behind, not the front. And I also knew who was likely to kick me and who wasn't, so took the necessary action. I was always willing to take a whack in or around the box, anyway, if we got a penalty or free-kick.

On top of that, I was very good at not going in for a 50-50 ball. Steve Guppy always used to wonder why fans gave him such stick for not tackling flat out – they would shout "Guppy you coward" – but I could get away with it. I told him about the art of making a 50-50 look like a 70-30 against you by seeing something before it happened and getting there a little bit later. It is not that you pull out of tackles; you are just covering up the fact that you can't tackle. I don't think he ever got the hang of it.

As for the way I looked on the pitch, it was all a matter of feeling comfortable. It was the same with the variety of old boots I used to mix and match. Different ones felt better at different games. I liked my shirt out and my socks down because it was how I grew up and how I felt comfortable. I don't recommend it to kids today, especially with cut-off shinpads, but I do recommend that they should be themselves and true to their personalities.

But back to the game today. Of course, pitches and facilities are so much better now, thanks to all-seater stadia. That is one big benefit of all the money that has come into the game. One thing I can't be having, though, is the call for technology to be used on decisions.

There has been a clamour, in fact, for the use of goalline technology to determine whether a ball has crossed the line or not. It should not, some people say, be left to the eye of a linesman – and I'm afraid I still struggle to call them assistant referees.

But tell me this: if I time my run, get across my marker, meet a cross and head it home, only to have it ruled offside wrongly, how is that error by a linesman any different? Or a dead-cert penalty being turned down? Those are mistakes, too, and if you are going to use technology to address one area, you have to use it for all and that is impractical. The game is spontaneous and to stop it too often would be to lose its appeal.

As would taking human error out of the game. Most goals come from mistakes. That's the whole point about football. It encompasses human talent, but also human frailty. And cup football differs from league football. Knockout competitions should be decided by vagaries; that is what makes them so exciting. But no league is ever going to be determined by one mistake or one decision.

One big drawback of the English game these days, so many people are saying, is the amount of overseas players in the Premier League damaging the national team's prospects. I don't believe it. We used to have plenty of English players in the 1970s for example, and a lot of Scots, Irish and Welsh around the place, but we didn't have great England teams then, did we? We didn't even qualify for the World Cups of 1974 and '78.

I would hate it if we tried to limit overseas players in the Premier League but I can see a case for restrictions being brought in at youth team level. It is a free European market and there should be free movement these days. Our kids just have to learn the dedication needed to compete with them, and our coaching has to get better. Now they have decided to go ahead with it, the Football Association should now put plenty of effort into the national centre at Burton to improve our whole developmental system – one that has fallen so far behind over the last decade.

We should still be able to produce an elite squad of 23 players who are competitive at the highest level, who can qualify for European Championships and World Cups and who can do well when they get there. This thing about there not being the depth of talent now is a red herring. There are still enough players of the highest quality.

We actually, in my opinion, have the best England squad in my memory and have done through the Sven-Goran Eriksson, Steve McClaren and now Fabio Capello eras. It is just that our players have received some poor coaching and management and the team has not been set up properly.

Would we, for example, say the Greece side that won Euro 2004 was better than England, or even the Italy side that won the last World Cup? Would you pick any of the Greeks ahead of any of the English or Luca Toni ahead of Wayne Rooney? It is just that Greece and Italy came together better as teams under their respective managers – Otto Rehhagel and Marcello Lippi – at those times and that is what we have been lacking.

And if it was just about the quality of players, with the management of them less important, how come Israel can end up with the same number of points as England in their ill-fated Euro 2008 qualifying campaign?

Like the rest of the nation, I was hoping that Capello could finally make them live up to their potential at the World Cup finals in South Africa before it was too late for this generation. He did have a good qualifying campaign, apart from that defeat in Ukraine, after an iffy start in friendlies, but I still worried about him making the team better in really big games.

The main problem is that we are not producing coaches and managers in this country and it is a shame that we can't see an Englishman getting a big club in the next few years. But Rafael Benitez struggled for a long time to get close to winning the Premier League for Liverpool. So why go for another foreigner? If not how is any Englishman ever going to get the CV Capello has got?

That is not to say I didn't want an Italian, even if I have had a bit of a problem with them ever since I got chased as a teenaged Liverpool fan at the European Cup final of 1984 against Roma in Rome. I just wanted the best man for the job.

Personally, my ideal formation is 4-4-2 with wide players who work hard up and down the pitch. For me, width is vital to a team, even if you see Arsenal and Brazil not always having it. Technically gifted as they are, they don't always succeed do they?

You also need two central midfield players who can cope and who are industrious. I don't think it matters if one is a stayer or an attacker. That's why I think Gerrard and Frank Lampard can play together. If you have good players working hard, everything takes care of itself.

Of course you need to be flexible and I have used 3-5-2 to good effect in the past if the squad at your disposal calls for it. You still need to maintain the basic rules, which to me are putting square pegs in square holes – that is, players playing in their right positions, rather than just being accommodated – and retain width and balance. I can't stress enough the need for hard work, though, at any level. Fans are often looking at what players are doing with the ball. I, and most professionals, are looking at players to see what they do when called on to defend.

Systems should simply be about getting 11 players in their right positions or as many as you can. The system should complement players, not the other way around. I like players who can affect the result, who are effective with the ball and without it. The team has to carry a serious goal threat or else it will lack belief. If you don't have that threat, you won't believe you will win.

I do think my strength is in looking at the overall picture of a team or a game. In other words, I am more of a manager than a coach, though I can lay on a session and have been through all my badges over the past four-and-a-half years, starting at Level One, which I did at Newbury army barracks. To be honest, it was a bit like Gordon Ramsay going on a course to learn how to do beans on toast.

A lot of the fortnight course was about subjects like child protection and first aid, which are all necessary for the sort of people who were on the course from all sorts of jobs and who were basically in charge of amateur age-group teams. Some of them were so overweight they couldn't even take part in the physical sessions. Pros should be able to start higher than this.

Then there was week-long Level Two, which is also the UEFA B licence, which I did at Cheltenham. There was so much course work and folders and writing that I almost lost the will to live.

After that was the A licence, which I did at the old Lilleshall national sports centre in Shropshire, it being a fortnight's residential course that cost me a fortune out of my own pocket. After my earlier experiences I thought it would be purgatory, but I actually enjoyed it, even though I was the only bloke who managed to find a maggot in his food.

This was more like the proper stuff. There were a lot of ex-pros on the course, including Roy Keane, Gareth Southgate and Martin Keown, and it was fascinating sitting down to talk with them. Not that there was all that much time for that. You were working from 9am till 9pm. None of them was stand-offish and all were willing to share their experiences in the pro game. It is one thing that makes football people. They love to talk about the game and swap views on formations and comparing and contrasting Manchester United, Arsenal and Chelsea; Ferguson,

Wenger and Mourinho. It was fascinating, even if we were knackered after such long days.

A lot of the work was still quite basic, though some who were not ex-pros still struggled. For example, the tutor would ask you when in the build-up to a game you would work on patterns of play and when you would work on free-kicks and set-pieces. The answer seemed too simple to me – pattern of play on a Thursday, set-pieces on a Friday – but, not surprisingly, the ones who had not been in the pro game got a bit left behind.

Despite all that, I do believe that every pro who wants to be a coach or manager should have to do these qualifications. I have had well-known ex-Leicester players on to me, for example, during recent times when Milan Mandaric has been freeing up the manager's job there regularly to ask if I think they should go for it. I ask them whether they have got the qualifications and they don't even think they need them.

There was controversy when Gareth Southgate was given Premier League dispensation to do the Middlesbrough job, but I don't have a problem with that. As long as a manager is working towards his qualifications, then he should be given time to get them. I still believe force of personality counts for a lot in management, but part of that personality is being able to stick at these qualifications. It's the same if you are a player. You may have the basic skills and aptitude, but you still need to learn your trade and the game.

So many people dropped out of the Lilleshall course because they couldn't hack it. I was proud to have seen it through – and, hopefully, I am on course to receive my Pro Licence – even though I have been very busy these past few years, not just with playing and managing but also with all the media work.

I think one of the problems these days is that too few ex-players want to put in all that effort – or put their heads above the parapet and take management jobs, even if they are willing to go through all the hassle of getting their coaching qualifications.

At the top level, they have made enough money never to have

to work again and it is only the really driven ones, like Roy Keane, Tony Adams and maybe Alan Shearer, who seem to be willing to go for it, though there seem to be a few who fancy it for a while but for the wrong reason – that the money is good these days, with the top managers finally getting near to what the top players get. It is a bit like the old dotcom boom, with people making a pile before getting out.

Also, there are those who have made decent livings and who can get jobs as youth-team coaches that pay well. They don't want the hassle that comes with being in the spotlight. Personally, I like it. It's the buzz that makes life worth living. Football ensures that you don't live a boring, staid existence and you have to take the criticism. In fact, I can thrive on it and can also give as good as I get.

The spotlight is certainly on football like never before. There has been a huge media explosion in the game these past 20 years and that is good for someone like me, who now makes a living from it. But I detect more unhappiness in the game than there was 20 years ago. People were more genuine then, I believe. Now there is a lot of superficial glamour about the game, all caused by more people being involved on the periphery who are trying to make money out of it because, let's face it, there is plenty to be made.

I do think the game was easier to love when I started out and there wasn't so much pressure. Everything now can bring you down if you let it. In this fast-food, multi-channel, video-game culture, people have shorter attention spans and, if things don't go well, even if only for a few games, they want change more quickly. It can be unforgiving with all the press comment, phone-ins and message boards. I know the latter have particularly upset some managers, because people can get away with making outrageous claims anonymously. I don't even look at them.

Some people may say that as a media critic I am part of it. But I never make things personal, even if I have history with certain figures, and instead merely give a professional opinion and one that is honest. I think players and managers are all right with that.

I know I was. I do think at times, though, too much stuff about people's personal lives is plastered about, along with personal comments that have little relevance to their ability to do their job. And I don't think that, just because people are being paid good money, it should mean they have to take all the rubbish. I always try to judge as I find, because there is so much phoney gossip in the game. I should know. I have been a victim of it.

Footballers are role models, yes, but only to a certain extent. Off the field, it annoys me when people say that as sporting heroes, footballers are responsible for kids' behaviour. That job, quite simply, is for parents. Your mum and dad should be your heroes, with respect also for teachers, and it is up to them to set the example and to teach right and wrong. Look at all the violent video games out there and the pitfalls of the Internet. Footballers aren't responsible for allowing kids access to all of that.

I would agree that footballers have a big responsibility on the field to lead by example. It should come from the way they conduct themselves on the pitch – with respect, yes, to referees and to their fellow professionals – and around their communities. But it is a passionate game and in the heat of battle there are going to be excesses on the field, whether in tackling or things that are said and that has to be accepted. As for off the field, some young men are going to get into situations they shouldn't. They do in other walks of life after all, and footballers should be cut some slack. They are only human beings.

I had my own tribulations when I found myself in Coventry Crown Court in the Spring of 2008 on a charge of dangerous driving and the whole affair really put the wind up me as, shockingly, I came close to going to jail.

The case went back to December 2006 when I was driving back from Blackpool having scouted a player for my column in the *Guardian*. As I was coming round the M42 near Solihull, I suddenly got the urge to go to the toilet so pulled into a middle lane, then to an inside one ready to get off the motorway at the first chance.

The next thing I know, I have got flashing lights in my rear-view mirror, so I pull on to the hard shoulder. I get out of the car and a traffic policeman is getting out of his unmarked police car, the driver staying where he is, and coming towards me. I ask if I can disappear down an embankment to have a pee and after first turning me down he eventually agrees.

After that, I get into their car, where one of them recognises me and the other doesn't. It is all reasonably good-natured, but the upshot is that they consider I was driving dangerously and that I would be hearing from them in due course.

When I received the summons, I could barely believe the detail of their statements. It said that I had come up behind them at over 100 miles an hour in the outside lane, that I had undertaken them and three other cars, then tried to get back in the outside lane before dodging into the inside lane, at which point they pulled me over.

Furthermore, the statement added that it was dark and the motorway was wet due to rain. On top of all that, I am supposed to have said, "Don't you know who I am?"

Now this all took me aback. I was driving a Peugeot 307 1.8 litre, which would have had trouble doing 100 mph. My recollection is of driving at around 75 mph, undertaking at most two cars when those in the outside lane wouldn't pull over before getting into an inside lane ready to get off at the next exit. Neither, as I recall, was it wet nor dark, since the M42 around junctions three and four are all lit up. As for using that old "Don't you know who I am" phrase, it is simply not me.

I couldn't let it go and had to contest it, although I would come to wish that I hadn't.

When it finally came to court 17 months later, I quickly became disappointed in my barrister as he seemed unprepared and did not challenge the statements of the two police officers as I would have wished. It became my word against theirs, with me believing that they had been mistaken. It was a concern of mine, for example, that the camera on their dashboard that records incidents had run out of film just before the incident.

In the end, after a two-day trial, the jury were going to go with the two policemen and I was found guilty of dangerous driving. Judge Peter Carr summoned me back to Birmingham Crown Court a month later for sentencing and made it plain that I could be facing a custodial sentence, despite there not being an accident and despite the fact that nobody was injured. My heart almost stopped. It was one of the worst moments of my life. He was taking into account the nine points on my licence, though I drove 50,000 miles a year and was pleased that I had not had any points for around 18 months.

It took the best efforts of my solicitor Steve Nelson to direct the judge towards the character references of a couple of friends and two charities for whom I worked before he relented. In the end, I was given a six-month jail sentence suspended for two years, a one-year driving ban, costs against me of £1,645 and 150 hours of community service. That involved me cutting grass and gardening near my home. I had thought they might have been a bit more inventive and got me to do some coaching in schools as a more constructive payback, but transport for me was a problem to organise, apparently.

In the end, it was a relief that I didn't go to jail, and I managed to hold on to my work with the BBC when I could have lost it had I gone inside, but I still wonder how it got to that stage. It wasn't my best piece of driving, but I didn't think it was so serious that it could have warranted jail. Still, I accepted my punishment and got on with the community service.

And I get on with life outside the game for the moment. Now that I am no longer a player – always open to offers, mind, and always will be – I get the best out of working in the media and am fortunate that there has been an explosion of outlets that offer work to ex-professionals who used to have to set up sports shops or keep pubs. I have to admit, though, that while I get a kick out of my new career, it can never really take me to the levels of excitement that football did. There is no limit to that. There might be real depths but there are also big highs.

But it is all part of a life beyond all the boot camps I have been at. It is all about change and progress. And there has been plenty of both.

6.3 Changing Man

I gambled, I have to admit, and I did get into some scrapes here and there. Some, shall we say, unusual situations also seemed to befall me. To be honest, I regret a lot of it, but you can't go back. What was done, was done. I am just a bit sad that people still seem to think I am something I am not and that they remember things about me from 20 years ago while other people's misdemeanours are forgotten within a couple of weeks.

Perception seems to count for a lot in the game and this image of scattiness and unreliability has dogged me for a while now. To be honest, I think a lot of people are a bit disappointed when they meet me. By the look on their face and their body language, I think they were expecting someone a bit more outrageous.

I have always thought of myself as a lovable rogue, nothing more. I've never stitched anyone up or done anything nasty. I'm just quick to see an opportunity, either to help people or do a deal with them. I've just grown up.

I think part of the reason I got the reputation I did was because I owned up to the gambling. It was not so much that it was out of control or that I was losing more than I could afford, but at times it did preoccupy my mind a lot of the time and meant that I didn't turn up for training as early as I do now for the commitments I have in my life, be they work or personal.

I contributed to my own image at times, I suppose. I always

used to joke about the gambling, for example, even though it caused me a lot of pain at times. And I did have a serious habit once upon a time and lost plenty. I used to think that I needed to bet to have some spark in my life. It took my mind off a lot of things. And some of the stories around me started to develop a life of their own.

I was once down at Cardiff for one of the playoff finals and was reading an article in the programme about me by the Sky presenter George Gavin. Apparently I once told him that I sold a two-bedroomed house in Luton and put the proceeds on a horse at Cheltenham. I was annoyed with George for telling the tale, and sought him out to tell him so. It wasn't a two-bed terrace I told him, it was a three-bed semi.

Luckily the horse won, but it had caused me untold worry. I had backed the horse ante-post and it had bled from the nose on the morning of the race, meaning there was a doubt about whether it would run and, therefore, a chance I could lose my stake. Fortunately it recovered. That's the sort of thing I am talking about – both me joking about it and the anxiety it all caused me.

It became a millstone for a while, something that was bearable for certain periods and overwhelming at others. I would go into a betting shop, or place a bet over the phone, certain that I was going to win, but then I started to get to the stage where I was hoping my bet would lose, because then it would be easier to give it up. Winning just keeps you going.

If certain accounts were too much in the red, I would just open new ones and shuffle the money around in the hope that things might change. It took me a while to realise that although you might be stopping the activity, you are not stopping the opportunity. It is always going to be there.

There has been a lot of publicity about players and managers betting huge sums of money, and some of it does sound obscene but, to be honest, it can be easily done. I once asked a bookmaker at the end of a day how much business I had done. He told me it totalled a staggering £554,000 with everything staked, won and lost.

Now that seems an astonishing sum, I have to admit, but it's all just paper figures these days – or numbers on a computer screen – because so many footballers bet over the phone or on the Internet to retain their anonymity. In fact, I had gone in the shop with "only" around £25,000, but when you are making plenty of bets – winning £60,000 on one race, maybe losing £50,000 on the next – it all adds up on a balance sheet.

At the height of my gambling, for example, I remember getting a phone call from the bloke at Ladbroke's who was looking after my account.

"Do you want the good news or the bad?" he asked.

"Go on," I said with some trepidation.

"Well, totalling up all your bets, this past year you have won 11.7 million quid."

I was wondering why I was so poor when he told me. "Unfortunately you have lost £12.5 million." I was £800,000 down.

Against all that, I remember winning £90,000 one day and went out and bought three cars. I knew that if I didn't spend it, I would just give it back to the bookmaker the next day. And so I got a car for Mandy, a runabout for myself and an expensive one for longer journeys.

Most bookies I know, by the way, don't mind you winning now and then and are happy to pay out. If you lose too much, after all, you knock it on the head and they don't want that. They don't mind losing to win. They want a steady flow. It is only when or if you start taking them for tens of thousands that they put the block on it. That doesn't happen too often, mind. You might have a good day or a good week, but you're not going to have a good month or a good year.

It's the old saying, isn't it? For every payout window in a bookmaker's shop, there are three taking money. The other thing that bookies who are losing might do is leak details to the press of a player's gambling habits, which means that he will settle his debts – if he can – rather than have to put up with the ongoing publicity.

Gambling stopped being a problem for me on Derby day, 4 June 2005. I had been going through a painful time, having just finished at Wycombe after an unsettling period and in that time before I got the Millwall job for those 36 days. Then aged 39, I was starting to think about my future, particularly because it was becoming less easy to find clubs.

I went into a bookies to put a bet on a horse I fancied at Epsom that day, but thought about it and just watched the race instead. The horse got beaten. Had it won, I might have kept gambling. Instead, I thanked my lucky stars and got out – both literally on the day, and for the future.

The day was no different from any other. I wasn't feeling better or worse than on any similar occasion. Everything just came together. There was more to life, and more important things in life, I decided. I had just had enough of the madness. The struggle was over and it all came as a huge relief. I gambled for a while longer, just occasionally, but these days I have cut it out completely.

With age comes a bit of wisdom and I look back and can understand some of my behaviour so I know how to change it. In fact I went for a couple of day visits to Tony Adams's addiction clinic, Sporting Chance, at Liphook in Hampshire, and met with Peter Kay, the chief executive. He was very good on how to recognise the signs and feelings that trigger you wanting to have a bet, and how to manage those feelings and cope without the gambling in your life.

When I went to China to do that reality show, for example, I had no trouble keeping away from gambling, even though it is a betting-crazy country. It is supposed to be illegal to gamble there and, of course, there are no High Street bookmakers, but betting takes place everywhere, on mahjong, cards, anything. In fact, it was nice to be the only one not gambling for a change.

Horse racing, rather than football, was more of a problem for me really. I still like going to the Cheltenham Festival for the atmosphere with a group of mates, but now it's just about the fun rather than looking to make money as it used to be.

When it comes to football, I know more about that but, even so, I have stopped gambling on it. A while back, for example, I had a bet on East Fife to win the Scottish Second Division because I was working with Lee Dixon at the BBC in pre-season and he had a mate up there who thought they would walk it. I backed them at 11/4 and thought I was quids in when they were 12 points clear. They blew it, though. The next season they started at 5/2, but I wasn't going to get burned again. They romped the league this time. The same happened with West Bromwich Albion. I backed them to win the Championship the year before they did.

That's me: a really bad gambler. But then again, I don't know any such thing as a good one. I always think that if a manager is in a really bad run, he should finance me to have a bet on them to lose and they will win. If some rich owner wants to bankroll me and pay me a commission, I will bet on their side to get relegated next season and then they will win the title.

I think I realised that, if I wasn't careful, gambling could turn into a fully blown addiction that would take me over when I packed up playing. When I was at clubs, nothing came above playing, which is why, although I got through a lot of money, it never took me over or overwhelmed me because football always came first.

Also, these days, I have come to realise the value of money. When I was playing and earning well as a younger man, it could be easy come, easy go sometimes. Now I really have to work hard for it all, doing long hours around the country, and I don't want to squander it.

Besides, I am a father now and that certainly changes your priorities and your outlook on life as every parent will tell you. Mandy and I did have to endure some sadness first when she had a miscarriage back in 2006. It came five days after a car pulled out abruptly when we were on the M3 and sandwiched us between his and another car. She was very shaken.

This time, thankfully, the only problem came on the night she went into labour. She was very considerate, having waited until after the football results on a Saturday and for my shift at Setanta to finish, but did interrupt my trip up to Leicester for a friend's 40th birthday party. I dashed back down to Portsmouth and, after a false start, I took her to Winchester Hospital where she gave birth to lovely little Grace Elizabeth at noon on Sunday, 27 January 2008. I was present through the night for the whole experience and wouldn't have missed a second.

Now, I have become a ga-ga dad and, given that I am away a lot watching football during the evenings – which means I am an expert on daytime TV like *Cash in the Attic*, but know nothing about *Coronation Street* – I am happy to be the one that does the getting up during the nights. Looking back, I wish we had had children sooner, but then again I have moved around so much as a player with Mandy preferring to stay in Portsmouth that it would have been difficult.

My life changed with Grace's birth, and according to everyone else, so did I. She gave me a new focus. Before, I had had a void that could only be filled by playing football or, to a smaller extent, gambling. All of a sudden, I had a purpose and a responsibility I had been looking for.

As all the promotion and relegation issues were being fought over that spring of 2008, for instance, I thought for a little while that I might like to play again but then I realised just how difficult that might be, what with a baby and my TV and radio work. How was I going to train with a club, let alone play?

It was probably the last knockings of the grieving process I went through as my playing career wound down. That may sound strange, and it may be difficult for some to grasp that footballers can have such feelings, but it is a sensitive subject for many players and one that rarely gets addressed.

In cricket, we have heard about some players who even commit suicide after such a big part of their lives is over, but in football it is barely spoken about, probably because people don't think footballers are that sensitive. Believe you me, though, it can be very acute.

I think, looking back, I was going through it for those two years following my Millwall managerial experience when I bobbed from club to club, never getting the chance to settle again. I was in denial about how fearful I was that I was coming to the end, because I was still fit and driving myself hard and still had the competitor's will to win. The denial was because it was too painful to admit to.

Players are gripped by a massive fear when they realise that what has been their very reason for being – and all the camaraderie of the dressing room – is now coming to an end, leaving them potentially lonely and with time on their hands, and it came to me. I have been one of the lucky ones, though, who has managed to find another career. It has been nowhere near the nightmare that it could have been.

You can almost discern three groups of players when they retire, by the way. There are those who have made their money and who have given themselves the chance to make choices in their lives. Then there is a group who were not good enough to make the big sums and who have to do something else. And then there is a minority who have wasted their money and got themselves into trouble, like Paul Gascoigne. That is sad.

As my career wound down, my own sadness came in the realisation that life was never quite going to hit the same heights it had when I was in the Premier League with Leicester or winning Player of the Year twice at Portsmouth or promotion with Millwall.

It may well have coloured my attitude and contributed to the unhappiness I felt at certain clubs later and with the managers there. Not that I didn't believe I knew more or couldn't have done a better job than some of them.

A natural loss of innocence occurs with professional players and it does me good these days to go and do presentations to kids at tournaments and coaching courses. I love to see them enjoying the game and I tell them expressly to do that.

In a way, it is good that it has been so hard to let go. It means I believed it was worth having so much. And while I might fancy idly that I could still play in the Championship, or even Liverpool, might even believe that I could do well lower down for a club, there does come a time to let go, a time when I have to accept it is probably over.

I might play the odd testimonial if someone I like and respect asks me, but I could never just have a kickabout for fun, in five-a-side or on Sunday mornings. Playing as many games as I have, and being as competitive as I was, I would just find it too frustrating.

There has been another area of my life where I have let go, too. After *Tales from the Boot Camps* first came out, in which I told how I was adopted as a kid, my blood mother contacted me. She now lives on the Isle of Wight and I duly met up with her. She was a very nice lady.

But after giving it a lot of thought, that was it as far as I was concerned. I did not really want to meet her again, nor my blood brothers and sisters, because my real parents are Anne and Alan Claridge and my sister is Ruth. They brought me up and looked after me. I wanted for nothing and never missed out on anything.

I did not want to maintain a contact that might become complicated and painful for all concerned and I certainly did not want to risk hurting the people closest to me, especially my mum, Anne, who will always be my first lady. I think my blood mother also realised it could be tricky and was just happy to have met me.

Some other things never change, though. I still like to work as much as I can around football to keep my brain and body active. When I first got offered media work, I never turned anything down for fear that they might not ask me again. Now I am a bit more confident about getting work, but still do as much as I can.

I like to live life to the full to keep busy and I don't like sitting around doing nothing for too long.

I still eat fruit all day long, and prefer simple food with no sauces and as many vegetables as can be fitted on the plate, with more in reserve. My weight stays between 12 and 12-and-a-half stone. I no longer take a pill to control my irregular heartbeat since I gave up football, as it was nerves and adrenalin before games that also contributed to that, but I still have to take Thyroxin for an underactive thyroid gland that accompanies the condition.

I don't really have any hobbies, since football has been both my job and my hobby. I play the odd game of golf, though don't really have the patience for 18 holes, and I like a game of tennis now and then in the summer. I am still obsessive about running and go to the gym three or four times a week. I was talking about keeping fit with Tony Cottee recently and he said he has not done a day since he packed in playing. He looked happy enough.

Otherwise – and I never really liked to admit this because it might have attracted a lot of grief in the dressing room – I like to visit gardens and country houses like Beaulieu and Broadlands with Mandy or holiday beauty spots like Cheddar Gorge. I really enjoy a nice, simple day out. I've never been one for the pub, so having Grace won't really cramp my style. In fact, it will be nice taking her to these places.

And these days I won't run the risk of the embarrassment I once suffered at Cheddar. It was a summer years ago and I had just been on a lads' end-of-season holiday to Magalluf when I was with Cambridge United. I didn't think that Mandy would approve, so I told her we were going to Scotland.

Anyway, I was drinking very late one night out there with a bloke I met and that day at Cheddar, as coincidence would have it, he happened to be there with his wife at the entrance to the caves. I was trying to avoid him and not to make eye contact, but he spotted me. He reminded me of the late-night drinking and the laddish behaviour in Magalluf and Mandy was furious. I was gesturing, trying to get him to shut up, but he wouldn't. In the end, I just had to admit to Mandy where I had been, but the deed had been done, hadn't it?

Not that my days out in the country should give the impression that I am mellowing. In fact I think I am getting angrier and quite fancy a slot on that *Grumpy Old Men* show on television. I don't let anyone take liberties with me now and I challenge perceptions of me. I am as quick as anyone mentally and if they want to take me on they had better be careful.

For example, I was covering a Carling Cup tie between Chelsea and Leicester City at Stamford Bridge when in the press room I met Bill Anderson, who has been covering City for the *Leicester Mercury* since time immemorial, and he asked me what I was up to now.

I told him I was doing my UEFA A Coaching Licence and he came out with some smart-arsed remark about them handing them out to anyone these days. I felt patronised, as if he still thought I was just some dumb footballer who had passed briefly through Filbert Street. I made it clear to him that I was a different person to the one he thought he knew back in those days.

People always think I am a scruffy sod, as well. It comes from how I looked on the field, with one sock down and shirt out. I did that first to be comfortable and if the by-product was that defenders would underestimate me or think I was some kind of joke, then all well and good.

I have lost count of the number of times people say to me, "First time you have worn a suit and tie?" Actually they are the ones who usually don't dress well. I may like to hang around the house in one of the many tracksuits I have accumulated from clubs down the years, but I have always spent money on clothes and have always dressed smartly when I am out and about.

In fact, I get fed up with some of these myths about me and where once I might just have smiled and let them pass me by, now I try to nail them.

Someone in TV, for instance, once came up to me and said they had heard I had had a good night at the Setanta launch party. I asked them what they were talking about. Apparently I was dancing on the tables and was the night's karaoke king. In reality, I was at the party, but didn't drink and left early. I seem to have had this unbelievable life and one I know nothing about. Mind you, the one I have had has been lively and interesting enough. It is just that for every story about me that is true, there are ten that aren't.

All I can do is keep networking, meeting people and trying to change such preconceptions. As with a sporting dinner I did at Millwall when invited back by Jeff Burnige, with whom I am still in touch. I may have been unhappy with how Jeff left me out on a limb at the club, but I have always found him a good man and I wanted to go back to the New Den and hold my head up high, even though I had applied indirectly for the job again another time afterwards and not got it. I wanted to meet the chief executive Heather Rabbatts so she could see at first hand just how the reality stacked up against the myth. I think, and hope, she was a little surprised.

It was really interesting taking questions from the audience at the dinner. I had told them they could ask anything – about the gambling, about my 36 days at the club. But they were very respectful and even protective. It was like they knew I was one of their favourite sons and they only wanted to remember the good times and not hurt me with any of the bad. In return, I didn't want to come across as bitter and twisted. I just wanted to give them a quick understanding and move on.

They say management careers always end badly and ultimately in failure and that can be true. Managers can fall out with the club hierarchy, they can fall out with fans. But you get over things and bounce back. I still cared about the club and the fans still had a soft spot for me, as was shown that night.

They asked me if I would ever come back. I told them that I *will* be back. The manager Kenny Jackett was in the room and I said that he would do a good job for them, but that sometime in the future I would be back.

It is not that I have unfinished business with Millwall more than anywhere else. I just feel that I have unfinished business, full stop. Often when you ask ex-pros if they want to get back into the game, they will quickly say no because of the intensity of it these days. I have no such qualms. I love that intensity.

And I would dearly love for some enlightened chairman or owner out there to see past the shallow views of me; for one who doesn't buy into the gossip and bullshit to give me a proper interview for a management job. I am convinced I would do a great job for a good club.

I did get interviews at Peterborough and Oxford United when jobs came up there, and I was grateful for the chance to put across my ideas and personality but, at the time, the positions and timing weren't right for me or them.

Sometimes it doesn't make sense. I see some people in jobs who I knew when they were playing and who did not show anything like the same dedication to the game that I had always shown and who did not always give 100 per cent like I did. I must have had some talent, and worked hard and shown stickability, to have played more than 1,000 games, mustn't I?

There are also people working who have far more colourful and controversial pasts and backgrounds than I do. Certain things seem to be held against me, but I am someone with a real will to win and someone who never gives up, which means that I will keep plugging away and will get back into the game when the time is meant to be.

I think people will see a different me if and/or when that happens. I think, in fact, I may have become everything I once thought was mundane and boring. My most important goal in life is to make sure my family are provided for and my first thought is not for myself but them and their welfare.

If you ask me to describe myself now, I would say – and I never thought I would – that I am ordinary. And do you know what? I quite like it.

As I see it, football is the best career imaginable and being fully involved in this game in one capacity or another is the only life for me. Maddening at times it may have been, but more often it has been magical. And, as far as I am concerned, it is a long way from finished.

Postscript

Never go back, they say. I went back. And, as with many of the bad decisions I have made in my career, I blame Ian Ridley. To be fair, though, this one wasn't quite as bad as I thought it might be and I even ended up pleased, for a change, that I had agreed to one of his schemes.

Ian had also defied the 'never go back' advice by being persuaded to take over as chairman at Weymouth again towards the end of the 2008/9 season. He found the club in a terrible mess, the biggest the club had ever been in and way beyond what we had both encountered in our previous time there. After Martyn Harrison had departed as chairman, he handed the club on to a Bournemouth music promoter called Mel Bush, who lasted only a few months before selling out to a property developer by the name of Malcolm Curtis.

Curtis would later depart the club as it all started to turn sour, after setting up a company that bought the land around the stadium for £500,000 – the fans saying that it was too cheap – with the money going towards paying off debts, as he left the running of the club to chief executive Gary Calder. Still they mounted, though.

Many people will remember the 9-0 home thrashing against Rushden and Diamonds with a team of kids who were pressed into service due to the first-team squad not being paid and then not being insured to play, the monthly payment to the insurers having lapsed. Those were among the least of the club's debts, which totalled around £500,000, with £200,000 owed to Curtis, £150,000 to the taxman and the rest due to various creditors such as a coach company, the groundsman, programme printers and kit suppliers.

Anyway, when Curtis had had enough of it all and walked away, two local businessmen, Paul Cocks and Shaun Hennessey, took it off his hands and rang up Ian to head up a consortium. Ian then brought Dave Higson, an old stalwart of the club when his engineering company were the main sponsors, in as his vice-chairman, and it should have been a good local board. They could not stop the club being relegated from the Conference down to the Southern section, though, even though they brought in Bobby Gould, the old Wimbledon and Wales manager, to spice things up.

Over the summer, they restructured the club and brought in a young ex-Weymouth player in Matty Hale as manager, with Ian Hutchinson, who had been at the club and done well for me when I was manager before, as his assistant. But they only had a shoestring budget. All the money was going out to pay off the ex-players and other football debts.

Ian rang me after another bad early season defeat and told me that the club were about a week away from administration. They had appealed to local businesses to help raise £50,000 in return for sponsorship packages but the take-up was slow. He asked if I would consider coming out of retirement to help on two fronts: to add a bit of experience to a young side short on confidence; to get a bit of buzz and profile back into the club to help raise revenue.

I had been fancying playing again and was getting twitchy, I must admit. My media career was doing well enough, though I had lost some work with the *Guardian* and Setanta, but I always said that it would never quite satisfy me in the way that being in the game had. For now, I was just trying to accumulate some money through the media work to build up some funds and to spend more time with Mandy and baby Grace until I was ready to try and get a manager's job again.

But while I fancied another game, coming back to Weymouth did not appeal to me after the way I had been sacked then been treated by a section of the crowd when I went back to cover that FA Cup tie against Nottingham Forest for TV. It didn't appeal to me much either when Ian told me that the club had no money to pay me if I did play.

He kept on at me, though. He can be persistent like that. In fact, he wore me down, and to shut him up I agreed. And so I found myself one Thursday night driving up to Bath University to train with the team, then meeting up with Ian on a September Saturday at Rownham Services on the M27 to go down to Weymouth for their home Blue Square Conference South game against Bromley.

That tortuous journey through the single-lane roads of Dorset didn't get any better and it was slow going again. It didn't help that it was the day of the Great Dorset Steam Fair and the County Show and every caravan in England was on the move. Even on a good day, though, it has been the reason why so many players decide against signing for the club or want extra pay or expenses to join, which has always been a problem.

I was worried about the reception I might get, I have to admit, but as soon as I got out of the car people were warm and welcoming to me. At that time, crowds were well down on the 1,500 average we were attracting in the Southern League when I was there last time around, which meant that only the real hard core were attending.

They were the ones who had been supportive to me, with the ones who had a go at me mainly just casual supporters. The club had been averaging around 650 for its last few home games. Today there would be 792 so they would take about £1,200 more than normal through the gate. Every little helps.

The team, basically young and green with just a few older hands around, were fine with me, taking me at face value as just another player, which was how I wanted it. And we made a good start to the game, with big centre half David Obaze heading home from a corner. That was where the good news ended, though. By half time we had conceded four. In the end, we lost 5-1 to a decent but not brilliant Bromley side.

I enjoyed it in its own way and lasting 90 minutes showed that I was fit enough. I was never match sharp, though, and after a reasonable curling shot not too far wide in the first half, I let a couple of half chances get away from me in the second. I was never tempted to say anything to the manager because it was down to him to sort it all.

I could see why the club was in so much trouble, though. The team was lacking confidence and Matty Hale was struggling in his first managerial job, from which he would resign soon afterwards. There was an air of decline around the place and it was sad when contrasted with the fun times we had had around six years earlier. Ian had his work cut out, I could see that.

At least, I felt, if this was to be my last professional game – my 1,009th – at the age of 43, then it had been for a club that had played a big part in my career, one where I first made my name.

The supporters were good to me throughout – and there was even a banner on the stand saying 'Welcome Back Steve' – and they kept encouraging the team, because their expectations now were low after everything the club had been through, unlike the massive expectation around the place the last time I was there. I also enjoyed spending time up in the lounges with fans and sponsors after the game.

First time around, it should never have ended for me at Weymouth the way it did, but this had helped me lay some ghosts and move on without the resentment there had been in me before. Now I could let it go.

And at least the benefit could be seen in the next couple of weeks as the club duly raised the £50,000 it needed immediately on the back of some good publicity in the national papers. There were even people pledging money from America and Denmark, I heard.

Sadly, once some debts had been paid off, it did not go far, and the club was soon back in trouble and staring at administration again. Ian resigned, with the problems too much for him to sort out and not enough money coming into the club, and they had to look for new owners and investors.

I was always willing to go back to help, but it turned out to be a one-off appearance – before the game it was being billed as a comeback; afterwards it was a favour. It did feel like the end, with me unable to commit properly to playing regularly what with my media and family commitments now. I don't like doing anything half-heartedly, least of all playing.

Never rule anything out, though, as my career has always shown, and while playing again might be far-fetched, a return to management is still very much in my mind. You never quite know where the next opening might be. So many clubs, so much unfinished business out there . . .

Index

289